NOT AFRAID

NOT AFRAID

THE EVOLUTION OF EMINEM

ANTHONY BOZZA

DA CAPO PRESS

Hachette Books
Hachette Book Group
1290 Avenue of the Americas
New York, NY 10104
hachettebookgroup.com
twitter.com/hachettebooks

First Edition: November 2019

Hachette Books is a division of Hachette Book Group, Inc.
The Hachette Books name and logo are trademarks of Hachette Book Group, Inc.

The publisher is not responsible for websites (or their content) that are not owned by the publisher.

Library of Congress Control Number: 2019947388

ISBNs: 9-780-306-92297-8 (hardcover)
9-780-306-92296-1 (ebook)

Printed in the United States of America

LSC-C

10 9 8 7 6   5 4 3 2 1

To my mother, who has loved and supported me, unwaveringly, for my entire life. I try my very best to make you proud. I love you with all my heart.

Contents

Preface   ix

Introduction: The Storm, October 10, 2017   xv

1. A Ton of Bricks   1
2. Never Enough   14
3. Everybody Has a Private World   35
4. Shady's Kids: A History of White Rap   69
5. Going through Changes   115
6. See You in Hell   144
7. Rap God   168
8. Do You Believe?   195
9. Energized Like a Nine Volt   233
    Conclusion: Greatest in the World   264

    Epilogue   273
    Acknowledgments   279
    Index   280

Preface

There are few artists in the history of hip-hop who have managed to establish a legacy, maintain their integrity, and achieve longevity. One of the true pioneers, LL Cool J, has reached commercial heights as a rapper, TV and film actor, label owner, and author and has done so consistently for over thirty years. In 2017, he became the first rapper to receive the Kennedy Center Honors for his lifetime contribution to American culture. LL was Marshall Mathers's first childhood hero and inspiration; it was his music, before N.W.A, Naughty by Nature, and Onyx, that Marshall blasted in his Walkman as a teen walking down 8 Mile. Over the years, the two have formed a friendship of mutual respect. The following is an interview with LL Cool J exclusive to this book.

In 1998, I was in the studio experimenting with Dr. Dre on the song "Zoom" and quite a few other songs. When we took a break, he played me a few tracks by a kid named Marshall that he was producing. It was dope. I loved the sarcasm, the cockiness, the arrogance, the creativity, and all the shit talking. It really resonated with me in a strong way. There were a few lines that I thought were very good, but he had this one—"How can I be white, I don't even exist" ("Role Model"). That one stayed with me.

When I first met Marshall, I ran that line by him, and I think it took him by surprise. I had no idea how much he was into my music growing up. I was glad to discover that he's a humble guy, that he saves it for the music, and that in person he's none of what he is on record. We've met on quite a few occasions since then; we've talked and vibed, and we have a great friendship. Marshall is a real talented guy, a great writer; he's witty and willing to take risks, which is important if you're going to have a long career in this business.

If you do what we do and you get that break and become a successful artist, you go through the honeymoon phase. At that point you're so popular and the public is so in love with you that you can take a shit on a fucking cookie, and everybody will love it. Enjoy that, because after the honeymoon is over, you actually have to stand up and make something that tastes good. That was the true test, and Marshall passed it.

When I look at what it means to be a true artist, it's not about the first five, seven, or even ten years. To me, it's what you're doing after that, if you're doing anything at all. The biggest challenge is to not be above it all, to keep caring if you're successful. Hip-hop is funny because the more successful you become, the less people think you care about the art itself, especially if you start to display the trappings of success. In hip-hop, present-day success can cannibalize your future success. Let me be specific with you: if you're purely living in hip-hop culture, you won't have an issue. But if you're successful in rap music and don't continue to live in hip-hop culture, you'll run into trouble. Subconsciously, hip-hop fans recognize this when they see it because hip-hop is an attitude; it's a mind-set, and it's a way of life. KRS-One said it best when he said, "Rap is something you do; hip-hop is something you live." If you're successful and continue to live within hip-hop culture, you'll be fine. Step too far outside of where you're from, and you'll definitely get spanked.

Em has done a good job of staying close to what he is and what he believes in. He hasn't deviated from who he is, and he's made some creative choices as a rapper. He's ventured outside his base, but he's always circled back. He's had the normal ups and downs of any post–honeymoon phase rapper and come out fine. He's still doing big shows and touring the world. He's got a real career, and you gotta respect that. He's never followed, and he's trusted his own creative voice and vision; those are the keys. When the metric for success is your love for the project and the inspiration it creates, for others as well as for you, then you're in good shape. When you start paying too much attention to what people are writing or saying about you or your sales or streams, you're in trouble. At that point you're not an artist. You're a song maker; you're a hack. It's better to be an artist who hasn't sold a million but is supremely respected by your peers. If you get both of those things, great, but it's about being true to your art. Do that, and believe me—the rest follows.

Em got both.

But we can't ignore the level that his career has gone to simply because he's white. There are certain states in America, media organizations, corporate sponsors, and doors that are opened for him because of his skin color. Those doors were not and will not be opened for me or other black artists. It's not everybody, but certain organizations feel a certain way about black artists that they don't about white ones. This isn't new, and it hasn't changed.

When Run-DMC, Beastie Boys, and I were all coming up together, Beastie Boys were being played on radio stations that wouldn't even consider playing my stuff even if it was the same shit. And in some ways, it was because we were all on the same label and Rick Rubin produced all of us! Em can attribute a great portion of his success—the more commercial side of what he's done—to that little extra turbo boost he gets from being white.

That being said, it would be unfair to even suggest that his color is the only reason he's successful and that he has no talent. It's nothing for black artists to be bitter about because that can disturb your creativity, which goes against everything I believe in. But if we didn't recognize it, we would all be liars.

Put it this way: look at Jay-Z and the great things he's done. But what if he was white? Trump had something to say to Snoop; he didn't have shit to say to Em—probably because he knows that fanbase is a lot of who votes for him. America is my home, but it is funny here, man. Em has opened doors for more artists, and he has expanded the genre of hip-hop and taken it to new heights. But it's kinda like Motown. All of white America knew about Motown, but they didn't go out of their way to support the individual artists. It took Michael Jackson thirty years to reach those heights! He started at eight years old and had to be the most talented motherfucker in the world to do it.

All that aside, at the end of the day, Em is an incredibly talented artist. He is a dope MC, a bad motherfucker on the mic, and a bad motherfucker on stage. He has done amazing work, and he continues to do so. He has made lyricism important, and he has taken the gospel of hip-hop around the world in a big way. He's done dope shit he didn't have to do, like paying it forward, putting 50 Cent on, and doing what he did with D12. And *8 Mile* was beautiful, artistic stuff. He is legitimately talented as a rapper by every measure: voice, flow, content, everything. I have supreme respect for Em. I love him, he's a good dude, and he will always be important to hip-hop because he's a big piece of this story that continues to be told.

And that is because Em is connected to the essence of hip-hop, which is always being true to your roots and where you come from. That's the secret, and it's simple and beautiful. I got into rap music to feel empowered, feel good about myself, boost my self-esteem, do dope shit, and have my voice be heard. If I stay in that mode, I can't go wrong. When I start talking about my fancy watch and car too much, my shit goes a little haywire. I love the aspect of truth at the root of hip-hop culture. I love it when KRS is true, and I love how Rakim can wear his gold chains, but he remains true. And I love Em because no matter what he does, he is true. No matter how big hip-hop has become—regardless of the money, the fame, the stadiums, and all that—empowerment is still the heart of hip-hop. Picture it like a series of concentric circles: when you're being true, you're standing inside that center, in your core. No matter how many layers or circles of success your career has to it, what can anyone say as long as you stand in that core, staying true to your bull's-eye?

Introduction: The Storm, October 10, 2017

It was, in every way, your average modern-day awards show. Prevailing favorites won their categories, and the nominee lists were slightly off, embodying both the paying public's tastes and the media's self-congratulatory ones. That said, since its debut in 2006, the BET Hip Hop Awards has remained one of the better shows out there for a few reasons: it is focused on one genre, it is in step with and tied to a dedicated culture, and it remains conscious and celebrates the music's history. Unlike, say, the Best New Artist Award at the Grammys, the BET Hip Hop Awards typically celebrates artists that make a splash in the actual year they win the award rather than the year the voting members of the board finally choose to acknowledge them. These qualities make the show entertaining and current. Plus, in award-show terms, it's short, clocking in at around ninety minutes. That's as long as the Oscars Red Carpet show alone.

There was a significant upward tick in the viewership of all live televised awards shows in 2013 and 2014, when the general public, famous and not, became enamored with social media, particularly live-tweeting. With so much rich fodder to opine over in real time, awards shows became events both on and off the internet. But all that faded, perhaps as our political and social climate darkened, taking the tone of much social media with it. Whatever the cause, from the Grammys to the Oscars to the Emmys to the MTV Music Awards as well as to BET's longer-format, broader-focused namesake BET Awards, audiences have thinned drastically. In 2018, the Grammys hit a nine-year low, with 19.8 million viewers (down 24 percent), and the Oscars hit an all-time low of 26.5 million (down 20 percent from the year before), while ratings for the beleaguered MTV Video Music Awards (VMAs) slumped from 9.8 million in 2015 to just 5.23 million in 2018, a loss of nearly half its audience in three years.

By comparison, the BET Hip Hop Awards is doing well. Its ratings have dipped significantly from the 2015 peak of 6.26 million viewers but have remained stable at around 1.6 to 1.9 million viewers ever since, a number that doesn't account for abundant streams of the event on the BET website, as most millennials don't believe in paying for cable (or anything else consumed via screen). This is also due, no doubt, to the fact that as of 2017, according to Nielsen, for the first time, hip-hop has become the most popular genre of music consumed in the United States, powered by a 72 percent increase in on-demand audio streaming.

BET's Hip Hop Awards gets things mostly right. In 2017, Kendrick Lamar deservedly took home a few trophies (he holds the record for most awarded artist, with three more than Jay-Z and one more than Drake), as did breakout star Cardi B and host DJ Khaled. At a time when a sea of facially tattooed, rainbow-dreadlocked "lil' yung" rappers sipping lean and dropping Xanax have made their way off Sound-Cloud and onto the *Billboard* charts, it was refreshing to see a mainstream outlet like BET continuing to honor the pillars of hip-hop. Shows like the now-extinct *Freestyle Friday* celebrated battle raps, pitting two rappers against each other in a two-round competition. Many of the contestants were signed to record deals after their appearances, and at least one, Jin, went on to star in *2 Fast 2 Furious*. At the Hip Hop Awards, the *Cypher* series continues this tradition, allowing emerging and underground artists to deliver bars alongside established stars. The cyphers are divided into groups, with ten to fifteen rappers participating on average, with the footage screened throughout the show. It's always a highlight and one of the mainstays that true fans look forward to because it's a chance to discover someone they may have heard about more than heard or an opportunity to see an artist they already respect prove their skills.

The 2017 BET Awards featured a round of cyphers with artists like 6lack, Fat Joe, Belly, Conway, Axel Leon, Ball Greezy, and more. Those were great. But then they aired a cypher that stood out from the regularly scheduled programming. It was just one rapper, a cappella, no beats, no DJ. You couldn't call it a cypher; it was a one-sided battle rap between Eminem and an absent opponent, Donald Trump, the forty-fifth president of the United States, a man who spits more lies in a week than a rapper with his first platinum chain and no record deal. In the eleven-year history of the show, the producers had never given one artist the mic to be so overtly political. Then again, these times are unlike any we've ever seen, and the chance to air what they did doesn't come around every day.

Stalking an invisible opponent, pacing in an invisible ring, his hood up, his hands punctuating his words, Marshall Mathers's bold-eyed aggression burned a hole in the camera. This was more than a battle rap; it was a true freestyle, made up on the spot, off the top of his head, for four minutes. He started and stopped, changing rhyme schemes to emphasize each verse's message, all of them painting a picture of just how terrible and dangerous Donald Trump is to America and the world.

From his endorsement of Bannon
Support for the Klansmen
Tiki torches in hand for the soldier that's black
And comes home from Iraq
And is still told to go back to Africa
Fork and a dagger in this racist 94-year-old grandpa
Who keeps ignoring our past, historical, deplorable factors.

His performance was arresting. As a lyricist and a battle rapper, he is, without question, one of the greatest of all time. But more importantly, at a moment when freestyle rap had been labeled old school or had come to describe "improvised" verses that are performed live but not featured in the original recording, Eminem revitalized the essence of the art form. If a "freestyle" is now just a new verse, it's more of a bonus track, an added solo, most likely prepared beforehand. This wasn't that at all. Sure, every rapper has a few lines in mind to start a spontaneous cypher, a couple of couplets in their pocket to get the ball rolling. Today's popular rappers, many of whom are skilled at writing lyrics and practicing their delivery, would never think to attempt a true freestyle, because they know their weakness would be revealed. Consequently, few can deliver machine gun–fast rhymes off the top of their heads about current events and our president the way Eminem can and the way he did.

"The Storm," as that slam poem has come to be called, isn't Eminem's greatest work, but it wasn't intended to be. It was a telegram to the White House and to Eminem's widespread fan base. That said, there are moments of brilliance and virtuosity in those four minutes. It was recorded on the eighth floor of a Detroit parking structure on a Friday morning a week before the BET Awards as employees of Comerica and the Wayne County government shuffled into work. Backed by colleagues Royce da 5'9", Kid Vishis, and newly signed Shady Records artists Boogie, Westside Gunn, and Conway, plus a few classic Detroit cars from the '80s, Eminem did about eight takes.

As usual, Eminem was called out for being a white man in an African American game. Rapper Vince Staples shot off a number of negative tweets, among them one calling Eminem's verse "garbage," and he later told *Pitchfork*, "My favorite thing about the Eminem freestyle is the wall of dark-skinned black people behind him. That was great." While Staples may have been right when he said that if he, as a black rapper, delivered some of the same lines, he wouldn't be taken seriously, he also completely missed the point. Eminem didn't do the freestyle to show off new verses because, let's face it, he's proven himself capable of so much better. What he did was utilize his privilege—if you want to call it "white," that's fine—but I'm talking about his privilege as Eminem. He made a choice, as an internationally iconic artist, and yes, a white one, to take a stand and make a point in as big a way as possible. As we would see in the months that followed, he was just getting started. But that night, on BET, on the Black Entertainment Network, the point he chose to make was more important. Beyond taking Trump down in a hailstorm of poignant insults, the fieriest portion of his cypher was focused on turning his white privilege on its ass. The final and most vehemently delivered lines in "The Storm" have nothing to do with Trump at all; they're aimed at his fan base.

And any fan of mine who's a supporter of his
I'm drawing in the sand a line, you're either for or against
And if you can't decide who you like more and you're split
On who you should stand beside, I'll do it for you with this:
Fuck you!

As a white rapper from a broken trailer park home, it's safe to assume that Eminem has his fair share of fans in Trump's America. Factor in his anger, his honesty, and his rebel stance, and it's not crazy to assume that there are plenty of poor, red-blooded red state voters who preparty for Trump rallies by blasting "Lose Yourself." Eminem knows this, and it was at them, as much as at Trump, that this cypher was aimed.

Eminem has enjoyed massive success as an artist and is financially set for life, so one could argue that alienating his Trump-loving fans was a relatively low-risk gamble. But again, that's not quite the point. He did two things in this freestyle: he called the president of the United States a racist, in effect referencing the institutional racism that still plagues our country, and he blatantly challenged his fans to reassess their loyalties and their values. As he stared down the camera, all verbs and vitriol, he was glaring at them as much as he was Donald Trump. He had every right to use his platform as he saw fit, and if he made a right-wing fan question or change his or her mind, then his cypher was a success.

As someone who knew Marshall Mathers way back when, who carefully chronicled his rise and most essential years and has ever since always watched his evolution, I found this moment to be significant. I saw the seeds of something that, to be honest, I'd almost written off. I never dismissed Marshall as an artist, but I had put him on pause. I'd listened carefully to every one of his records and was up to date on all his movements, but I'd noticed a shift in his work artistically that I understood but was not always riveted by. Over the course of the past fifteen years, since I wrote *Whatever You Say I Am: The Life and Times of Eminem*, Marshall went through ups and downs equally as traumatic as his childhood. He reaped the benefits of commercial and artistic success, but he also suffered greatly, losing his best friend; going through divorce, remarriage, and redivorce with Kim; and almost succumbing to his chemical demons. Yet somehow, through downward spiral and rebirth, he carved out a niche that went beyond his skills as a lyricist and rapper. He created a sound whose origin story could be heard in his early work but that had come into its own. It was as emotional and confessional as early tracks like "If I Had" and "Rock Bottom," but sleekly crafted and reimagined as shots aimed more for the charts than the heart. And they worked. They really did: "Love the Way You Lie," "The Monster," and "Not Afraid" all peaked at number one, as had *Recovery*, *Marshall Mathers LP 2*, *Relapse*, and *Revival*. All those albums and all those singles are great and equal to what had initially caught my ear. Personally, I've always been more engaged by the wise-ass rhymes in "Drug Ballad," the blistering sing-song ferocity of "Kill You," and the songwriting genius of "Stan." That was Mr. I Just Don't Give a Fuck, the word-obsessed rebel with an endless clip of rhymes to fire and nothing to lose.

No artist worth his or her weight in platinum ever remains the same; that is not the nature of an artist. I never expected it of Eminem, nor did I criticize any of his choices in the years to follow (not even *Encore*—as bizarre as it got, the accents were hilarious). I simply didn't find myself as moved, but all that changed as I watched his freestyle cypher that night on BET. Maybe I was seeing what I wanted to, but it felt to me that this was, in real time, the rekindling of a fire in an artist who is one of the greatest of all time but is also more than the sum of his skills. By nature of his race and backstory, he's both an unwitting icon and a symbol of American culture in our lifetime. Quite simply, Marshall Mathers is a mirror of the America that made him—the America we live in. His journey embodies the divisiveness, flaws, and widespread afflictions that make this country, and our biggest export, our culture, what it is. Even today, as critics self-appointed and actual declare him an artist past his peak, Eminem is one of the most commercially successful and polarizing figures in global pop culture. Like America itself, he's undeniable, even if he's not exactly adored right now.

When I wrote my first book, based on my first cover story for *Rolling Stone*, the first national cover story on Marshall Mathers anywhere, Eminem's story was still new, still evolving, still resonating from the back-to-back release of three classic albums and a star turn in *8 Mile*. He was the most popular and influential musical artist of the era, and that book told his tale from all angles, from his background to his rise to his significance as a signpost in American culture. It was more than a biography of the man, because understanding such a polarizing figure requires more than just covering the events on the timeline. One must study the influences, the people and places that made him. This book is no different, though the artist and his times have drastically changed. It is a study of an artist who shot to the top so quickly that fame almost took him too soon. It is a story of a rare talent coming back to a very different playing field and finding his way in a whole new inner and outer world. Ultimately it is a story of survival, of being true to yourself and not afraid.

It had been fifteen years since I was inspired to think deeply about Eminem's significance as an artist, a figure, and a mirror, but when I saw him perform "The Storm," fully engaged, righteously angry, and honestly letting fly at Trump from the top of his head with a full round of oral ammo, I was energized. In that moment, I knew that he is still a concentrated filter of our times. He never lost his talent, but he had lost his closest friend, his way, and nearly his life. He had been through so much, and though he'd already come back, this was his real return. I saw a new man, not perfect, not trying to be, but no longer a boy. I saw someone who cared enough about his country to use the leverage he had to make a statement that could not be ignored, denied, or misinterpreted. He had nothing to lose, except the fans he no longer wanted. I saw a man who had survived his upbringing and the rocket ship ride to success that I witnessed firsthand back in 1999. This was him not giving a fuck, all grown up. His skills were sharp, his perception was clear, and his message that night was sent from the source—biting, bold, and heavy as a winter Detroit sky.

Chapter 1

A Ton of Bricks

On March 23, 2003, four years and one month after the release of his first major label album, *The Slim Shady LP*, along with Luis Resto and Jeff Bass, Eminem won the award for Best Original Song at the Seventy-Fifth Annual Oscar Awards, held at the Kodak Theater in Hollywood, California. The song was "Lose Yourself," from the original soundtrack to *8 Mile*, the semiautobiographical film in which he starred. When he won, Eminem was at home in Detroit, asleep in his bed, with his daughter beside him, unintentionally joining a list of stars like Marlon Brando, Elizabeth Taylor, and Katherine Hepburn, all of whom famously won but didn't attend the ceremony for reasons ranging from outright boycott (Brando) to disinterest in prizes (Hepburn). Marshall Mathers's motivation was different.

"I was sleeping," he said. "I was home with my daughter watching cartoons . . . I felt like I had a snowball's chance in hell of winning. At that point in my life I felt like rap never got a fair shake at anything."[1]

In a very short period of time, over the course of three studio albums plus the soundtrack and film, Eminem had gone from a popular and polarizing outcast to the prism through which many uninitiated around the world came to understand what hip-hop meant and what it meant to America. The message was spread further and wider because Eminem put a white face to the culture, and the Hollywood treatment of his life's story made it even more universally digestible.

The racial implications of Eminem's success are something I discussed in depth in my first book, *Whatever You Say I Am: The Life and Times of Eminem* (Three Rivers Press, 2004), as have many others since then, but that aspect of his story should never be brushed aside no matter how many times the tale is told. He got more headlines because he was white for three reasons: (1) he was an outlier skilled enough to win the acceptance and respect of the gatekeepers of hip-hop culture; (2) the color of his skin made him mainstream white America's entrée into the most influential African American cultural movement of contemporary times; and (3) because he was white. Eminem didn't campaign to be that tour guide, but he served as one nonetheless. He never wanted to be a leader, envoy, or example. In fact, he would have been happy with a respected, modestly successful career that never rose

---

1. "Eminem on Behind the Boards—Part 6 of 12," interview by *Behind the Boards*, video, 10:00, July 27, 2009, https://www.youtube.com/watch?v=qV4tG-3V3do &feature=player_detailpage#t=173s.

above the underground, as long as it provided him a living that could support his family.

Today he has several glass cases full of them, but Eminem has never cared for trophies or accolades. Back in 1997, he participated in the Rap Olympics not to walk home with bragging rights but because he needed the prizes ($500 and a Rolex). He nearly skipped the Forty-Second Annual Grammy Awards ceremony at which he received three nominations and took home two wins, for best Rap Solo Performance ("My Name Is") and Best Rap Album (*The Slim Shady LP*). Since then he has been nominated forty-three times and won fifteen, landing him in rarefied company with Jay-Z and Kanye West for the rap artists with the most wins. Aside from memorable musical performances, Eminem has kept his presence and acceptance speeches at award shows to a minimum, because as bombastic as his musical persona has always been, and as hard as it may be for many to believe, he is not that way in real life. He's a straightforward, no-nonsense blue-collar kid from Detroit, content to mind his own business. He's funny, he's mischievous, he's witty, and he's genuinely taken with every aspect of creating verses and being an MC.

He's also never been preoccupied with fame; authenticity and integrity have always meant more to him than accolades and popularity. He eschewed the typical musician success story of relocating to Los Angeles and joining the paparazzi targets posing at events, opting instead to build his world in suburban Detroit, in a gated community, in a nine-thousand-square-foot compound where he wants for nothing and can enjoy some semblance of privacy.[2] This decision wasn't a calculated middle finger to the system or what was expected of him; it was a strategy necessary to his survival, because Marshall Mathers nearly died from the side effects of success. As he said in 2002, "Fame hit me like a fucking ton of bricks."[3]

"It takes an incredibly grounded person to survive the impact of fame," says Dr. Donna Rockwell, a clinical psychologist who specializes in mindfulness and celebrity mental health. "Fame is like hitting a wall to a human's psyche, emotional presence, and understanding, and it causes drastic changes in their interpersonal relationships. It would be good for a person to have had a nice, well-grounded childhood, but that does not create any sort of barrier against having the same things happen to them after fame hits."[4]

The concept of celebrity is nothing new; in fact, the concept of people being known because they are popularly recognized, as opposed to being famous for their achievements or positions of power, dates back to eighteenth-century London. At that time, the city displaced the royal court as the preferred site of society's social scene. A new-money consumer class emerged, fostering forms of urban leisure through interest in theater, coffeehouses, novels, and journalism. As a result, mass curiosity arose surrounding the individuals tied to these disciplines. Rather than follow the royals, the

---

2. In addition, the rapper purchased a twenty-two-room, 17,500-square-foot house on six acres near the former CEO of Kmart to use for family getaways. He sold it in 2017 for less than half of the purchase price.

3. "Is Eminem the New Elvis?" *Sydney Morning Herald*, December 18, 2002.

4. Donna Rockwell, interview with the author, 2019.

monied, nonaristocratic elite and Londoners of all economic strata became consumed with the intimate stories of their favorite actors and writers. The cycle continued and grew in the mid-nineteenth century, when Paris's world-famous department stores placed fashion at the center of celebrity by making what a known person was seen wearing as important as the fact that they were seen. Then, in the same era in New York City, society glamorized industry and wealth of any kind and institutionalized the gossip column, creating a new means for the known to be commodified. But it wasn't until the twentieth century, after the World Wars, that celebrity became a defining presence in the lives of everyday citizens. In his book *A Short History of Celebrity* (Princeton University Press, 2010), Fred Inglis, emeritus professor of cultural studies at the University of Sheffield, states that radio, television, and Hollywood worked to "restore immediacy and intimacy to human narrative at just the moment when mass modernity made everything in city life seem so anonymous and fragmentary."[5] This was the dawn of a new age, one in which celebrity as we take it for granted today was truly born. Dispersed through these new avenues, media created a contradictory marriage of intense familiarity and distance in those who consumed it: stars were now beamed into people's homes more easily than ever before, making them as familiar as a neighbor yet as remote and untouchable as the supernatural.[6]

---

5. Fred Inglis, *A Short History of Celebrity* (Princeton, NJ: Princeton University Press, 2010), 10–11.

6. Inglis, *A Short History of Celebrity*, 155.

At this point in the history of humanity, the impact of radio and network television is downright quaint compared to how the internet has altered the consumption of media, reality, and the figures celebrated and created therein. The number of available avenues alone, from YouTube to Instagram and Twitter to Facebook, has worked to magnify the sense of familiarity with strangers to a microscopic level. When it comes to the institution of celebrity, I would argue that the same paradox of intimacy and distance that Inglis suggested applies, but the scope has drastically changed. Today, celebrity is allowed no mystery because consumers demand their experience of the famous to be both relatable and attainable. It isn't enough to be fans; they also need to be friends. Relationships between fan and famous are created through voyeuristic sharing of moments on social media that has become omnipresent in the lives of everyone who chooses to open an account. These relationships with public figures, no matter how intimate their sharing, are simply not real by nature, but they are taken as such now more than ever. Similarly, the sense of distance that once cast the celebrity in an otherworldly, unattainable light has changed by disappearing altogether. The immediacy and constancy of social media has murdered privacy, especially for the famous. In its place is a symbiotic relationship with a power-hungry, hive-minded public that is quick to opine and judge because they regard intimate knowledge of every detail of a celebrity's life as their right. The public's sense of otherness when it comes to celebrity has also been replaced with the belief that since the nonfamous are just like them, anyone could be—and should be—famous if they get enough followers on YouTube or Instagram. If Andy Warhol were alive today, he would no doubt be selling fifteen minutes of fame bundled with a new phone and an unlimited data plan.

"Everybody is famous now," says Dr. Rockwell. "Everybody has their own network, whether it's YouTube or Instagram or a podcast. The effects of fame are going to impact a larger percentage of society who will fall victim to the same psychological effects of fame and celebrity that our famous people do. The mental health effects of all of that attention are not going to be good for society. There is going to be an increase in narcissistic characteristics, which will leave the person feeling all of the negative symptoms of narcissism: isolation, not being able to feel a sense of satisfaction, boredom. All of these things will be occurring more frequently in the population, and at some point that is going to need to be dealt with."

According to a study conducted at UCLA in 2011, preteens listed fame as their top priority, followed by achievement, popularity, image, and financial success.[7] These are individuals who have yet to experience the emotional/psychological roller coaster of puberty or the pressure of high school cliques. This is the legacy of reality television and the like-and-follow culture of the internet. Even so, the general consensus remains, even among those who should know better, that being famous means having it made: fame is the goal achieved. The assumption is that fame comes with fortune and therefore financial security, which it often does, but less

---

7. Yalda T. Uhls, "Kids Want Fame More Than Anything," *Huffington Post*, April 26, 2012.

time is being spent pondering the side effects of fame, particularly in cases where it wasn't actively sought or expected. Overnight fame might sound like a dream come true to many, but like anything that sounds too good to be true, it isn't. It is a sudden change, with lasting psychological side effects that are difficult to navigate at best and lethal at worst.

Rockwell, who is also an adjunct professor at the Michigan School of Professional Psychology, has conducted thorough studies on the effects of fame for the past ten years, in which time the nature of the fame cycle has changed immensely. She has interviewed figures in entertainment, sports, government, business, law, publishing, television, and news and has found more than a few commonalities when it comes to the psychological toll of being famous. Participants in her study experienced "character splitting," seeing themselves as the people they were expected to be rather than the people they really are. This leads to a dangerous degree of self-consciousness, general mistrust of others, and deep feelings of isolation that often coincide with the heights of her subjects' greatest achievements. "You will continue to be the person you always were pre-fame," she says. "You'll have the same neurology and same emotional history. When people become famous, they should get right into therapy so that they know how to tolerate the fame experience and how to cope with what they're bringing to it. It's very difficult to navigate, and it makes preexisting conditions worse by taking away the normal mirroring we get from our environment. There are now so many sycophants and yes-men that any chance of actually knowing or being able to do 'the right thing' becomes more elusive."

This is the ton of bricks that hit Marshall Mathers in the 2000s, and he reacted like a proud, scrappy, smart-mouthed kid who isn't afraid of a fight: he worked too hard, partied even harder, and flew off the handle when tested. He behaved the way he did when he had nothing to lose, not realizing that he now had everything to use. He pistol-whipped a man he saw kissing his estranged wife, Kim, and landed in court—and nearly jail—for carrying a concealed weapon. He endured what seemed like an endless stream of lawsuits, most of which were settled out of court for undisclosed sums. There was his mother's $10 million suit (she was eventually awarded $1,600 by the court), his ex-wife Kim's defamation suit following her suicide attempt, and another $10 million suit brought by French pianist Jacques Loussier against Eminem, Dr. Dre, and Interscope over an uncleared sample/ interpolation of Loussier's song "Pulsion" in "Kill You" from *The Marshall Mathers LP*. There was even one from D'Angelo Bailey, the junior high school bully Em called out in the song "Brain Damage" on *The Slim Shady LP*. This ludicrous lawsuit ended in perhaps the most humorous moment Eminem has ever enjoyed in court. Bailey filed the $1 million case in 2001, claiming that Eminem ruined his reputation and any chance he had at achieving success in the music industry. When Bailey's case was thrown out by Judge Deborah Servitto in 2003, her thirteen-page opinion on the matter included a rhymed verse: "Mr. Bailey complains that his rap is trash so he's seeking compensation in the form of cash. Bailey thinking he's entitled to some monetary gain because Eminem used his name in vain. The lyrics are stories no one would take as fact, they're an exaggeration of a childish act."[8]

For his assault and gun charge, Eminem was handed three years of probation, including court-ordered sobriety and regular drug tests. It was a wake-up call that taught him that his life was no longer his own and that he had to be careful of his every move. He could afford the fuck-you money he paid lawyers to handle the lawsuits, which have continued to this day, costing him an estimated $4.7 million annually in legal fees, but no amount of money was going to keep him out of jail for breaking the law.[9] Mathers responded by cleaning up his act and diving into his work. He threw himself into producing artists on his Shady label, dropping guest verses, and starring in *8 Mile*. "I just got caught up in the drinking and the drugs and the fighting and just wilding out and doing dumb things I shouldn't have been doing," he told the *Sydney Herald* in 2002. "But I came out of them and I conquered it . . . I'm proud of myself now for not only my accomplishments but for pulling through all that—my criminal cases, my divorce. If I was still on drugs and still living the life that I lived three years ago, I would be a fucking failure."[10]

---

8. Andrew Dansby, "Judge Drops Eminem Rap," *Rolling Stone*, October 20, 2003, https://www.rollingstone.com/music/music-news/judge-drops-eminem-rap-183834/.

9. Editors, "Eminem's Courtroom Rap Sheet—10 of the Best," *LawFuel*, May 3, 2017, https://www.lawfuel.com/blog/eminem/.

10. "Is Eminem the New Elvis?" *Sydney Morning Herald*, December 18, 2002, https://www.smh.com.au/entertainment/music/is-eminem-the-new-elvis-2002 1218-gdfzf1.html.

The film's demands had a positive effect on Mathers, though he likened the schedule to boot camp. He got in shape, and he devoted himself to making sure every detail rang true to the time and place in which it was set. "It was anywhere between thirteen and sixteen hours a day, six days a week. It literally gave me enough time to go to sleep, get up and come back and do the movie."[11]

After the film, it seemed that Eminem had found stable ground and that he had dealt with the onslaught of sudden fame. Though he hadn't quite befriended it, he'd found a way to coexist. After quite a long and steady run of projects, he threw himself into production work for others. He produced twelve of the sixteen tracks on *Loyal to the Game*, the posthumous Tupac Shakur record, and he executive produced *D12 World*, the second and final studio album by his closest Detroit rap associates.

The controversy, of course, didn't stop. In 2003, he was accused of being racist by *The Source* magazine based on a cassette tape from 1993 that featured a young Eminem depicting black women as dumb gold diggers. He admitted to making the song and publicly apologized, explaining that it was "something I made out of anger, stupidity and frustration when I was a teenager. I'd just broken up with my girlfriend who was African-American and I reacted like the angry, stupid kid I was. I hope people will take it for the foolishness that it was, not for what somebody is trying to make it into today."[12]

---

11. "Is Eminem the New Elvis?"
12. "'The Source' Accuses Eminem of Racism," *Billboard*, November 21, 2003, https:// www.billboard.com/articles/news/68082/the-source-accuses-eminem-of -racism.

The Source wasn't the only institution questioning Eminem's motives: in December 2003, the US Secret Service confirmed that it was looking into allegations that a leaked song, "We as Americans," was a death threat aimed at President George W. Bush, based on the following lyrics: "Fuck money / I don't rap for dead presidents / I'd rather see the president dead / It's never been said, but I set precedents." Ultimately, the investigation was dropped.

Another vote of disapproval came from Michael Jackson in 2004. A week after the release of "Just Lose It," the first single off Eminem's fifth studio album, *Encore*, Jackson called into Steve Harvey's radio show in LA to let the world know how unhappy he was with the song's music video, which parodies Jackson's lowest moments: the child-molestation allegations, his rhinoplasty, and the 1984 Pepsi commercial shoot during which his hair caught fire. He personally asked stations to stop playing the video, and many of his friends and supporters including Stevie Wonder spoke out against it, with Harvey proclaiming, "Eminem has lost his ghetto pass. We want the pass back." While BET pulled it from their rotation, MTV continued to air it.

Neither Mathers nor his label, Interscope, seemed to mind the controversy, as it was sure to translate into album sales. They issued the following statement to media, contingent on the fact that it be printed in full: "Eminem's video for 'Just Lose It' was taken off the air today by BET. Michael Jackson requested that the station no longer play the video because he found it offensive. We are sorry that BET made this decision. Eminem's new album, *Encore*, will be released on November 16."

Later that month, they released the video for "Mosh" a week before the 2004 US presidential election. The video depicts an army of Bush-administration victims marching with Eminem on the White House. The video ends with a message to vote on November 2. After Bush was reelected, however, the ending was changed to Eminem and his crowd of protesters invading the White House during the president's State of the Union address. This was the first time that Em spoke out on the state of American politics. As expected, the controversy benefitted commerce: *Encore* sold 710,000 copies in its first three days and went on to sell 1.5 million in its first week. A month later, it had sold four million copies in the United States alone. Nine months later, it had sold eleven million copies worldwide.

As he had done in 2002 and 2003, Eminem planned to promote the album on the Anger Management world tour. The show was poised to go on, though in the press he'd begun to hint that *Encore* might be the last the world would hear from him for a while. He'd grown weary, and according to many, he had taken Slim Shady, his aesthetic, as far as it could go. He seemed ready to join his mentor, Dr. Dre, in a life spent behind the mixing board, crafting the careers of others. What he got instead was a storm he couldn't weather, leaving him emotionally marooned, in self-imposed exile.

Chapter 2

Never Enough

The Anger Management Tour 3 was set to be the concert of the summer in 2005, boasting a roster of hip-hop's finest hitmakers: Eminem, 50 Cent, Lil Jon, G-Unit, D12, Obie Trice, plus Stat Quo, the Atlanta protégé that Eminem and Dr. Dre had cosigned to Shady/Aftermath. But the twenty-date, five-and-a-half-week tour, which kicked off on July 7 in Indiana, got off to a rocky start. A tour bus crashed during the first week, seriously injuring Alchemist (Eminem's DJ), Stat Quo, and five others, as well as eleven civilians who were involved in the ensuing six-vehicle pileup. Later in the tour, after playing Madison Square Garden in New York City, two members of 50 Cent's G-Unit—Lloyd Banks and Young Buck—were arrested for gun possession. Thirteen others in their entourage were arrested as well when the van carrying them was pulled over for running a red light. Upon inspection, officers found two guns—a .357 in the possession of a man named Steven Roker and one loaded .40 caliber handgun sitting on the floor of the van.

Everyone in the vehicle was arrested and charged with criminal possession of a concealed weapon for the unclaimed .40 caliber, and another passenger was charged with resisting arrest and disorderly conduct. It likely didn't help that Young Buck had ended the group's set that night by enticing the crowd to join him in an enthusiastic chant of "Fuck the police!" The authorities got the last word: all thirteen were held overnight but luckily released early enough to allow the two rappers to perform at the tour's second sold-out night at the Garden.

Reviews of the tour generally praised Eminem for bringing a proper show with sets, videos, a narrative, and a theme that echoed *Encore*. Nearly every critic distinguished him as the stand-out talent on the bill, the true artist who deserved his mega-selling status and regard. The consensus was that 50 Cent was more of a marketing machine than an MC, someone fans liked for his songs rather than his persona. He was often criticized for bogging his set down with constant plugs for his product endorsements with Vitamin Water and Reebok as well as his *8 Mile*-style film *Get Rich or Die Tryin'*. The other theme among reviewers across the country was that Eminem seemed tired and that *Encore*, though it sold through the roof (1.5 million copies in the States in its first week alone), was uneven—less focused and the product of an artist who had lost his fire. "In his lyrics, Eminem is always second-guessing his career, his celebrity, his persona; 'Encore' is full of sighing complaints, as if he were feeling ready to quit. (Onstage, he lampooned the newspapers and magazines that have claimed he is planning to retire, but he also didn't promise to stick around)," wrote Kelefa Sanneh in the *New York Times*.[1]

Rumors circulated of his impending retirement, based not only on the title of the record but also on Eminem's zeal to promote D12 and the artists on his label rather than himself. It didn't help the word on the street that *Encore* and the film that introduced Em's set on the tour featured him in a suit and tie in the same setting as he is pictured on the *Encore* album cover, taking a bow alone on a stage. In the video, he seems to be preparing for the show, but instead he shoots himself off camera. Each night he would take the stage in the same outfit just as the gunshot sound rang out and the video ended. All this speculation in the press and in fan forums was given a degree of validation when the *Detroit Free Press* published a piece in early July citing anonymous sources in Em's camp who claimed that the rapper was going to retire after the Anger Management Tour's last date, at Slane Castle outside Dublin, on September 17, 2005. They claimed that he was tired of the limelight, of touring and performing, and would spend his time focused exclusively on his label and signing and developing new talent.

The story was picked up and recycled by multiple news sources, necessitating an official comment from Eminem. "I'm not retiring," he told *MTV News* a week later during an Anger Management Tour stop. "When I say I'm taking a break, I'm taking a break from my own music to go into the studio and

1. Kelefa Sanneh, "A Hamlet of Hip-Hop and His Pal, Dance Man," *New York Times*, August 10, 2005, https://www.nytimes.com/2005/08/10/arts/music/a-hamlet-of -hiphop-and-his-pal-dance-man.html.

produce my other artists and put their albums out. That's called 'taking a break' for me. When I know my next move, I'll tell everyone my next move. Not some reporter who writes a story about 'This is Eminem's last album.' I never said it was my last album. I never said anything yet. I don't know what I'm doing yet. Nothing is definite, you know what I'm sayin'? Nothing is written in stone."[2]

When questioned about it in subsequent interviews, Paul Rosenberg would only say that *Encore* "certainly put the cap on this part of his career."[3]

It was clear what he was referring to: though *Encore* was Eminem's longest studio album to date, there were clues in the music that he had reached a creative plateau of sorts and perhaps a natural stopping point. Since 1999, his trajectory had been nothing but upward without looking back, as if he were driving a car with the accelerator pinned to the floor and he'd tossed the rearview mirror out the window. From the start, Marshall Mathers had a lot to prove, and he used this endless well to drive his creativity. *The Slim Shady LP* was the Trojan horse he rode through the gates of hip-hop culture to show the world rap skills were color-blind. *The Marshall Mathers LP* was the flawless follow-up that cemented his validity and took mainstream pop culture by storm. *The Eminem Show* centered on his battle with this newly found fame and proving that he wasn't affected by it. Then *8 Mile*

---

2. Rob Mancini, "Eminem: 'I'm Not Retiring,'" *MTV News*, July 21, 2005, http://www.mtv.com/news/1506087/eminem-im-not-retiring/.

3. Charlie Amter, "Eminem Prepares 'Curtain Call,'" *E! News*, October 10, 2005, https://www.eonline.com/news/50856/eminem-prepares-curtain-call.

increased his star status and widened his appeal by revisiting the past to re-create his creation story for the masses. *Encore* was what came next. For the first time, with no hurdles ahead of him, Eminem sounded unsure of what to write in the next chapter of his story.

Taken as a whole, *Encore* is an analysis of Eminem's entire life and career from the perspective of a man with nothing left to prove and no mountain left to climb aside from those he creates for himself. By the time he got to *Encore*, it was as if Eminem's narrative points of view (Slim Shady, Marshall Mathers, the rap god Eminem) had added another character, an unnamed yet omnipresent observer, who throughout the album commented on Slim, Marshall, and Eminem and where they'd ended up by teaming up. It was as if, with no fit competition in sight, the greatest battle rapper alive could only look back to settle a few already dead beefs, recount past victories, and shadowbox with himself. The opener "Evil Deeds" details his origin story once again, albeit with more than a few lines devoted to criticizing an outsider's perception of what his mother Debbie's "Satan spawn" had become: "Woe is me, there goes poor Marshall again whinin' about his millions / And his mansion and his sorrow, he's always drownin' in / And the dad he never had, and how his childhood was so bad / And how his mom was a dope addict, and his ex-wife, how they go at it." Later in the song he takes the other side, explaining how all he'd like to do is take his daughter to the mall without getting mobbed. "Yellow Brick Road" is similarly a nostalgic look back, contrasting it with yet another nagging issue in Eminem's present: the accusations of racism and the beef that wouldn't end between Eminem and *The Source* magazine, driven wholeheartedly for maximum exposure and profit by the magazine's cofounder, subpar rapper Raymond "Benzino" Scott.

Throughout the album's ninety minutes—by rap standards an epic—and amid some of Em's most complicated wordplay, there was also a song that signaled a step forward in his craft when it came to epic pop-chart-bound tracks. "Like Toy Soldiers" is a call to end the unnecessary violence in hip-hop and one of the few moments on the record where Eminem seems comfortable with his stature as an influential voice in the culture. The lyrics are from the heart, and the track is a continuation of the sonic formula of "Lose Yourself," employing a well-known pop music sample to a drastically different end, in this case Martika's "Toy Soldiers" (1989). Though the original song deals with drug addiction, the relatively upbeat ballad takes on a different tone under the brooding beat and Eminem's flow. Later examples didn't rely on a sample to anchor the song, but this was the start of a style that would come to define the string of pop hits like "Not Afraid" and "Love the Way You Lie" that came years later. In that vein, "Mosh" was Eminem's first well-aimed shot at the political system in this country. He had grazed the right wing in "White America," but the message in "Mosh" was undeniable.

More than any of the studio releases that came before it, *Encore* is a very wordy record. The music, it seemed, took a back seat to Em's lyrics, his rhymes dictating the rhythm rather than the soundtrack directing the pace of his flow. Every song sounds as if he recorded it a cappella and created the tracks afterward. It often has the feeling of an artist going through the motions, but frankly Eminem is still such a talent that even the painfully visceral Kim diss "Puke" has its moments. By this point, Eminem had killed Kim repeatedly in song ("'97 Bonnie and Clyde," "Kim"), called out her infidelity ("Soldier," "Sing for the Moment," "Say Goodbye to Hollywood") and drug addiction ("'Till I Collapse"), and even attacked her for being a bad person in "Hailie's Song," a track dedicated to how much he adores their daughter. "Puke" is a comedic take, including him as part of the toxic puzzle, with Em claiming that she still has such a strong hold on him that he pukes every time he thinks of her. He also doesn't miss an opportunity to call her "a coke-head slut" and tell her that he hopes she dies.

The Anger Management Tour's last American date took place in Detroit on August 12, 2005, and it was scheduled to recommence on September 1 for thirteen dates across the United Kingdom and Europe. That never happened. Eminem pulled out of the tour, canceling the shows, citing exhaustion. "My homie is a little tired, man," Eminem's closest friend and confidant Proof told *MTV News*. "He feels exhausted out here. It's crazy . . . We actually been running for the last seven years, but nobody sees it that way."[4] Three days later, Eminem was hospitalized to undergo treatment for dependency on sleep medication. It was the beginning of a recession from public life and the first inkling of a substance abuse issue that had been growing in tandem with his fame.

---

4. Corey Moss, "Eminem Cancels European Tour Due to Exhaustion," *MTV News*, August 16, 2005, http://www.mtv.com/news/1507755/eminem-cancels-european -tour-due-to-exhaustion/.

"Temptation is a very difficult thing once you become famous because everything is available to you. You have access to everything you want," says Dr. Donna Rockwell. "This leaves the celebrity to their own devices without help or guidance. I think that the use of substances by famous people is to help create, sadly, a more healthy boundary that they feel is livable, where they will have some sense of their own private space and their own control over this world."

Eminem retreated to his Detroit compound, working in the studio with D12 and Stat Quo for the rest of the year. He stayed out of the public eye, unwilling to discuss his rehab stint or anything else. At the end of 2005, Interscope released *Curtain Call: The Hits*, a collection of his biggest singles plus four new less-than-great tracks. "He still comes across as uncomfortable with both stardom and his standing as a white rapper, and in a recent MTV interview, he seemed unhappy with this compilation's track list. This isn't his art—it's his commerce," wrote Sean Fennessey in *Pitchfork*.[5] The release was still wildly successful, earning Eminem his fourth straight chart-topping debut. It went on to sell seven million copies in the United States alone.

In January 2006, Eminem remarried Kim, surprising everyone but the closest friends who knew that the pair had been reconciled in one way or another for some time. "They were always breaking up and making up," Proof said about them in 2002. "That was just Em and Kim." As if on cue, the reunion didn't last: Eminem filed for divorce just eighty-two days

---

5. Sean Fennessy, "Curtain Call: The Hits," *Pitchfork*, December 5, 2005.

later, and by year's end the couple reached an out-of-court settlement. They agreed to shared custody of their daughter, who was eleven at the time, as well as Kim's twelve-year-old niece, Alania, whom they'd adopted, and three-year-old Whitney, Kim's daughter from another relationship.

Marshall Mathers had retreated from the spotlight and found a version of domestic bliss, some type of shelter from the storm, a degree of normalcy that he never had growing up. It didn't work out with Kim, but he did find solace in caring for the girls.

That said, nothing could prepare him for the shock of losing his best friend, DeShaun "Proof" Holton, a few short months later, on April 11, 2006. The thirty-two-year-old rapper was murdered, shot three times at an after-hours club, during a dispute that started over a game of pool.

It is hard to emphasize how important Proof was to Marshall Mathers. He was his best friend, his brother, his muse, his collaborator. He was the rock that Marshall counted on in both his musical and personal life. He was the one who got him into the rap game and the only person he trusted to keep him sane. It had been that way since the day they met. Proof more than encouraged Marshall to rap, he demanded it, the way a wise coach coaxes the personal best from his players. "Proof and Em and I go back all the way to being teenagers," says Denaun Porter, who rapped under the name Kon Artis in D12 and produces under the name Mr. Porter. "All three of us had our own chemistry together and with each other. We are family. Proof did for Em what he did for all of us: he took care of us, encouraged us, he was a leader, a peacemaker, all that.

When we did a D12 show, me and Proof did soundcheck, put the show together, that was all us. When it came to Em, Proof did that for him since the start all the way back to when they was just touring with a DJ. And he continued to make sure the stage and show was all set for Em all the way to the level it is now. That's how much and for how long Proof has had his back."[6]

Marshall wasn't the only rapper in Detroit who benefitted from Proof's selfless devotion to the art form and the scene; he gave all of himself to see that hip-hop and everyone in his orbit did the best they possibly could. Proof was a tireless and omnipresent figure in the Detroit scene. By his own admission, he rarely slept, spending his days and nights in the clubs and studios where rappers known and unknown would congregate. Long before the success of Eminem and the Shady Records family, he organized rap battles and shows and encouraged local talent in every way he could. The first release on his Iron Fist label was called *Hand 2 Hand: Official Mixtape Instruction Manual* and featured MCs who would never have been heard outside Detroit if it weren't for Proof. He also used his fame to encourage local musicians to join the Detroit Federation of Musicians, which could provide them with pension plans and disability insurance.

Proof never bragged about any of his efforts, nor did he boast about his mentoring of Eminem and Obie Trice, though he was a key factor in helping both artists select the instrumental tracks that suited their skills. He was in constant

---

6. Denaun Porter, interview with the author, 2019.

contact with Eminem, each and every day, inspiring him at all hours by texting couplets and rhymed phrases. They had a continuous creative conversation that made each of them better lyricists and artists. In *8 Mile*, Proof's essential role in the Eminem story was represented in two ways. He acted in the film, appearing as the MC who caused Eminem's character, Rabbit, to choke in the very first rap battle scene in the film. But his spirit and, more importantly, significance in Eminem's life was portrayed by Future, the character played by Mekhi Phifer, who organized and refereed the rap battles. Future encourages Rabbit to find his voice, just as Proof did with Marshall Mathers.

Proof was a nimble, witty freestyle MC, with a ferociously curious mind. He loved all styles of music, from Miles Davis to Jimi Hendrix. He was a gifted and giving anomaly—a rapper who cared for art over materialism, who did all he could to bring wealth to others. The easiest way to understand Proof is to ponder the fact that he had the skills and smarts to pen chart hits, but on the heels of his multiplatinum success with D12 and his association with Eminem, for his major-label solo studio debut, he chose to release *Searching for Jerry Garcia* (2005), an introspective record inspired by the philosophy of the Grateful Dead front man.

DeShaun Holton's father was in the music industry, producing records for acts including Tower of Power. In interviews, Proof said that and little else about his father, alleging that both he and his mother were very involved in drugs. Proof attended the private Gesu Catholic School before enrolling in Osborn High School on Detroit's east side. He formed his first rap group, the 5 Ela with his friends Thyme and Mudd, then the influential Goon Squad, which featured Stylz, Trick Trick, and DJ OC. Proof's greatest legacy, however, was the role he played at designer Maurice Malone's Hip Hop Shop, where he MC'd freestyle sessions on Saturday afternoons. Local and national talent from the Notorious B.I.G. to Redman and Method Man passed through to sling verses with the finest players in Detroit's underground. Proof was the consummate diplomat, a friend to everyone, the type of character who fit into all manner of scenes. He was also the only one who saw potential in the rhymes of a smart-ass white kid named Marshall. Proof didn't care about the color of his skin—he saw a diamond in the rough—and taught Mathers to hone his observations and tighten his phrasing. In so doing, he prepared him for battle. He then began sneaking him into the Osborn High School cafeteria to battle rap at lunch hour.

Proof was the kind of person who was always looking out for others. As Mudd of 5 Ela recalled at his funeral, "He was my big brother, he taught me how to rap, how to talk to the ladies, he taught me to kick game. This is who he was: when my first child was about to be born, I was telling him one day how worried I was about providing for my family. The very next day, without a word, he dropped off a huge bag full of all his family's old baby clothes."[7]

Proof's murder was not a cut-and-dried affair by any means. The initial police reports, most of which were immediately disseminated to the press, portrayed Proof as a thug rapper

---

7. Mudd, interview with the author, 2006.

who killed a war hero. They alleged that he started the fight, then pulled a gun, shot first, and was then shot by the club's bouncer, who also happened to be the cousin of the man Proof allegedly shot.

The CCC Club was a stout red building with a gray roof, a thick gray steel door, and no windows. It was located on a barren corner of 8 Mile Road across from a giant yellow Mega Pawn store. In 2006, 8 Mile still marked the border between the city and the suburbs, between the haves and have-nots, between black and white. The CCC Club was on the black, city side and had been a hotbed of crime and violence since 1996. "Since that year, there have been eighteen incidents in the club that have resulted in police reports," said deputy chief James Tate, spokesman for the Detroit Police Department, the next day. "These incidents range from a fight to a stolen vehicle and one raid."[8] In 2005 alone, a total of 337 violations were issued at the club, resulting in twelve felony arrests, sixty-eight towed vehicles, and twenty-four confiscated firearms. A few months earlier, in February, a bouncer was shot twice in the torso. "We've been trying to get the place shut down as of late," Tate said. "All we can do is issue tickets. The courts decide the rest. When you have a location that is a magnet for trouble, we do what we can to see the situation resolved. When you have owners operating illegally, they're setting the tone for whatever occurs from that point on."[9]

8. Anthony Bozza, "Proof Positive," *Guardian*, May 21, 2006, https://www.theguardian.com/music/2006/may/21/popandrock.eminem.

9. Bozza, "Proof Positive."

Proof arrived at the club with a group of friends after an evening of bar-hopping to play some pool before calling it a night. He got into an argument with Keith Bender Jr., a thirty-five-year-old Desert Storm veteran who had recently returned from duty. According to the police report, the two got into an altercation, attracting the attention of Bender's cousin, the club's bouncer, Mario Etheridge. Within a few minutes, both Bender and Proof were fatally shot—a bullet to Bender's face took his life eight days later (the same morning Proof was buried), while Proof was killed instantly by two shots to his back and one to his head. Further details indicated that Proof pistol-whipped Bender, then shot him in the face, at which point, while Proof stood over Bender threatening to shoot him again, Etheridge shot Proof three times.

Etheridge then drove Bender to the hospital without revealing his identity, phoned the police en route to report a shooting at the club, but then avoided detectives for several days thereafter. As the investigation slowly drew closer to him, he turned himself in with his lawyer present and gave testimony similar to what, by then, local papers had gleaned from the police report. The general consensus in the wider media was that this was just one more example of senseless hip-hop violence perpetrated by a thug rapper.

Nowhere was it reported that, as some witnesses claimed, the fight that ensued in the bar involved a number of men, not just Proof and Bender, nor was it reported that others at the scene claimed to have seen guns fired by several people. The police initially reported that Proof brandished a gun that was licensed to him, and initially Etheridge was not charged

with murder. Instead, he faced two counts of possessing
and discharging a weapon without a license. In a preliminary
hearing, he pleaded not guilty to the charges, because in
Michigan, if an individual fatally shoots someone while coming
to the defense of another, it is not considered murder or
manslaughter.

Sixteen days after the incident, the Detroit police changed
their tune. They announced that Proof did not enter the CCC
Club with a firearm. They also stated that Etheridge did not
arrive with a pistol either, but rather grabbed a gun during
the ensuing brawl. Though this version is closer to the truth,
according to H. Mack, a very close childhood friend of Proof,
it's not quite right. Mack was near enough to the action that
night to be shot in the hand by a stray bullet and treated at
the same hospital where Proof was pronounced dead. "It was
fucked up," Mack said. "The fight wasn't just the two of them,
everyone in the club was involved. Guns started going off.
P hit the guy, and then his cousin Etheridge fired shots into
the ceiling. I do not believe P shot the man—he'd never shoot
nobody unless they fired first. That's who he was. Yeah, they
were fighting over some bullshit but he would never, ever
shoot someone over some bullshit. It was all just fucked up."[10]

Another witness who was at the CCC and asked to remain
anonymous when I covered these events for the *Guardian*
echoed this far more chaotic version of events. "Once
Etheridge started shooting in the air, we all got down on the
floor behind the pool table," he said. "We were just trying to

10. Bozza, "Proof Positive."

get out of there, but Proof and Bender started fighting again."[11] He told me that the club was cleared while Proof's lifeless body lay on the floor, then, a few minutes later, well before the authorities arrived, it was deposited outside the club's back door, with his money and jewelry gone.

Over the next weeks and months, Proof's estate was sued by the family of Keith Bender following Bender's death, and both sides continued to debate who shot first and where the guns used to kill both men had come from. Etheridge's lawyer claimed that the bouncer took someone else's gun and used it to defend Bender, while Wayne County prosecutor Kym Worthy told reporters that witnesses saw Etheridge in possession of two guns and confirmed that he shot into the ceiling with one of them in an attempt to stop the fight between Proof and Bender before turning the gun on Proof. In May, the CCC Club was ordered closed for a year by the Wayne County prosecutor, which required the installation of new locks by the owners, who then turned the keys over to the prosecutor's office. The club never reopened and was eventually sold and turned into a clothing store.

In the end, a jury decided that Mario Etheridge acted in lawful defense of his cousin and was not charged with murder, only weapons violations, which carried a possible sentence of nine years. In September, after a three-day trial, Etheridge was found guilty on two weapons charges after a number of conflicting witness accounts were heard in court. The judge told the jury that Etheridge was involved in two incidents

11. Bozza, "Proof Positive."

that night: the first being the shots he fired into the ceiling, and the second being the shots he fired in defense of Bender, which killed Proof. For these two actions, he was convicted of carrying a concealed weapon and discharging a firearm in a dwelling or occupied structure. A month later, on October 17, Etheridge, who had no prior convictions and had been in jail since the April 11 incident, was sentenced to time served, given a $2,000 fine, and set free.

Proof's funeral was every bit the send-off the Detroit legend deserved. The wake was held at the Fellowship Chapel on West Outer Drive, where four thousand fans passed through the doors to pay their respects on April 18, a week after his death. They arrived early, beginning at about 8:00 a.m., and those who didn't manage to get inside were sent home twelve hours later, as the stream of human traffic never stopped. Proof was laid out in a twenty-four-carat gold-plated casket fit for a king, dressed in a beige suit, a matching Kangol cap, and a pair of brown Seamless Edition Air Force Ones. A Detroit Pistons jersey, signed by his friends and fans on the team, was draped over his body. Floral tributes lined the room: one spelled out the word "Daddy"; another was fashioned into a large orange *P*; another read "8 Mile" in red roses, next to another in the shape of a white heart with a golden ribbon emblazoned with the motto "Spice of Life."

A four-hour-long memorial was held the next day in the chapel that seated two thousand, with loudspeakers placed outside for the throng that had filled the parking lot to the point of overflow. Proof's blood and rap family sat in the front rows: Dr. Dre, Xzibit, Lloyd Banks and Young Buck of G-Unit,

Treach and Vinnie of Naughty by Nature, as well as D12 and local luminaries like members of Slum Village, 5 Ela, Goon Sqwad, Promatic, and more. Eminem sat between his manager, Paul Rosenberg, and 50 Cent in the second row just behind Proof's mother, wife, aunts, children, and cousins. The loss visibly weighed on him. Wearing a black suit and a black T-shirt featuring Proof's likeness, he moved slowly, hunched over, a shadow of his usual self. He repeatedly embraced members of Proof's family—his wife, Sharonda; mother, Sherallene; and grandmother Myra—crying with them, hugging them, and rocking back and forth, racked with sorrow. He had lost the best friend he'd ever known, the only person who had stood by him since his teens, his right-hand man, both on stage and off.

A number of Proof's associates gave heartfelt tributes, and when it came to his turn, Eminem took to the proscenium, looking shell-shocked, as if he'd never addressed a crowd of people before, or never dreamed he'd be doing so for the reason he was that day. "Without Proof, there would be a Marshall Mathers, but there would be no Eminem, there would not be a D12, and there would not be a Slim Shady," he said. "This is the man I knew: he came to me one day when I was living in my house on the east side and threw a pair of shoes at me. 'Put 'em on,' he said. I said, 'Why?' 'Because I'm tired of you wearing those same dirty-ass shoes.'"[12]

D12 member Obie Trice, who had himself been a victim of gun violence on New Year's Eve while driving home from

---

12. Bozza, "Proof Positive."

a party, resulting in a bullet permanently lodged in his skull, paid his respects while calling for an end to the gun violence that had plagued Detroit for years. "I want to talk to the black men in here," he said, choking back tears. "We been comin' up in this struggle and we killin' each other. Yeah I know—you 'hood, you gangsta. We all from the 'hood. Detroit is the 'hood. We are killing each other dawg, and it's about nothin'. We are leaving our kids, our mamas, our grandmamas over nothin'."[13]

Proof's casket was led by a white horse–drawn carriage to Woodlawn Cemetery, a two-hour trip that tied up traffic across town. His final resting place is beautiful, resembling a park more than a collection of gravestones, complete with lush, manicured foliage and a pond populated by ducks and geese. At the grave site, the casket was opened once more for his nearest and dearest to once again bid him goodbye, giving him one last kiss on the cheek or forehead. As he was lowered into the earth, a flock of white doves was released into the sky.

Afterward, confidants gathered at the Good Life Lounge to do what more than a few of them felt Proof would want them to do—have a party in his honor. A huge spread of soul food—barbecue, mashed potatoes, greens, mac and cheese, and biscuits—was laid out, liquor was poured, and old-school hip-hop like Eric B and Rakim and N.W.A boomed from the system. The occasion was grim, but Proof's spirit had once again brought everyone together, and the memories that

13. Bozza, "Proof Positive."

were shared were inspirational. As the night continued and the dance floor eventually filled, D12 songs like "Purple Pills" and Proof's solo work were met with hoots, hollers, and the spraying of beer.

"He gave me my name," Obie Trice said of the slain rapper. "When I met him at the Hip Hop Shop, my name was Obie 1. Proof was about to introduce me and he looked at me for a while and said, 'What's your name? Your real name, no gimmicks.' He introduced me as Obie Trice. He gave me my name. He did all that shit, man. He was the pioneer of Detroit hip hop music."[14]

Mike D, manager of the famed St. Andrew's Hall, immortalized in 8 Mile's rap battle scenes, knew Proof for years and saw how little he was affected by the money and fame he earned with Eminem. He recalled a night not long before Proof's death when the rapper drove up to the club in a new BMW 750—a gift from Eminem. "It was not the kind of car he'd roll in," Mike said. "I was like, 'Nice car.' He threw me the keys and said, 'Take it for a ride. You know I don't care about material shit.' He really didn't, he'd drive anything."[15] Proof's currency and concern was the people he knew. In Detroit he was a ringleader, a social butterfly and Peter Pan rolled into one: on any given night, going from place to place, he'd accumulate a posse of twenty or more, hosting a roving party, everyone drawn by his magnetic spirit. "I've never met anyone like him," Mike D said. "He'd be at our club nearly every night that he went out. He didn't care what kind of

14. Bozza, "Proof Positive."
15. Bozza, "Proof Positive."

band was on, he just wanted to see the music. He used to take my entire staff at St. Andrew's out to breakfast if he was still there at closing time. I'm talking thirty, fifty people—all of my employees, the DJ's, everyone."[16]

Proof was Detroit to the core, which is why he didn't think twice about going to the kind of club that other platinum-selling rappers might think twice about stepping into. He didn't see it that way; he was just out and about and wanted to play some late-night pool. He was as authentic as his city: complex, proud, loyal, and confrontational. He was an artist who was consumed with supporting the people and place that weaned him, and ultimately and tragically, a man who was consumed by the same.

Losing that kind of friend, that kind of copilot and creative light in his life, was devastating to Marshall Mathers. It was the last vestige of trust, of socialization, of the part of his past that had worked. Proof was the family Marshall chose, the one person who encouraged him and nurtured him when he needed it. Proof believed in him when no one else did, even Marshall himself. Life had become increasingly isolated for Marshall Mathers. Proof was his anchor, his lifeline. With that tie severed, he was alone and adrift on a sea. And deep inside him, a storm was brewing.

---

16. Bozza, "Proof Positive."

Chapter 3

Everybody Has a Private World

After he got home from his two-week rehab stint in 2005, Eminem was sober for just one more week. He'd done drugs and drunk alcohol recreationally for years, some years more than others, but they'd never gotten the better of him. He'd somehow always managed a balance. Then when his career took off, the pressure of fame, lessons learned from probation and his escapades in court, plus the demands of an international audience awaiting his next move required that he tone it down. He was happy to have finally made it and to be so busy that he didn't have time to get wasted and party the way he did when he had nothing to lose. But there was a devil on his shoulder. Over the years, drugs and booze had filled the void and numbed the pain caused by the trauma in his life, but more than anything, they helped curb the insomnia that had plagued him since he was a teen. An overactive mind is the enemy of sleep, and even without the rap career, the events of Mathers's upbringing and personal life understandably equated to hours of staring at the ceiling.

He had been relying on over-the-counter sleep medication like Tylenol PM for years. He even rapped about it on "If I Had" on *The Slim Shady LP* and regarded it as part of his routine. As his career elevated, so did his lifestyle, and though he has never been the type to amass the flash accoutrements of celebrity life, he did take advantage of something every famous person gains easy access to: better drugs. When faced with the grueling sixteen-hour work days for *8 Mile*, shot at locations an hour or more away from his home, Eminem reached for something cleaner and stronger to make sure he got some rest each night. He procured a prescription for Ambien, which did the trick so well that he kept it up after the movie wrapped, entering a cycle of dependency that continued for several years. Coupled with the painkillers and drinking, he'd strapped himself to a serious chemical merry-go-round. He entered rehab in 2005, at the behest of those close to him, because they had noticed him losing his edge, his focus, and they were worried.

"When I came out of rehab, I was clean for I think three weeks, total. I only stayed in rehab for two weeks because when I went to rehab it felt like everyone else was ready for me to go, but I wasn't ready myself," he confessed on the Dutch hip-hop show *101Barz* in 2009. "So I stayed for two weeks. I detoxed, I tried to work the program, but everything they were saying, in the back of my mind, I knew, man, that once I got out of there, I was going right back to what I was doing. There was like a little devil up in there telling me that's what was going to happen. After maybe a week home, I started taking Vicodin again. I think at that point in time I still thought, 'I can juggle this, I can do this, I can take it, you know, today. And maybe tomorrow I won't.'"

When it comes to substances, 40–80 percent of those who go to rehab will relapse within a year, with addiction to opiates, nicotine, and alcohol having the highest rates of relapse.[1] Eminem was one of them. "Statistics vary because addiction is not a simple thing. It sometimes takes people one or two times, sometimes more," says Dr. Tina Galordi, a clinical psychologist who has been working with addiction and trauma for twenty years. "It all depends on how entrenched they are in it. It depends on the reasons why somebody is addicted in the first place. Some people have a genetic disposition; some people have just been doing it for long enough that brain changes happen. They have been living in those patterns for so long that they are reinforced and it's much harder to stop because they become part of their belief systems and part of their identity. This is changing, but one of my big issues with the music industry is that it's so much a part of the whole rock star identity."[2]

"My routine was Ambien at first, but then Valium or anything else to get me to sleep, and then basically Vicodin to get me through my day, or whatever," he told me in 2009. "When I went to rehab I wasn't ready to go, so when I came out, I relapsed pretty much right away, within a week. I was still writing and trying to do my producer thing, but when

1. "The Truth about Relapse Rates and Addiction Recovery," Beach House Rehab Center, January 4, 2017, https://www.beachhouserehabcenter.com/the-truth-about-relapse-rates-and-addiction-recovery.
2. Tina Galordi, interview with the author, 2019.

I was sitting in rehab, that's when I canceled the last leg of Anger Management. I canceled in Europe, and I was feeling pretty shitty about having to do that. And I reflected on that in rehab, and I didn't like myself for that. I just needed to pull back from the spotlight. You could blame the drug problem on genetics, you could blame it on my career and the way it took off, or you could just blame it on me. My career certainly played a hand in my drug use and how bad it actually got, but it was also my own doing. I felt that I needed to pull back from the spotlight, but I wasn't going to retire. I felt that I could go and do the producer thing and feel comfortable doing that. I thought I was starting to get good at producing records, so working with artists on my label basically seemed like my way to pull back a little bit."[3]

Eminem threw himself into production, starting around the time of *Encore*, working on tracks for himself and for artists on his label, including members of D12, 50 Cent, Stat Quo, Ca$his, and Akon. He also executive produced *Eminem Presents: The Re-Up*, an album intended to be a Shady Records mixtape featuring the label's signings and raw street-level production values. Em enjoyed being holed up in the studio so much that he spent the better part of two years working on that record, giving it a much too high-end aesthetic for release as a mixtape. Behind the board, Eminem took a huge cue from Dr. Dre, lending Eminem's tracks the bombastic scale typical of his mentor's style. But they had a more claustrophobic quality, suffused with synth strings and

---

3. Eminem, interview with the author, 2009.

plunky keyboards reminiscent of early Wu-Tang. Eminem was developing his own sound but was criticized by some for production and loops that were repetitive and simple. "It's a crew album—of course it sucks. The depressing thing is how much," wrote Robert Christgau in his two-star review in *Rolling Stone*. "The boss's beats tend toward ominous rock-key marches a la 'Mosh' and 'White America,' with gunshots scattered here and there like pepper spray. But not only is this mode less fresh now, Eminem doesn't develop it, and the rhymes don't nearly justify its declamatory pomp."[4]

Eminem is noticeably absent throughout the record, appearing as the lead on just five of a whopping twenty-two tracks. The fact that he was more content to stay behind the board and take the necessary time to draw the album cover himself shows you where his head was at. "Like a neglectful party host, he keeps disappearing, leaving you to have your ear bent by some crashing dullard," wrote Dorian Lynskey in the *Guardian*. "Despite his own talent for psychologically elaborate lyrics, he favors MCs whose emotional range runs the gamut from A to B, or rather guns to hos. They don't even paper over the cracks with charisma a la Snoop Dogg. Listening to plodders such as Stat Quo, Ca$his and Bobby Creekwater, you wonder with a shudder how characterless the rappers he didn't sign must be."[5]

4. Robert Christgau, "Eminem Presents: The Re-Up," *Rolling Stone*, December 28, 2006.
5. Dorian Lynskey, "Eminem Presents the Re-Up," *Guardian*, December 7, 2006, https://www.theguardian.com/music/2006/dec/08/popandrock.urban.

"During the time when we did that album, you have to excuse me, because my memory is a little blotchy from those four years, which is probably understandable looking back on how much I was actually using," Mathers says of the project. "We did that album. You know what it did and how it came out. I was getting content with that process. But I was still recording songs for myself. I never stopped doing that, the problem was that I got writer's block for the first time in my life."[6]

This issue started after *Encore*, and Mathers feels that there truly was a degree of burnout after taking his triple persona of Slim/Marshall/Eminem as far as he felt it could go. But the drugs certainly had a lot to do with it too. "If a creative person has an overly critical inner voice, they often turn to a substance, an anti-anxiety medication or a drink for example, to silence that critical voice enough so that they can get into the flow of their creativity," says Dr. Galordi. "If they don't have any other ways to get rid of that part or to not believe that part of themselves without substances, trying to be creative when that block is there is going to be really challenging." At this point, Eminem's drug use had increased so much that he had done more than silence his inner critical voice; he'd essentially begun to silence his creative voice as well.

Jumping into production allowed Em to remain creative and feel productive without facing the deeper issues that were impeding his natural gift for wordplay. "It was a combination of the writer's block and me being lazy, because I

---

6. Anthony Bozza, "Being Eminem," *Guardian*, May 16, 2009, https://www.the guardian.com/music/2009/may/17/eminem-urban-music-relapse.

just didn't want to write rhymes anymore. I didn't want to sit down and write them out and work on them the way I always had, so instead I started to do the Jay-Z thing and go in and freestyle off the top of my head. That's how Obie Trice does it too. He's great at that. He will have a line and he will say, 'Okay, I want to lay this,' and then he will stop the tape and do it again. That's what I started to get into."

Looking back now, he enjoyed rapping off the cuff but realizes that his greatest verses have always been the product of studied practice and revision, of tightening a concept and interlacing multiple rhyme patterns to create a tapestry of language. "Freestyling like that took a lot of pressure off. So it was kind of fun for me to do that, but in the meantime, I was still trying to write and record new songs for myself the way I always had. But the problem was whenever I tried to write anything down, literally I just couldn't write. I couldn't write a rhyme to save my life. I mean I could write them, they just weren't any good. Nothing was up to my standards. I was trying, but I couldn't think, I couldn't get them out. This went on for two or three years."

Marshall Mathers has always been a wordsmith. Starting in eighth grade, he would sit, nightly, with the dictionary, looking for words that appealed to him. He wasn't searching for meanings, just the words themselves. He would write them down; then, as if building a family tree, he would list words that came to mind or that he sought out for the rhyme. From there, he built his couplets and verses and learned to tell stories. The root of Eminem's lyricism is an acrobatic appreciation for the construction of words. Being cut off from something that had been second nature to him for most of his life was akin to losing a limb. "I felt like shit," he says. "There had never been a time when I wasn't writing. When I don't write all the time, like if a couple of weeks go by and I'm not writing, I feel shitty. I have to write constantly, at least making rhymes as little exercises, in order for me to feel like I'm doing something."

The narcotic cocktail of benzodiazepines (Valium), sedatives (Ambien), and opiates (Vicodin) wasn't helping Mathers much either. Taken individually, each one has a number of incapacitating side effects, ranging from paranoid and suicidal ideation to impaired memory and judgment, dizziness, slowed breathing, irregular heartbeat, drowsiness, nausea, lethargy, impaired mental and physical performance, fear, anxiety, moodiness, skin rash, hearing impairment, and muscle pain. Taken in tandem, the downsides are compounded as is the possibility of overdose and accidental death. Eminem's drug diet was a ticking time bomb. "Part of what forms over time is a Jekyll and Hyde situation where a person develops an addict personality that puts the healthy part of them in the background," says Dr. Galordi. "They begin to identify with the addict personality, and it's beyond just using—it's how they begin to think. There is a desire to never feel uncomfortable, which they'll achieve by manipulation, lying to get away with things, whatever it takes to avoid feeling uncomfortable."

"The pills I was taking, they had my mood really fucked up," he says. "It was making me depressed and, you know, it just became a vicious cycle of depression." Feeling creatively bereft and physically numb, he didn't see any way forward for himself as an artist. He had yet to acknowledge that the drugs were an issue. In fact, they had played a significant part in both his creative process and his lyrics. Eminem wrote a good deal of *The Marshall Mathers LP* in Amsterdam, where marijuana was legal and top-notch Ecstasy was easy to score.[7] When they got together in the studio, he and Dr. Dre would sometimes pop Molly before embarking on a marathon recording session. But those drugs are very different than what Eminem had exchanged them for. Depleted serotonin is one thing, and it certainly causes both short- and long-term depression, but that is child's play compared to opiate and benzodiazepine withdrawal.

"As if my drug problem wasn't already bad enough, you know, the Proof thing happened and then it was like . . . son of a bitch, what am I going to do now?" he says. He takes a long pause to collect himself. "I went through a lot when Proof died. It was just . . . really just fucked up, you know? It was the worst thing that could have happened. It was a really fucked-up time in my life. And that happening, it gave me a real excuse. I just thought, 'Well, I have got a legitimate excuse to use drugs now.' Some days I would just lay in bed and take pills and cry."

"I didn't know how bad he was because at the time I had moved to California and was working as a producer," Mr. Porter recalls. "So I wasn't around when the pills were getting bad. But after Proof I moved back home, and I was in a bad way too. I was going through my own thing: I was super overweight, not healthy, I had a heart condition and something

---

7. *Amsterdam* was, in fact, the working title of the album until well into the production process.

wrong with my eyes. I was not taking care of myself. When Proof happened, I got so depressed I didn't work for a couple of years. No desire to make music or do anything. I didn't even want to be here. I wish I'd been in a better space so I could have been there for Marshall. I remember going to see him one day, and he was doing drugs but he was keeping shit from me because he knows I'm a worrywart. I knew he was doing them, but I had no idea of the extent."

Eminem's intake escalated as he spent more and more time out of the public eye, eschewing interviews and public appearances more than ever. He gained a significant amount of weight, and during the few appearances he made to promote *The Re-Up*, he was noticeably out of sorts. On BET's *106 and Park*, on December 4, 2005, performing with 50 Cent, Lloyd Banks, Ca$his, and Tony Yayo, Em was capable on the mic and delivered his verse expertly, but during the ensuing interview, he was a shadow of his normal self. His speech was slow, his eyes vacant, his face puffy, and his answers to simple questions somewhat rambling. In the past, during TV promo tours for his albums, he was always on point and present. Like the greatest class clowns, even when he didn't want to be there, he found a way to make it entertaining.[8] On BET that day and during the other promo stops, 50 Cent wisely picked up the slack, coming to Em's aid whenever he started to drift off

8. A very early spot on MTV's *TRL* shared with Mark Wahlberg comes to mind, back when too much ado was being made of Mathers's skin color. Appearing alongside the man who, as Marky Mark, did much to damage the credibility of white rappers was too much for Em, who couldn't help making the quip, "We'll all just stand together like a happy, fun bunch!" For more on the backstory of that awkward *TRL* moment, see the first book in this series, *Whatever You Say I Am*.

in conversation. At one point on BET, 50 even acknowledged that he was answering for Em, saying, "I'm security," and referencing how hard the past few months' events had been for Em to bear. When the show's hosts, Rocsi and Terrence, tried to press the man himself for an answer, 50 told them that Em was saving all of it for his next album and that they'd have to wait to hear him discuss what he's been going through. It was clear that all was not well. Em's normally alert, keen eyes were slanted and hazy, and he moved slowly, like a drunk man in a pool of warm water. Years later, he watched the appearance and had no recollection of it at all.

"I took more pills and the more I said, 'Fuck it,' and took more pills, the higher my tolerance got; the higher my tolerance got, the more I needed pills in my body just to feel normal, so I wouldn't be sick. It was a vicious cycle." Part of the cycle included eating mostly fast food in an effort to wash the narcotics down with something that would help insulate his stomach lining. "I got up to between 200 and 230, about 80 pounds heavier than I am now. I was going to McDonald's and Taco Bell every day. The kids behind the counter knew me—it wouldn't even faze them. Or I'd just sit up at Denny's or at Big Boy and just eat by myself. It was sad. I got so heavy that people started to not recognize me. I remember being somewhere and overhearing these kids talking. One of them said, 'That's Eminem,' and the other said, 'No, it's not, man—Eminem ain't fat.' I was like, 'Motherfucker.' That's when I knew I was getting heavy."[9]

9. Josh Eells, "Eminem: On the Road Back from Hell," *Rolling Stone*, October 17, 2011, https://www.rollingstone.com/music/music-news/eminem-on-the-road-back-from-hell-249093/.

The already private and elusive MC isolated himself even further by eliminating anyone from his orbit that questioned his health or state of mind, tightening his circle down to its very minimum, where it has remained to this day. "People tried to tell me that I had a problem, and I'd always say 'get that fucking person out of here. I can't believe they said that shit to me. They know nothing about my fucking life. Are they out of their fucking mind?'" he said in the 2013 documentary *How to Make Money Selling Drugs*. "I'm not out there shooting heroin; I'm not out there fuckin', you know, putting coke up my nose; I'm not smoking crack. You're struggling with the argument of do you have a problem or do you not have a problem? Can you control it or can you not? And I literally thought I could control it."[10]

His abuse reached its apex in 2007, when Mathers bought methadone from a dealer in an effort to curb the stomach problems that were beginning to plague him from consuming, by his account, up to thirty Vicodin and forty to sixty Valium per day. "My everyday regimen would be, wake up in the morning and take extra-strength Vicodin. I could never take more than one and a half because it tore up my stomach lining. So I'd take the one and a half and it'd kind of be Vicodin throughout the day. Then, as evening crept up, around 5:00 or 6:00, I'd start with a Valium or two, or three, or four. And every hour on the hour, I'd pop four or five more. The Ambien would put me over the top to go to sleep. Towards

---

10. *How to Make Money Selling Drugs*, dir. by Matthew Cooke, Eminem, Susan Sarandon, "Freeway" Ricky Ross (Tribeca Film and Bert Marcus Productions, 2013), documentary.

the end, I don't think the shit ever put me to sleep for more than two hours . . . two, three times a night, I would get up and take more."[11]

He was told the methadone was just like Vicodin but easier on the liver, a common justification for opiate addicts who switch to heroin, looking to deescalate the devastation to their internal organs caused by pharmaceutical drug abuse. "I thought, 'It looks like Vicodin, it's shaped like Vicodin—fuck it.' I remember taking one in the car on the way home, and thinking, 'Oh, this is great.' Just that rush. I went through them in a couple of days, then went back and got more. But I got a lot more."[12]

For the remainder of that December, Mathers continued to take the methadone he had bought indiscriminately until he was spending most of his days in bed. During one of those layabout marathons, he collapsed in the bathroom, got up, fell again, and was unable to get up. He was rushed to the hospital and woke up in the ICU connected to IVs and monitors. He was told that he had ingested the methadone equivalent of four bags of heroin and that when he was brought in he was about two hours away from dying. "My organs were shutting down, my liver, kidneys, they were going to have to put me on dialysis, they didn't think I was going to make it. My bottom was going to be death," he admitted in *How to Make Money Selling Drugs*.[13]

---

11. Eells, "Eminem: On the Road."
12. Eells, "Eminem: On the Road."
13. *How to Make Money Selling Drugs*.

"It was Christmastime, and I was in the car driving with my dad," Mr. Porter says quietly. "I knew something was going on, because I couldn't get in touch with him, so I called Paul's assistant, and I could tell by her voice that everything was not okay. At that point I was already crying. I was terrified because losing Proof was all I could take. I told my dad I didn't know if I'd be able to carry on if my other best friend was taken from me. Even now talking about it, I'm choked up because he's my best friend and the only person from my childhood that is still my friend. Everyone else is gone in one way or another. I can remember so many times, those were the guys I could be myself with and nothing more than that. He's still the only friend I've got that with. It still bothers me to this day because I wish I'd been there. I didn't know the way it happened but I felt it. I swear to you I got this feeling that something was very wrong that day."

After a week in the hospital, Mathers returned home, but his trouble was far from over. His body ravaged and not thoroughly detoxed, he was weak, listless, and in a fragile state. He accidentally tore the meniscus in one of his knees while napping on a couch. He landed back in the hospital for surgery, and upon his second return home, he had a withdrawal-induced seizure, necessitating a third hospital stay. Despite all these clear signs that he was in dire shape, Mathers was soon using again. "Within a month I had relapsed and shot right back up to the same amount of pills that I was taking. I just remember walking around my house and thinking, every single day, 'I'm gonna fucking die.' I'm looking at my kids and thinking, 'I need to be here for this.'"[14]

"With addicts, realistically the substance becomes their best friend, their lover, the only unconditional relationship they've probably ever known," says Dr. Galordi. "It's hard to tell an addict that they need to stop when they have no skills to deal with that. People logically understand that they'll die if they continue to use, but when the emotional charge is strong enough and that craving high enough, it takes over the logical part of the brain. In that heightened emotional state, the consequences fall away. The logic isn't online when the emotional impulse is there."

Mathers tried going to a few AA meetings but found himself shutting down and not wanting to return when inevitably someone asked for an autograph. Instead he sought out a rehab counselor and began to see him weekly. He also reached out to Elton John, one of the first people he called when he wanted to get clean, who became his sponsor. The two started on a program of weekly check-ins and grew very close. As a fellow musical superstar with nearly thirty years of sobriety under his belt, John was the perfect mentor to help guide Marshall through the myriad adaptations ahead. He began a routine, he started working the steps, and slowly but surely, Mathers began to make real changes. "The hardest thing about getting sober is breaking it down into 'just today,'" Dr. Galordi says. "What you can do just today and learning what triggers you.

---

14. *How to Make Money Selling Drugs.*

It's like learning a new language. They need to look at their trauma, developmental and otherwise, they need to look at how they manage stress, and they have to break situations down to the very micro level of what motivates choice at any given moment so they understand where their motivations are coming from and how to go about making healthy choices for themselves." To combat his natural insomnia and overactive mind, Mathers started running obsessively once his strength returned. He dropped weight and ate better and began gaining pleasure from everyday details of his life that he had ignored or taken for granted during his years in a drug haze. Soon after that, as his mind began to repair, his synapses found new paths to his pleasure receptors as his dopamine and serotonin levels started to even out. Slowly, his mind began to clear. And when it did, the writer's block that had held him down for so long lifted like fog when the sun burns through. "When creative addicts get sober, they have a lot more courage than most people because they are now facing things in themselves that are pretty hardwired," Dr. Galordi says. "All of these inner things, their demons that they've been medicating or pushing down, they're all still there, but now they can't hide from them anymore. It's like being in a nightmare where they've been running away from a monster but now they've made the choice to turn around and face it."

"I came out of all that, the shit that was cluttering my mind, and as I came up out of the haze from the pills and everything, shit started to get clearer," Mathers says. "My mood elevated, my mood changed, and the subjects that I was writing about or had been trying to write about became different.

And somewhere along that timeline, as my mood was getting better, I came up with the concept of *Relapse*. The word, the actual word, just hit me one day. I guess, you know why that might be on my mind, but I wasn't, like, trying to write an album about all that. I'd just been through it; it was all new to me still. But the word just hit me when I was in the car, and it got the wheels turning a little bit."

As Mathers began to write and collect material, he realized there was only one way to know if he'd returned to form. Writing rhymes and sketching song ideas were one thing, but making them a reality in the studio was quite another. He had never been living a completely sober life during any phase of his recording career, and many of his songs—many of his best songs—had actually been recorded under the influence of one thing or another. He was nervous and insecure to try it at all. In an effort to avoid triggers that might cause him to slip into his old ways, he didn't want to record the new material in the home studio where he'd spent too much time high in the past few years. "Everything around us influences us," Dr. Galordi says, "so there is a whole behavioral pattern to break which involves distancing yourself from people who identify a certain way if you no longer want to. It's like breaking a habit. You don't go to a pizza parlor if you're trying to stop eating pizza."

Em was going to need guidance. He was going to need moral support. He was going to need Dr. Dre. "Dre and I had gotten together in the studio five or six times within the past couple of years and literally left the studio with nothing," he recalls. "I was nervous to try again. We planned a trip to get into the studio in Orlando. You know, so when that word hit me, I called Dre and told him about it. This was a couple of weeks before the trip when the word 'relapse' and the beginning of the concept came to me."

Mathers wasn't sure what to expect out of the trip. "I was really nervous about it," he says. "I was just like, 'Oh, man, am I not going to have anything for him again?' I didn't know if I was going out there to try to help him with his record or to try to do mine.[15] It was never really decided what we were going out there to do." Em is the first to admit that at the time he was still far from what he now knows to be himself. And his writing wasn't there either because in relearning a new normal, he was still coming to terms with his creative process. His skills were reduced to limited bits of rhyme that were nowhere close to the complex, long-form narrative style he is known for. "This trip happened when I was pretty new in my sobriety. I was only a few months clean at that point," he says. "But my mood was elevating, everything was starting

---

15. Dr. Dre's *Detox* is the Sasquatch of contemporary hip-hop: clues have been discovered, but its existence has yet to be confirmed. Dre has supposedly been working on it for nearly twenty years, with a number of all-star collaborators like Mary J. Blige, Game, Nas, Jay-Z, Eminem, and Lil Wayne, as well as various Aftermath artists like Eve and protégés who have come and gone on his label, like Bishop Lamont. In 2010, he released three singles, "Under Pressure," featuring Jay-Z, "Kush," and "I Need a Doctor," complete with official music videos and a million-dollar marketing campaign that included billboards in LA to promote the album that never materialized. In 2011, a number of prominent tracks, including "Syllables," featuring Eminem, Jay-Z, Dre, and 50 Cent, were leaked and later revealed to have been recorded for *Detox* in 2007. In 2015, Dre announced that *Detox* was officially shelved because "he didn't like it." However, in January 2018, while visiting the Golden State Warriors practice facility, he hinted at the possibility of a *Detox* release, saying that he was "working on a couple of songs."

to get clearer and I was writing more and more. I told Dre I had been writing songs without beats. I was just kind of like hearing beats in my head, making them up in my mind so I could write. I think I wrote a couple of songs, but they weren't real songs, just loose verses that could have been used for whatever. I was getting back in shape, but what I told him were songs was me basically, in hindsight, doing mind exercises." Ready or not, regardless of what he had on paper, Eminem felt compelled to call Dre. "I was like 'Yo, homie, I think I'm starting to come out of this writer's block,'" he says with an uneasy laugh. "And Dre said, 'All right, that's what I like to hear.'"[16]

When the pair got to Orlando, Eminem was able to dust off his anxiety and insecurity and, with them, the creative cobwebs. His clarity returned, and with Dre at the wheel, the duo slipped back into the comfortable collaborative relationship that has brought the world so many platinum hits. "We stayed in Orlando for around two weeks," Em says, "and we recorded eleven songs, and when we came out of that batch of songs, they kinda felt to me like our stuff on the first two records did. That's what it was feeling like, and when I left, that title—the word 'relapse'—kept playing over and over in my mind. That word as the title for this record was the only thing that made sense."

Of the songs they recorded during that trip, one in particular got him inspired more than any other. "I think the song 'Underground' was the one we recorded that made me say to

---

16. Bozza, "Being Eminem."

myself, 'Fuck it. This is what this album is going to be.' That particular song felt like, *this* is it." "Underground," like "Still Don't Give a Fuck" on *The Slim Shady LP* and "Criminal" on *The Marshall Mathers LP*, follows in a tradition of Eminem ending his albums with a serious show of verbal dexterity and extremity. All three songs also start with the phrase, "A lot of people ask me." Like those songs, "Underground" is a reassertion of just how little Shady gives a fuck, how offensive he can be, and how much he represents Mathers's demons. There are multiple images employed: Shady being brought back from the dead, the underground, after falling and breaking his legs—a metaphor for "falling off." It addresses rehab, gleefully relapsing, and slasher-movie psychos (who are nothing compared to Shady), and it makes ample use of the homophobic and misogynist slurs that distressed so many advocacy groups when he first arrived in 1999.

As is Eminem's trademark style, the intensity of the interlaced rhyme schemes builds and comes to an apex in the third verse, where Eminem characteristically pulls out all the stops:

Straight jacket with a hundred and eight brackets
And a strap that wraps twice around my back
And they lack it; cut your fuckin' head off
And ask where you're headed off to
Get it? Headed off to? Medic, this headache's awful!
This anesthetic's pathetic, so is this diabetic waffle
And his prosthetic arm keeps crushin' my hard taco.

"Dre always says that I climax on the third verse," he says. "I don't intentionally do it; it just comes together that way. Once I get on a subject, I get more in depth by the third verse. By the end of the first verse and once I'm halfway to the second I've locked on to my subject that I'm going to rap about. By the third verse it just gets a little more open. Ideas come in that I don't expect sometimes."

"Underground" might have gotten Em feeling comfortable inhabiting his old clothes, so to speak, but he had his doubts about whether or not this outfit was still in style. "I'd had several conversations with Dre over the years when I wasn't really feeling creative, you know, over the couple of years that went by while I was gone. We would talk and I would ask him, 'What do you think people want?'" he recalls. "That question was even more on my mind because I was hearing all these different things like, 'If Em comes back he needs to reinvent himself. You know, he needs to be a completely different person.' So I talked to Dre about it a lot, and after a while Dre was just like, 'Man, people want to see you, they just want to hear you wile the fuck out again.' I definitely took that into consideration, and then after he'd said it the first, second, third time, it just clicked with me: You know what, he's right, I don't need to reinvent myself, I just need to go back to doing what made me in the first place."

Returning to Detroit after that trip, Mathers worried that his creativity and momentum would remain with Dre back in Florida. "There were a couple of songs that got me feeling that inspiration again, but after the trip was over and I was heading back to Detroit I was anxious, like, 'Oh shit, I'm going back home. I won't be inspired to write. I'm going to need to get out again in order for my mind to expand or whatever.'" That didn't happen—quite the opposite. It was as if the cork had been pulled on his dormant creativity, and now he couldn't stop the flow. "It just never stopped. Once I got sober and got kind of comfortable being sober, man, it was a whole shit storm. There were these thoughts I could not control, and that really made me feel like me again. I was laying down to go to bed and I'd think of three lines and need to get up and write them down so I wouldn't forget them in the morning—that sort of thing. I felt like me again."

"He wasn't relying on substances to be creative, so he had to force himself to do shit," Mr. Porter says. "He'd always been a writer, but it changed. Once it started up for him again, it was like he was addicted to writing more than he'd ever been addicted to anything else. It was all day every day, and I watched it grow. He went through a mourning period and then he went through a healing period, changing everything until he was a new version of himself. I saw him change from using substances to become inspired to becoming the substance that inspired him. That was the biggest step he took."

Em was glad to have one habit back, but he had to ensure that he didn't regain any others. He decided to change his recording environment and production and engineering team for this album, and for good. In 2007, Marshall had purchased Effigy, then a three-year-old, state-of-the-art recording studio in Ferndale, where he rebuilt the control room to his specifications, adding a few extra one-thousand-watt, eighteen-inch subwoofers. With recording technology moving ever further into the digital realm, Effigy is, by anyone's standards, the type of sonic palace that is no longer built from scratch. The design and construction alone, to refit a manufacturing plant, was

$1.5 million, and the gear at least double that.[17] Previously Em had recorded at 54 Sound and then F.B.T. Studios, the facility designed and owned by his longtime collaborators the Bass Brothers, with whom he had done quite a bit of partying through the years, particularly in the early days. Effigy became his new recording headquarters outside his home studio, and when he made the switch, he left the old squad— the Bass Brothers team—behind. "I started working again, but at first I didn't like recording vocals at the new studio. It took me a while to break it in, but once that happened, I was like, 'All right, this is it. I like this better now.' I started doing everything in the new studio."

Aside from the song "Beautiful," which Eminem produced and recorded in 2007, when he was still deep into his drug abuse, the resulting album was produced in its entirety by Dr. Dre, the first time Eminem's mentor had ever done so.[18] "Everything else besides 'Beautiful,' which I produced myself, was made by me and Dre together, but it was more Dre than me. Everything on the album is Dre, which was a relief to me in the sense that I didn't have to worry about the beats. It left me to strictly focus on the writing. That was great for me personally at the time because it took a lot of the stress off me. I could just focus on what I needed to focus on."

Over a period of what was supposed to be two months, Dre and Em holed up at Effigy but got into such a creative

---

17. Brian McCollum, "Ferndale Studios at Epicenter of Detroit's Music Recording Industry," *Detroit Free Press*, January 19, 2014.

18. Dre produced or coproduced six tracks on *The Slim Shady LP*, six tracks on *The Marshall Mathers LP*, two on *The Eminem Show*, and eight on *Encore*.

groove that the sessions lasted on and off for nearly a year. They then moved again to Orlando as the amount of material they were amassing was enough to fill two full-length albums. In keeping with the necessary changes he'd made to his lifestyle, Eminem's creative approach changed too. Rather than nimbly manipulating the flow of his delivery to fuse preexisting songs to a given beat, he opted to select beats from Dre's vast catalog to suit the songs he had already written. Coming off a period when he'd pushed himself to create the track as well, he felt liberated. After all, he was choosing instrumentals from arguably the most coveted unheard library in hiphop. While Marshall worked on the words in an isolated wing of the studio, Dre and his engineers and musicians worked on the music. When the two teams had reached a high-water mark, they would get together, dedicating a day or two to laying vocals on as many songs as they could, their stopping point being when Mathers lost his voice, at which point he'd go back to writing and Dre and Co. would go back to music making.

Relapse marks the start and end of two trends in the evolution of Eminem's delivery and lyricism. Let's first acknowledge that Eminem has never really gone away. Even when he was as far as he could be from the public eye, he continued to record, dropping verses on other artists' records even when he was unsure of what direction his own music would take. During his deepest drug addiction, when he chose to freestyle without preparing lyrics, choosing to record one line at a time, Eminem developed a penchant for accents. They were random, strange amalgams of Indian,

Middle Eastern, Scottish, and Jamaican. They freaked everyone out, because they were so far from anything he had done before that no one was sure if this was a new character(s), a momentary fixation, or a subtext lost to us. It was a way to bend language further, making it expand to ridiculous proportions.

It began on *Encore* with "Ass Like That," which, granted, was a response track to Triumph the Insult Comic Dog and thus deliberately juvenile and overly cartoonish. Still, over a Bollywood-style beat, when Em raps lines like, "The way she moves, she's like a belly-dancer / She's shaking that ass to the new Nelly jams / I think someone's at the door but I don't think I'mma answer," he sounds like the Canadian rapper Snow crossed with the Maharishi.

If you look at Em's delivery on all his major label records before *Encore*, his split persona cast of characters (Slim Shady/Marshall Mathers/Eminem) was more clearly defined. Shady is insane; he's a maniac with a nasal delivery, a split personality inside an antagonist persona. He's the ultimate black-hearted Bugs Bunny. He'll steal your girl, take all your drugs, prank phone call your mom, don a disguise, and get away with it all. Then there's Marshall Mathers, whose delivery is as close as you're going to get to what it's like to have a conversation with the man himself. His cadence is Detroit hip-hop through and through, and his voice is middle of the road as he tells you exactly what it is to be him. And then there's Eminem, the space where the two halves meet, where Marshall Mathers strives to entertain, to be the best songwriter and entertainer he can, and becomes the superhero rapper, the one who speaks to us, the one who inspired us with "Lose Yourself."

These well-defined modes got completely screwed up during Eminem's darkest times. When the writer's block hit, he lost the plot and was unable to write rhymes as any of the three personas he'd skillfully established for himself. He was left staring at a blank page and resorted to making things up, one sentence at a time. The drugs, the drama, all of it landed him in a dire place indeed. The accents were a lazy way to make language work for him, another layer that eschewed grammar, allowing him to bend vowels and consonants to his will.

Eminem's style is one of the most intricate in the history of rap music. Linguistically, he has done it all, but in general he enjoys assonant rhymes, lacing vowels together within sentences surrounded by a different set of rhymed patterns. It allows him options. It is a true language lover's party.

Eminem's accent phase was born of his inability to create lyrics in this vein. If you think about it, given his natural penchant for playing with the sounds of words, it makes complete sense. He wasn't at his best; in fact, he was at his worst. He was the furthest from writing and crafting intricate verses that he had ever been. He was incapable of doing anything but what came to his mind every time he found himself needing to rhyme, and the accents were his way of making it all fall into place. With all meaning stripped away, he was able to simply play word games.

During his lost years, Eminem estimates that he recorded three or four albums' worth of material, none of which he considered good enough to see the light of day. Out of that batch of what could be as many as sixty or more songs, "Beautiful" was the only one he deemed worthy of release. "That's the only one that I actually could listen to and feel like, you know, it took me to a time when I was really depressed and down, but at the same time, it reminded me of that space and reminded me of what never to go back to. There is a lot of honesty in that song, so I didn't want to just throw it away. The first verse and half of the second verse I actually started writing when I was in rehab, going through detox. I didn't have a beat, only one in my head, so I wrote the first verse and I knew I wanted it to be a bounce style or whatever. I wrote the first verse in rehab and finished it when I got out—after I'd relapsed and gone right back to taking pills."

The song is a stand-out moment on the record, and it's the only one that wasn't recorded sober. There's an honesty to it, a sadness to it, and a theme that recalls "Rock Bottom" from *The Slim Shady LP* and the most intimate moments on *Infinite*. "If you listen to that song and how it starts off, I'm just so fucking depressed," he says. "I remember exactly where I was, sitting on the edge of that bed in detox, and I wasn't fully going through with it. Obviously they give you the medicine to make it easier on you, and I wrote that in the first two days. I remember the feeling like it was yesterday. I didn't even know if I wanted a career anymore because the shit I was going through was too much. Just like, 'This right now is not worth it.' That song is a little time capsule."

It is important to remember that Eminem's life, as much as he's made it fodder for songs, still isn't entirely public. The fact that he'd made this record at all after going through rehabs and relapses and surviving a rough childhood is something that shouldn't be ignored. Just because he became the biggest artist in the world doesn't mean that he wanted to be. He never campaigned to be Bono, and though he's donated money to help the underprivileged, he's honestly done his best to be left alone.[19] The world just hasn't let him. He's become some type of distorted pop star by lampooning other pop stars but has never strived to be anything other than the off-kilter, incredibly gifted artist he's always been. Consider the fact that after his time away, with the music business and pop culture in general waiting to see how he would return, when he organically turned to the least palatable source of inspiration one could imagine, he didn't try to hide it.

"I was watching everything I could on serial killers," he says. "And that came through on this record. I've always been intrigued by them, in the movies, documentaries, all that shit. I kind of went back through my DVDs and went back to watching them, and it sparked something in me. The way a serial killer's mind, the psyche of them, the way they think and plot, it's pretty fucking crazy. I was inspired by that. But not everything came from those documentaries; the shit that came from my mind was scary enough."

Relapse's conceit is a masterful continuation of the multilayered metaphors that make Eminem's oeuvre conceptually erudite even at its basest moments. In his relapse as Em, the

19. Conviron Altatis, "Eminem Keeps His Charity Works Secret, Marshall Mathers Foundation Secretary Says," *International Business Times*, October 28, 2015, https://www.ibtimes.com.au/eminem-keeps-his-charity-works-secret-marshall-mathers-foundation-secretary-says-1478533.

artist, he slips back into his earliest and "worst" form, Slim Shady, which is also a return to form, to what made him a household name in the first place. It signifies a return to the start of the cycle that aided and abetted his drug abuse, the roots of the relapses he had just endured. And like a relapse, which is often fatal, the album sees Shady behaving more violently than ever. In a word, this metaphoric relapse into Shady might kill Marshall. The album is every bit as intricate as the rhyme style and metaphoric interplay that made Eminem famous—that too often was misunderstood.

It was also, deliberately or not, the greatest homage Eminem could ever give to the underground scene that birthed Slim Shady. In a word, *Relapse* is the greatest horrorcore album ever recorded.[20] It is the *Dark Side of the Moon* of the genre, elevating what is a viscerally interesting, metaphorically based aesthetic to something that speaks to so much more than its intended end. *Relapse* is a disturbingly gritty album about drug abuse made by a recently sober person who, at the time, wasn't capable of speaking about what he'd been through in any way other than turning it into something far from his actual reality. It is the sound of a prankster facing his fears by reliving and becoming the absolute worst versions of his impulses. As a major label artist, as the Eminem who had entertained for so long, he needed this return to his musical roots. The album was more horrorcore than he'd ever

---

20. Horrorcore is a genre of hardcore rap that uses slasher film–style hyperviolent scenarios as metaphors to discuss the angst of urban blight, mental illness, and drug abuse. It originated in Houston, Texas, and Detroit, Michigan.

been before. Considering what was expected of him, I respect his decision.

Disappointed critics, who were expecting more of a confessional and thought *Relapse* was retreading old ground, missed the point. He wasn't far off enough from the traumatic events that inspired this record to directly speak of them yet. Although his persona might indicate otherwise, Marshall Mathers is a sensitive man, and he's been carrying heavy bags since well before the world decided that he was the greatest thing since Elvis and sliced bread. He's used rap the way therapists use puppets to get children who have lived through trauma to open up. On *Relapse* he once again turned to Slim Shady, the embodiment of his darkest impulses, to tell the world what he'd lived through, because he wasn't ready to talk about it without a thick artistic filter.

Even so, he did share some honesty in two songs: "Beautiful" and "Deja Vu." Taken together, as they are sequenced on the album, they recount the overdose that nearly claimed his life and the moment that he realized he needed to make a change, even though it took him quite a while to make it a reality. Taken as one, the two songs are chilling—one written when he was sober and the other written when he wasn't; one recounting the gritty reality of what happened and the other a snapshot of someone miserably crippled by his addiction. This is the moment where the facade is stripped away, where Shady is done peacocking, and Marshall, for a moment, is revealed. These two songs are so good that they make the rest of the record, which is strong, seem like horseplay.

"All of it came together in the relapse concept: On this album what if I'm relapsing back to the old me, and I kind of relapse in a rehab facility or something like that, and I kind of just black out and fucking kill everybody? I don't know if I was trying to create a triple meaning for myself with the title, like relapsing literally, going back to the old days, and also relapsing and blacking the fuck out and just killing everyone. I wanted to go in depth a little more than I ever had. I wanted to paint a picture with the story. I wanted you to feel like you're in it. I wanted to make the listener be able to picture what is going on in each song as it progresses."

Relapse is Slim Shady's true encore—*Encore* wasn't. This album is an artist looking over his shoulder, making sense of the recent past that nearly killed him, before he's strong enough to turn around and take a long hard look. Personally, I think he gave his other half the send-off he deserved: Shady had never been given so much rope, and that fiend ran with it.

What Em/Shady/Marshall didn't count on was that while he was away things had changed. His faithful were steadfast, and *Relapse* was the top-selling hip-hop album of the year, as it should have been—it is an amazing Eminem album. But it wasn't the cultural earthquake that the other records were. In fact, the aftershocks had grown less and less with each passing release. The media, those who didn't understand him as Shady, wanted to coddle him as Marshall and idolize him as the entertainer Eminem. They weren't sure what to do with how he'd returned to the party. Once again, opinions were polarized.

> *Relapse* is the latest episode in a soap-opera career that has always mingled confession, melodrama, comedy, horror, media baiting, craftsmanship and tabloid-scale hyperbole on every front.[21]—*New York Times*
>
> If *Relapse* were Eminem in Michael Myers mode, it would be fantastic, but instead he's gone Mike Myers or even Robin Williams, subjecting us to "wacky" accents and a delusional sense that he still has a grip on what's edgy.[22]—*Pitchfork*
>
> The further *Relapse* strays from narrative veracity, the more one suspects his fan base feels he's tapping into his bottomless well for horror-show grandstanding.[23]—*Slant*

"Horror-core songs are so outrageous, they're impossible to mistake for acts of advocacy. No one will think Eminem plans to lynch Lindsay Lohan with 66 inches of extension cord in 'Same Song & Dance.' But please, all those 'inch' sounds don't make this witless fantasy as interesting—never mind laughworthy—as any of Eminem's songs on his previous albums."[24]

This period marks another change in Eminem's evolution. He would never admit it, but this was the first time that the opinions of his fans and critics affected him and tempered his

21. Jon Parales, "Get Clean, Come Back: Eminem's Return," *New York Times*, May 21, 2009, https://www.nytimes.com/2009/05/24/arts/music/24pare.html.
22. Ian Cohen, "Eminem, Relapse," *Pitchfork*, May 19, 2009, https://pitchfork.com /reviews/albums/13034-relapse/.
23. Eric Henderson, "Review: Eminem, *Relapse*," *Slant*, May 15, 2009.
24. Robert Christgau, "Eminem: A 'Relapse' of Horror?" *All Things Considered*, NPR, May 20, 2009.

decisions when it came to releasing new music. The intent, as per Em and Interscope, was to release the remainder of the songs he'd recorded with Dre as *Relapse 2* the next year. When the album didn't connect the way he hoped it would, he opted to repackage seven songs and remix the rest of the album to be released as *Relapse: Refill*. The songs that stood out, that signaled an aesthetic change in style for Em, would become *Recovery*, which was an altogether different vision by a fully reborn artist.

"*Relapse* was like *The Slim Shady LP*; it was him and Dre connecting and was the last time Dre was in there heavy like that, start to finish," Mr. Porter says. "I was there, and it was the most amazing experience. To see those two work is the most inspiring thing I've ever been around. 50 came in too; it was just an incredible project to be around."

Regardless of what anyone said about *Relapse*, the truth lay in the sales. It debuted at number one in the United States, selling more than half a million copies in its first week, while logging in as a top seller across Europe and Canada. Globally, it was the best-selling rap album of 2009. This was the start of yet another trend in the history of Eminem, one that would become a dominant theme over the next ten years: he didn't need music journalists' approval or that of his most judgmental fans to top the sales charts. His popularity was (and is, as of March 2019) so widespread that he could release an album that topped the charts without the approval of the critics or, if critics are to be believed, a fair share of his fans. It was a shift back to what he'd thought he'd left behind: a peanut gallery of naysayers and a core group of those who believed. That core had multiplied and remained faithful. But hip-hop and the world as he knew it had become something different altogether.

Chapter 4

Shady's Kids: A History of White Rap

Before going any further, it is important to take a moment to better understand the musical climate into which Eminem resurfaced following his hiatus. Pop music and hip-hop in particular evolves quickly, with the average rapper being lucky to enjoy a career that spans a few years, half a decade at best. Tastes and styles change, and only the select few, those true artists who are able to establish themselves well enough at the highest level, can avoid being left behind the times. With the onset of singles-driven and now streams-driven music consumption, artists in hip-hop and pop are more disposable than ever as the vast quantity of available options has made fickle fans of the general public. Above and beyond the music itself, today's artists must do more to remain relevant to their audience, whether that means releasing less music more frequently, touring more often, or engaging directly with their fans via a social media network. During Eminem's hiatus, these trends and shifts, particularly in hip-hop, transformed the culture in several key ways, so that the public he returned to had different tastes than the one he had left a few years earlier. He literally had to find a new place for himself, in a climate and culture that he was elemental in altering.

It is a fair and safe argument to say that white rap did not properly exist as a bona fide commercially viable genre before Marshall Mathers. There were white rappers and plenty of white people in hip-hop, but before him, the concept of a white rapper with a white origin story, rapping about the trials and tribulations of being white in America, was at best a beautiful anomaly and at worst an insulting appropriation of the most important cultural identity in modern African American history. Before Eminem, when white rap connected commercially, it was rarely credible or authentic. He achieved the Holy Grail of platinum-selling records and unanimous respect from the taste-makers and gatekeepers of a fiercely protected and revered African American culture. In the post-Eminem musical landscape, however, these mores and a sense of integrity are being obfuscated by a generation of artists and consumers who choose, as it suits their needs, to disingenuously employ or altogether sidestep the racial implications of being white in hip-hop.

Technically, the first number one song to feature rapping was by an entirely white group. The year was 1981, the song was "Rapture," the group was Blondie, and the "rapper," who is really a singer, was Debbie Harry. The first proper white rap group of consequence was the Beastie Boys, who were signed to Def Jam Records in 1984 by Rick Rubin and Russell Simmons alongside future icons LL Cool J and Run-DMC, all while the pair were still running the label out of Rubin's

New York University (NYU) dorm room in Greenwich Village. The Beasties were a hardcore punk band who played downtown New York clubs, opening for acts like Bad Brains, the Dead Kennedys, and the Misfits, but they recorded a song called "Cooky Puss," based on a prank phone call to a Carvel Ice Cream store, featuring samples and rapping. It became a hit in New York underground dance clubs and inspired the band to incorporate rap into their act. They decided to include a DJ in their live sets and found a willing NYU student named Rick Rubin. The rest, as they say, is history. The band dropped their instruments and became a three-man rap group, Rubin signed them to his label, began producing their records, and a few years later, in 1986, the Beastie Boys' *License to Ill* became the first number one album in hip-hop history. Once again, charting rap had a white face.

There would be no other artistically worthy white rap group until Def Jam signed and released 3rd Bass's *The Cactus Album* in 1989. MC Serch and Pete Nice released only two albums (1991's grossly overlooked *Derelicts of Dialect* was equally fantastic), but they were hip-hop through and through, much more so than their white label mates, the Beastie Boys. Pete Nice majored in English at Columbia University and hosted a hip-hop show on the student radio station, while Serch performed at clubs and block parties, and the two were brought together by record producer Sam Sever, who, along with hip-hop heavyweights Prince Paul and the Bomb Squad, produced their debut album. In the early days, the Beasties reveled in shock tactics and controversy, like the inflatable penis featured in their stage show, and often incited the audience, going so far as to cause a riot at the Royal Court Theatre in Liverpool, England, in 1987. These antics suited their hardcore punk origins because, at the time, rap and the lifestyle that went with it were, for white kids from Manhattan, a more outrageous stance than punk rock. On the other hand, the members of 3rd Bass, like Eminem later, concerned themselves with establishing their credibility and roasting artists like MC Hammer and Vanilla Ice, who they correctly believed were selling out hip-hop culture.

3rd Bass and the Beasties were the beautiful anomalies, each worthy and significant in their own way. They were followed by a long, strange trip of cultural appropriation for commercial gain, beginning with Vanilla Ice in 1990. A Dallas-born, South Florida–bred entertainer and motocross competitor named Robert Van Winkle, Ice was the first to give white rap a bad name. His dance moves were good, and his skills weren't terrible by the standards of the 1980s (I'd say he was marginally better than MC Hammer), but lyrically Ice was as corny as they come, with a rhythmically stiff delivery that was whiter than ivory. It didn't help matters that his album *To the Extreme*, which spent sixteen weeks at the top of the *Billboard* album charts and sold fifteen million copies, was the type of diluted, benign hip-hop that newcomers to the music, and white middle-class Americans, could easily dance to. Winkle had written the lyrics to his biggest hit, "Ice Ice Baby," when he was sixteen, which is the only original thing about it: the musical hook was lifted from "Under Pressure," by Queen and David Bowie, without credit or permission, and in keeping with the cultural appropriation of his act, the chorus was swiped from the signature chant of the African American fraternity Alpha Phi Alpha. With a style that was, as he asserted, "like a chemical spill," Ice did damage. The only irony to this story is that Vanilla Ice's whitefacing of black music allegedly funded Death Row, one of the most notorious rap labels of all time. After several threatening "meetings," one of them on the balcony of an upper-floor room of the Bel Age Hotel in Los Angeles, Ice signed over $4 million of royalties from "Ice Ice Baby" to Suge Knight and his associate Mario "Chocolate" Johnson, who had done some production work on the track.

The least ironic aspect of Vanilla Ice's story and legacy is how he has continued to resurface in the public eye, never gone long enough, and each time "reinvented." He grew dreadlocks and became a Rastafarian, but after a failed follow-up album, a drug-binge period, and a failed suicide attempt, he switched gears and quit music. He then moved back to Florida from LA to pursue competitive Jet Ski racing, and in 1995 he was ranked number six in the world. He then got a real estate license, took up house-flipping, and joined a grunge band called Pickin Scabz. After a lackluster attempt at a raprock career, he has spent the 2000s doing reality TV on the HGTV network and anywhere else that will have him. These regular reappearances have continued Ice's aforementioned damage when it comes to white rap credibility.

Back in the pre-Eminem 1990s, Ice's emergence was followed in 1991 by Marky Mark and the Funky Bunch and their number one jock jam party anthem "Good Vibrations," which erased any doubt that white men were definitely doing it wrong. To begin with, a few years earlier, actor/underwear model Mark Wahlberg had been convicted of a hate crime for assaulting two Asian men while trying to steal two cases of beer from a convenience store in Boston. Unsurprisingly, Wahlberg has done everything he can to distance himself from that phase of his career.

Lucky for him, one year later in 1992, House of Pain's "Jump Around," which reached number three on the *Billboard* Hot 100 and was produced by DJ Muggs of Cypress Hill, took the crown. Ever since, it has been playing at sports events and frat parties near you. The musicality of the song is legitimate, and both Everlast and Danny Boy are able rappers, but once again, this is a case of white hip-hop artists trying to be something they are not. Despite DJ Lethal being of Latvian descent, House of Pain fancied themselves a group of working-class Irish American thugs far more Southie than any Wahlberg. Everlast and Danny Boy were both born on the East Coast, but they were raised in suburban Los Angeles, so when they began to dive deeper into their Irish heritage on songs like "On Point" from their second album, *Same as It Ever Was*, with lyrics like "Back in the days there were Irish ways / And Irish laws, stand up for the Cause," it all rang a bit false. Nonetheless, their music was a tougher white rap and in this way somewhat truthful: it is, after all, as rowdy, misogynist, and unhinged as a sports bar brawl on St. Patrick's Day in New York City. The song and the group certainly connected with white fans of rap who were ready to see someone other than pretty boys and well-educated Jews representing them. Touring with alternative rock bands at festivals, a savvy move to attract a wider audience (one that Eminem imitated in 1999), House of Pain represented a new chapter. This legacy continued when the band broke up after their third record: DJ Lethal became a member of Limp Bizkit, keeping the frat rock alive, and Everlast became a guitar-strumming rap-acoustic-rock solo artist, who began feuding, circa 2000, with Marshall Mathers via several diss tracks and was soundly served. As of 2010, the two have officially squashed the beef.

As hip-hop evolved and grew, its influence seeped into the fabric of pop culture, and its effect was felt far and wide. During the mid-1990s, via radio and more importantly MTV and BET, it penetrated even further into the middle of the country and around the world. The ground was laid for white rap, (mostly) warts and all, so what happened next was inevitable. Aside from truly gifted, authentic lyricists in the fertile underground scene of the time (more on them later), white musicians at a populist level stopped trying to make it as legitimate rap groups, instead opting to take rap and make it part of what they could easily sell to a broad audience: rock music.

Nowhere was this formula more successful, and for true fans of hip-hop more annoying, than in the nu metal stylings of bands like Korn and Limp Bizkit. At this phase, it was no longer cultural appropriation, it was shared cultural influence, but the roots of the music were lost as it moved from black to white. Hip-hop culture, like every single style of music that has become popular in America, be it blues, jazz, or rock and roll, began as an expression of the marginalized, ethnic, primarily African American voice in America.[1] Hip-hop drew in Hispanics through break dancing and graffiti, but black Americans were at the forefront of developing the music as DJs, rappers, and later promoters, producers, and executives. Hip-hop was a communal voice that told many stories, and as blues and jazz were before it, the music was the message, detailing what it was like to be disenfranchised in a theoretically free country. By the late 1990s, via hip-hop, black artists became a cultural force to be reckoned with, but the takeover was not yet complete.

As an educated white male from a privileged background, I can only theorize as to how it must have felt as rap-centric nu metal overtook the more traditionally rock (and white) grunge scene, because I felt uncomfortable watching white guys like Fred Durst and Jonathan Davis rap. It had little to do with their style or "skills" or the backdrop of distorted guitars and angst. What bothered me most was that they had co-opted an art form associated with a societally disenfranchised voice and selfishly used it to express their disenfranchisement of the soul. It felt like the ultimate appropriation and crime, one equating what this country has done to African Americans on a racial and sociopolitical level to middle-class ennui. It's very different to feel ostracized for being different, what Korn's Jonathan Davis called a "freak on a leash," than it is to be penalized for the color of your skin in a country that

---

1. It is generally accepted that the earliest recorded rock and roll song is Chuck Berry's "Maybelline," which was actually adapted from a Western swing tune called "Ida Red," popularized and recorded by Bob Wills and his Texas Playboys in 1938.

was built upon African slave labor following the murder and displacement of the Native Americans.

That said, you can't blame the nu metal hucksters for giving their audience what they wanted, which was a white face telling a story they could relate to, made edgier by its association with rap, which was still an outlaw medium in mainstream circles at the time. The hip-hop influence was elemental to these bands' success: they were rock and rap, and like House of Pain before them, easy to digest and even easier to listen to while being rebellious out in the suburbs. Back when being offended wasn't grounds for stopping traffic on the freeway, these bands rode a postgrunge wave of aggression and anti–political correctness that arose in tandem with a pop music soundscape dominated by girl and boy groups that were straight out of Disney.[2] It was upon this stage that Marshall Mathers emerged.

Before we talk about how he changed everything, though, let's talk about the one white rap group that cannot be classified as anomaly or embarrassment because they're a bit of both. They're the most polarizing act of all time when it comes to white rap. They are the Insane Clown Posse (ICP) and are more important to understanding Eminem's role in the white rap canon than anyone, including me, would like to admit.

ICP is a Detroit rap group founded in 1989 that has sold, to date, more than six million records in the United States

---

2. Britney Spears, Justin Timberlake, and Christina Aguilera (along with Ryan Gosling) all joined the cast of Disney's *The All-New Mickey Mouse Club* in 1993 and followed similar paths to MTV pop stardom.

and Canada. They wear black-and-white face paint and have a quasi-religious book of Revelation worldview, synthesized from a deck of Tarot cards and a Graffix Bong. They spray their audiences with gallons of Faygo soda and, by existing, say more about the poor white population of the Midwest than any other musical act currently working. They have a fanatical following called the Juggalos and a successful independent record label called Psychopathic, and they have even mounted their own festival, the Gathering of the Juggalos, annually since 2000. They also have a professional wrestling league in which both members participate. ICP and the groups they have developed, produced, and promoted (Esham, Twiztid, MC Breed, Cold 187um, and more) are the voice of the white trailer park population and the kings of a steadfast version of white hip-hop. They have never tried to change their style or message, elevate their skill, or evolve their art with the times in any way. Much the way it goes in hardcore and metal, the more they remain the same, the more devoted their fan base becomes. They are the white version of what hip-hop was intended to be: a liberated, colorful, superhuman expression of righteous frustration by its marginalized creators—one that society could not ignore.

ICP may no longer be poor (according to the often dubious CelebrityNetWorth.com, they are each worth $15 million), but they've never strayed from their roots, and so they've kept their original audience and seen it grow over time. Perhaps their secret to success is that they don't regard themselves as artists with a need to develop, so their devotion to their self-proclaimed religion and its endless themed "cards" that dictate the motifs of their albums are effectively insurance against failing the devoted. Where the changing life circumstances of success have proven a snafu that has derailed many a rapper's career once they've elevated their game from the street to the boardroom, ICP is able to blissfully just continue. Perhaps it's because ICP sees itself as the leader of a congregation, a shepherd to the disenchanted, all of them making their way through this fucked-up world together. Whatever it may be, preaching to the faithful, the band has managed to create a Midwest empire of fans who consume every single ICP or Psychopathic Records release the way independent, artist-run rap labels with strong regional ties, like No Limit, have been doing since the 1990s.

In no way am I saying that Violent J and Shaggy 2 Dope have a place in a conversation about great rappers of any color. But nor am I saying that they should be ignored for their insane-in-the-membrane flow and brazenly low-brow aesthetic. Quite the contrary: the fact that they've unwaveringly remained in a Faygo-coated state that has continued to grow is a reason to pay attention to them, whether you like them or not. They represent a sizable, very real sector of the American public, one that is growing ever larger in Trump's America, and for this, they should be taken very, very seriously. After twenty-five years, the Juggalos are here to stay; in fact, since 2011, the FBI has listed them as a "loosely organized hybrid gang" in their annual intelligence reports alongside criminal operations like the Bloods and Crips. ICP has mounted an unsuccessful years-long legal battle to shake the designation, and in September 2017, the band led a march on the National Mall in Washington, DC, and held a concert afterward to protest the FBI designation. As of this writing, however, the label remains.

ICP is important in Eminem's story, not because they had a ten-year feud that began over a flyer falsely advertising an ICP appearance at an Eminem show in 1997, nor because of the diss tracks each made about the other, nor because the beef was eventually squashed over a friendly game of bowling arranged by Eminem's best friend and copilot, Proof (RIP). ICP is important because even though Eminem doesn't consider them contemporaries or their music true rap (a fair argument), they share more stylistic touchstones and influences than any other Detroit act he's ever been associated with—certainly more than his oft-cited peer Kid Rock.

ICP's metaphoric universe, the Dark Carnival, is a place where the rich oppressors and sexual predators get violently taken out by protagonist monster characters with superhuman sex drives. If their card decks are their Bible, the Dark Carnival is their God. For example, Shaggy 2 Dope told Mitchell Sunderland in *Vice* that the Dark Carnival first came into his life as a voice telling him that they should wear clown face paint.[3] The entire affair is B-level slasher film meets C-level gangsta rap to a backdrop of questionable rock with hip-hop beats. The clowns and the carnival are entirely ICP, but the grisly homicidal imagery is not; it is a continuation of horrorcore,

---

3. "Tears of a Clown: The American Nightmare That Created the Insane Clown Posse," *Vice*, April 29, 2015, https://www.vice.com/en_us/article/avyde5/tears-of-a-clown-insane-clown-posse-find-hope-after-a-life-of-struggle-and-trauma-456.

a style that arose in hip-hop in the 1980s as a reaction to the brutal realities of crack-era life in cities whose infrastructures were decimated with inhabitants living a frightful existence on the edge of utter poverty. It is this style of rap, which is particularly tied to Detroit, that equally inspired ICP and the birth of Slim Shady. Their alternate, bizarro-world take on reality is a reflection of the same poverty, drug abuse, violence, trailer-park dead-end living that Marshall Mathers emerged from. Like African American rap artists have since the dawn of MC culture, both ICP and Mathers created alter egos to express themselves in a larger-than-life fashion. Both rely on shocking, cartoonish imagery to make sense and make light of the intense, intolerable aspects of their feelings. Let me reiterate that Eminem and ICP are *in no way* equals when it comes to musical talent, but they do spring from the same well and mine some of the same territory.

The first group associated with bringing images of the occult, the supernatural, and of paranoid terror into gangsta rap was, of course, black. The 1988 debut album *Making Trouble* from Houston's Get Boys is full of grisly violence for the sake of it, particularly the song "Assassins," which recounts the narrator's detailed, boastful accounts of the women he has murdered for fun. It even ends with a disclaimer that the group is "just buggin," a concession Eminem and so many others have employed after their most offensive verses. The group's initial style was a clone of Run-DMC but later came into its own when Scarface and Willie D replaced founding members the Sire Jukebox, Raheem, and Sir Rap-a-Lot. What remained and what has characterized Scarface's solo work ever since is a penchant for exploring paranoia, mental illness, and other psychologically unsettling themes, all of which are in full effect on the group's biggest hit, 1990's "Mind Playing Tricks on Me."

Horror-film theatrics were a sign of the times in the rap of the 1980s, even reaching the mainstream in 1988, with the release of DJ Jazzy Jeff and the Fresh Prince's "Nightmare on My Street," a song that recounts the narrator's run-in with saber-fingered movie monster Freddie Kruger of *Nightmare on Elm Street*. But it was in Detroit that a sixteen-year-old rapper named Rashaam Attica Smith made horrorcore a viable genre with the release in 1989 of his debut *Boomin' Words from Hell* under the stage name Esham. The blood-soaked violence of his lyrics was inspired by his upbringing in the Seven Mile neighborhood on Detroit's east side, though his musical and rap style were strongly influenced by summers spent on Long Island with his grandparents, where he was exposed to East Coast rap and theatrical metal acts like Ozzy Osbourne and Kiss. Esham's album reflected the danger to be found on every corner in inner-city Detroit in the 1980s, where the city's murder rate topped the nation in 1985, 1986, and 1987. The two most alarming aspects of those facts were the high number of teenagers involved, both as victims and perpetrators, and the reasons for some of the crimes, such as an eighteen-year-old who killed a college student over eighty cents and an ice cream in 1986. "Detroit unfortunately has the reputation as a haven for the deviant and the criminal," Dr. Robert Trojanowicz, director of the School of Criminal

Justice at Michigan State University, told the *New York Times*. "And the bigger the problem gets, the harder it is to solve."[4]

Esham's music embodied—and disembodied—this night-marish reality. When the teenager rapped about Hell, he was talking about his neighborhood, and when he labeled his music "acid rap," it was because he felt like what he saw was as terrifying as a bad LSD trip. Esham still makes music today, and though his music has failed to gain a significant audience outside Michigan, he is considered a pillar of Detroit hip-hop because he was the first Detroit rapper to be nationally known. He also made a case for being entirely independent by establishing Reel Life Productions with his older brother Jimmy to release and distribute his music, exhibiting an entre-preneurial spirit that was a big influence on the Detroit scene as it began to develop.

Esham's legacy in defining the tone of Detroit rap is tre-mendous. Before him, everyone was trying to sound like a rapper from somewhere else rather than reflecting his own reality, one as garishly haunting as a horror film and as real as being caught on the wrong street after dark. The link between Esham and ICP is crystal clear: he appeared on their first record and eventually signed to their label for a time, and then ICP followed his lead when it came to establishing their own distribution network for their music. When it comes to Eminem, Esham was more of a reminder to stay close to home stylistically.

---

4. Isabel Wilkerson, "Urban Homicide Rates in U.S. Up Sharply in 1986," *New York Times*, January 15, 1987, https://www.nytimes.com/1987/01/15/us/urban-homicide-rates-in-us-up-sharply-in-1986.html.

Eminem was not the artist we know when he released his first record, *Infinite*, in 1995. His naturally rhythmic flow and lyrical skill are evident, but the album failed to connect with a large audience in his hometown or anywhere else because, aesthetically, it wasn't authentic. *Infinite* wasn't Eminem; it was Marshall Mathers trying to make a record he thought would be successful. Critics accused him of copying New York rappers Nas and, more specifically, his cohort AZ, and they weren't wrong. No one in Detroit was going to be excited about a local rapper who was trying to sound like he was from Brooklyn. Eminem almost hung it up after *Infinite*, but he went back to the drawing board one last time. After years of not being accepted in the hip-hop scene, of working dead-end jobs and struggling to feed his daughter, of coming up poor, he had nothing to lose. Slim Shady was born, and the rest is history.

Slim Shady was Eminem's vengeful alter ego, righting his wrongs and living out his darkest impulses. Through this alias, Marshall Mathers was also able to be truthful about who he really was, just as monsters in horror films represent an exaggerated but honest mirror of the human condition. Shady is every bit a product of horrorcore and in this way was a more truthful representation of Eminem as a Detroit rapper. Shady connected immediately, and on a larger scale than just Detroit, because the timing was right for Shady's brand of cartoonish violence on the mainstream stage, as this style of rap had been seeping up from the underground for some time. The Gravediggaz, a supergroup featuring RZA of the Wu-Tang Clan, iconic producer Prince Paul, as well as rappers Frukwan and

Poetic, released two critically acclaimed albums, 1994's *6 Feet Deep* and 1997's *The Pick, the Sickle and the Shovel*, which were the most mainstream horrorcore recordings before Eminem's. Def Jam Records even signed and released a horrorcore group, which is arguably the most bizarre and out-of-place listing in their label's catalog: the Flatlinerz and their 1994 album *U.S.A. (Under Satan's Authority)*. The fact that group member Redrum (Jamel Simmons) is label cofounder Russell Simmons's nephew might explain it.

As unlikely as it seems, when Eminem emerged as Slim Shady, via his alter ego, he was more truthful about his real life than he had been while trying to be his real self on *Infinite*. Through horrorcore, he expressed his rage and the desire for transcendence over his hardships and revenge. By creating Slim Shady, someone greater than Marshall Mathers, he also managed to be more authentically hip-hop: despite the violent tone of the message, at the core of his music, Mathers shed light on his story as a disenfranchised, poor white male. The most important thing to remember about Eminem and his legacy, not as a rapper but as a *white* rapper, is this: he achieved the impossible—commercial, popular, and critical success—in a genre that was never intended to be a form of expression for the race that is still the majority viewpoint represented in American culture.

Eminem's extraordinary talent made this possible, but it was his warts-and-all honesty about who he is and where he's from that won him the toughest trophy: true credibility in hip-hop. To achieve it, however, Eminem's skills weren't enough; he needed a cultural cosign by a black hip-hop icon to be taken seriously. That came in the form of his being signed and developed by Dr. Dre, which lifted him out of the white rapper pond in which every single white act aside from the Beastie Boys and 3rd Bass found themselves justifiably floundering.

Eminem's success changed the landscape, opening the door for a number of white rappers to get record deals and national recognition. And those rappers faced similar challenges being accepted as credible by hip-hop media outlets and audiences that weren't predominantly suburban and white. Some of them made some good music along the way, while others capitalized on the growing desire to take rap by white people for white people to its end game: a world entirely apart and deliberately mindful of avoiding black hip-hop culture. Something else has also happened along the way in the forty years since hip-hop's start and the twenty years since Marshall Mathers became a household name. The music industry, and the way music is created, has changed drastically, resulting in a generation of artists who care little for credibility or accountability and many who do everything possible to profit from rap and court the mainstream while demanding they not be held accountable for their choices. In their case, deference has given way to denial and entitlement.

It didn't seem so at the time, but the two biggest white rappers to be signed to major label deals in the immediate wake of Eminem's success have proven to be among the most authentic and least reprehensible while occupying opposite ends of the style spectrum. Houston's Paul Wall signed with

Atlantic Records and released 2005's *The People's Champ*, which debuted at number one on the *Billboard* 200 and sold 176,000 copies in its first week. It would go on to sell more than a million copies. Wall was backed by regional hip-hop cred: he had paid his dues working in the offices of his future label, Swishahouse, a well-respected independent rap label established in 1997, and as a street team member on the northwest side of Houston working for other southern labels like Cash Money and No Limit. Most importantly, though, he launched his career performing alongside his childhood friend Chamillionaire, with whom he released several successful, independently distributed collaborative albums.[5] Wall's second major label album, 2007's *Get Money, Stay True*, made less of a mark but nonetheless debuted at number eight on the *Billboard* 200, selling ninety-two thousand copies in its first week. Both albums featured a number of guest spots, cementing Wall's credibility in spite of his very white, Limp Bizkit–style goatee and flat-brimmed hat. Wall has continued to release albums on and off ever since, though none have scaled the heights of his debut.

Bubba Sparxxx was raised outside LaGrange, Georgia. His father was a school bus driver, and his mother was a grocery store cashier. He first heard rap music on mixtapes that his neighbor, who lived half a mile away, received in the mail from New York City. Inspired by 2 Live Crew, N.W.A, Too Short, and Outkast, he eventually moved to Athens, Georgia, and was discovered rapping after a University of Georgia football

---

5. *Get Ya Mind Correct* (2002) sold more than 350,000 copies with no major label distribution, which promptly drew the attention of said major labels.

game. His first album, *Dark Days, Bright Nights*, caught the attention of Interscope's Jimmy Iovine, who signed him and had the album re-recorded with the assistance of two very credible hip-hop figures: the multifaceted producer/rapper/ songwriter Timbaland and Atlanta production duo Organized Noize. The major label version of Bubba's album debuted at number three on the *Billboard* 200 in October 2001 and sold more than five hundred thousand copies. The album was very well received by critics, most of whom cited his producers' fine work and how well it highlighted Bubba's battered and fried white meat flow. He stood apart and was celebrated for the fact that he was linked to respected black figures, making him worthy of praise, where artists with similar rapping skills and style, like Haystak and Tow Down, were relegated to the novelty bin.

Over the next five years, Bubba released two more critically acclaimed albums, *Deliverance* and *The Charm*, which captured him alternating between more somber material culled from the harsh realities of southern down-on-your-luck living with more upbeat mainstream tracks aimed at a commercial crossover that never really came. He then took a seven-year hiatus, battled drug addiction, eventually got sober, and returned to a very different musical landscape. Bubba's success, along with that of Kid Rock (particularly his 1998 rap-rock chart hit "Cowboy"), inspired a school of white rap that could not be further from the black roots of hip-hop or the role of white rappers within it. It arose in the early 2000s, and looking back now at the endless tide of rappers who have launched their careers on SoundCloud and YouTube, it was an omen of what was to come. The country rappers were also the first to do something that is now common in hip-hop and rap-based music today: they skirted the question of authenticity and the whitewashing of a proudly black genre by circumventing the traditional hip-hop industry in order to sell themselves directly to white consumers. This created a white-dominated alternate world, where the music exists out of context, aware of its roots but dead set on ignoring them.

Sparxxx, like Paul Wall and of course Eminem before them, came from the class of white rappers who understood their role in the genre: one of respect and deference to the black origins of the art form. They had the skills to be in the game, but their credibility was tied to their connections. They were vouched for, their presence justified and celebrated because of their apt rap skills. So long as they remained authentic, these respectful white performers would be allowed to exist in a black man's game.

Country rap, or hick-hop, changed all that, particularly when it became a new spoke in America's most commercially successful music wheel—Nashville, Tennessee. According to a 2013 government study, Nashville's music industry provides $10 billion in annual income and fifty-six thousand jobs, nearly four times the number of music industry jobs as New York or Los Angeles.[6] As the traditional music business began to crumble in the digital distribution age, large management

---

6. "Music Industry Provides $10 Billion Impact on Nashville's Economy Annually," Nashville.gov, July 29, 2013, https://www.nashville.gov/News-Media/News-Arti cle/ID/1914/Music-Industry-Provides-10-Billion-Impact-on-Nashvilles-Economy -Annually.aspx.

firms and record labels either relocated or opened branches in Nashville because contemporary country remained a strong seller, and still is.

Aside from their cultural appropriation, most hick-hop artists have no connection at all to the roots of hip-hop. They exist outside the culture and care little for the acceptance of the black gatekeepers, whose approval they'd never get anyway. Artists like Ryan Upchurch, Moonshine Bandits, Colt Ford, Jawga Boyz, and more have planted a flag squarely in the dusty back roads of rural America, their music buoyed by twanging guitars and good ol' boy party lyrics over hip-hop beats. Many, like Upchurch, are politically conservative, some proudly flying the Confederate flag on stage and in their marketing, while others denounce it, realizing how glaringly inappropriate it is to use a symbol of slavery in a medium created and dominated by African Americans.

This context-free appropriation of hip-hop has gone so far as to see bona fide cowboy hat–wearing, acoustic guitar–strumming Nashville stars releasing tracks featuring black rappers as well as rapping in their own right. Jason Aldean scored a number one hit with "Dirt Road Anthem," a song featuring rapped verses and traditionally sung pop-country choruses. He even released a remix featuring rapper Ludacris, which the duo performed at the 2011 Country Music Television Music Awards. In 2012, Taylor Swift and rapper B.o.B. collaborated on a country rap song called "Both of Us," which is essentially a pop hip-hop track featuring banjos . . . and Taylor Swift. Also in 2012, pop country duo Florida Georgia Line recruited Nelly for a remix of their record-breaking hit

"Cruise."[7] The music video presents a very interesting reality, where Nelly cruises in his Ferrari convertible alongside Florida Georgia Line's pimped-out pickup truck convoy full of cowgirls, everyone singing along to the auto-tuned chorus like one big happy family. It should be noted that this wasn't Nelly's first foray into country music collaborations. If anything, he was ahead of the trend in 2004, when he tapped Nashville superstar Tim McGraw for "Over and Over," a duet that sounds like an attempt at a "Crossroads"-era Bone Thugs-n-Harmony tune . . . with Tim McGraw. "Over and Over" reached number three on the *Billboard* Hot 100.

All this points to a pop culture universe where the racial component—an essential element of hip-hop—has been eradicated like a meddlesome tumor. It makes sense in the country/hick-hop universe, because country music is associated with and tied to folks whose ancestors, in many cases, were slave owners. As much as rap has become a musical genre that has influenced generations who today are far from both institutionalized American slavery and the civil rights movement, the fact remains that it has been, for the past forty years, the essential pop cultural language of black America. It might not be excusable but it sure is understandable that someone in the money-making Nashville music system would be open to incorporating rap into their program to sell more records. In addition, rap music has always proudly

---

7. "Cruise" broke two major sales records in country music. It became the first country song to receive the RIAA Diamond certification, which denotes sales over ten million copies. It also became the best-selling digital country song of all time with more than seven million downloads and twenty-four weeks at number one.

been about the hustle, so it should be no surprise that artists like Nelly, Ludacris, and B.o.B., whose commercial successes outweigh their critical praise, have cashed in big.

There is one noteworthy outlier associated with the country rap genre, one who emerged from the inventible fusion of urban black and rural white southern culture with hip-hop as a common language, and that artist is Yelawolf. Hailing from the small town of Gadsen, Alabama, Michael Wayne Atha is part Cherokee Indian, part white, and entirely southern, bred on country, rock, and gangsta rap, with a musical style that floats freely between them. He sings, he raps, and he is musically astute enough to have produced most of his underrated sophomore album, 2015's *Love Story*, by himself. His first major label release, 2011's *Radioactive*, featured a number of notable guest appearances and was awarded a 4.5 out of 5 mics by *The Source* magazine, ranking it an "instant classic," but *Love Story* was more a showcase of Yelawolf's true southern rap-rock-country sound. The album is a revealing, soulful record that blends his influences into a sound entirely his own. He possesses the ability to write cinematic narrative-based tracks like "Sabrina," from 2017's *Trial by Fire*, low-down gangsta shit like "Pop the Trunk," from 2010's *Trunk Muzik 0-60*, and well-crafted, incendiary anthems like "Best Friend," from *Love Story*, all of them peppered with his nimble, rapid-fire flow. Eminem signed Yelawolf to Shady Records in 2011, which makes complete sense, because Yelawolf is a southern rap version of Em.

In simplest terms, country rappers, starting with Kid Rock way back in 1998, created an alternate universe where it was okay to take from a black genre and market it to white people without fear of repercussion. This has been happening in music since time immemorial, but hip-hop was different; hip-hop was controlled and created—and constantly refreshed—by capable, talented young black artists and entrepreneurs. Whether it was a case of time passing and people getting comfortable or just brazen white privilege rearing its head once again, this was a paradigm shift. It didn't seem to matter, because country rap is nothing true hip-hop fans would ever consider hip-hop. However, it mattered commercially and morally. The country music industry operates in its own world, and in the 2000s, cultural appropriation without consequence became the wave the next crop of white hip-hop artists rode straight to the bank. And they weren't alone. They were merely taking advantage of a generational tone that has undercut the pillars of a culture that has long struggled for its equal space in the American dialogue. That is the real shame, and the change that can't be undone.

There are other white performers who integrate rock into their rap, albeit in a different style, who have also used a direct-to-consumer marketing plan to succeed. Lil Peep, who died of an accidental overdose of Xanax and fentanyl at age twenty-one in 2017, spearheaded a brand of lo-fi emo rap that combined angsty, gloomy lyrics with catchy melodies and music influenced by alternative and emo rock bands like Fallout Boy, Panic at the Disco!, My Chemical Romance, Blink 182, and the Red Hot Chili Peppers (RHCP). Peep's touchstones weren't rappers at all; he wanted to be the next Kurt Cobain, and he idolized Anthony Kiedis of RHCP. He was devoted to music—he got a face tattoo at seventeen to motivate himself to make it his only viable career choice— and wrote openly about his struggles with drugs, depression, and suicidal thoughts. His goal was to give a voice to people who suffer from anxiety and depression and who have been abused, bullied, and misunderstood. Like most rappers who don't fit a mold, Peep gained notoriety online and through the free streaming service SoundCloud.

On the other end of the spectrum is Ohio rapper Machine Gun Kelly (MGK), who was signed to Diddy's Bad Boy Records in 2011 and whose biggest claim to fame was a brief beef with Eminem that began after he tweeted that Eminem's daughter Hailie was "hot as fuck" back in 2012 when she was only sixteen. MGK plays guitar on stage, worships nineties rock, is open about his love for cannabis and psychedelic mushrooms, dresses like he's in a Backstreet Boys revue, and strives for mainstream success. His music has never broken through, and it's telling that to date his most successful song is "Rap Devil," the track he released during his beef with Marshall Mathers. Luckily, rap is MGK's second career: he has proven himself a very endearing and capable actor with a number of credits under his belt, including Netflix's *Birdbox* and the Mötley Crüe biopic *The Dirt*, as well as Cameron Crowe's Showtime series *Roadies*.

Back at the turn of the century, when the music industry still relied on CD sales and traditional profit ratios, a handful of white rappers were snapped up much the way any band from Seattle with the right distortion pedals got a record deal in the wake of the grunge juggernaut that followed Nirvana's success. In fact, it briefly became fashionable for hip-hop collectives to sign and tout their white discoveries. The Wu-Tang Clan signed a Jewish rapper from Staten Island named Remedy, who released his debut, *The Genuine Article*, in 2001. Memphis rap clique Three 6 Mafia signed Lil Wyte and backed his debut *Doubt Me Now*. As Carvell Wallace wrote in a timeline of white rap history for *MTV News* in 2016, in the early 2000s, "'White Dude' supplants 'Mentally Unstable Dude' as clique-based hip-hop's hottest must-have accessory."[8]

That was when credibility and accountability still mattered, because this was a case of respectable black hip-hop collectives essentially buying themselves that season's trendy handbag. At the time, those white guys would mean nothing without their black backers, but that ceased to be the case in the years to come. Credibility hasn't died altogether, of course, but in contrast to the problematic new normal, those who carry the torch have made an authentic artistic choice that some see as quaint and nostalgic. The white rap that came next and that characterizes the current scene can be loosely divided into a few camps: frat rap, lyricists, rock rap, and pop. Perhaps it was inevitable, perhaps it's their fault, or perhaps the artists to arise in the past few years are just symbols of how music fans' palates seem to crave nourishment akin to sugary breakfast cereal—short-lived flavor with no nutritional value. Blame the internet, blame the self-absorbed millennial bubble world that the personal computer, apps, sensitivity, and narcissism

---

8. Wallace Carvell, "A Condensed History of White Rappers," *MTV News*, July 14, 2016, http://www.mtv.com/news/2905399/a-condensed-history-of-white-rappers/.

have wrought, but today credibility and racial accountability are no longer popular. They are in no way a prerequisite for being a performer of any kind, which benefits the majority of white rappers and those who seek to make money from them. Today, all you really need are enough views, likes, and follows on social media to find yourself an audience willing to spend their money on your product. And this, in both the white and nonwhite rap world, has infinitely damaged hip-hop as both a musical genre and a culture.

There are no whiter rappers—because being a white rapper is different than being a white person who raps—than those associated with frat rap, a subgenre whose artists are preoccupied with college, partying, their own corny cleverness, and the banal ennui of a higher-educated middle-class existence. The poster boy for this rush class was undoubtedly Asher Roth. His 2009 debut, *Asleep in the Bread Aisle*, plays like a series of Facebook status updates from the average white college student. Take "Bad Day," a song that recounts the all-too-common challenges of flying coach ("Instead I end up sitting in 27C / An aisle seat, fine by me / But the guy that's inside's always tryin' to pee") in order to attend a friend's wedding in New York City. To his credit, Roth has never been dishonest about exactly who he is and where he's from: he's an upper-middle-class suburban white kid from Pennsylvania who loved college. That's fine, but to his discredit, no one has ever made partying sound so dull. The production is blunted and monotonous, and there is a general lack of wit that his smug self-deprecation and faux sentimentality can't season. Then again, how could it, when his wistful back-in-the-days remembrances are devoted to events that just happened? Everything you need to know about Asher Roth is revealed on his first album when Busta Rhymes faxes in a half-hearted verse on "Lion's Roar" and still outshines him.

Long Island native Hoodie Allen actually is a frat boy, having successfully pledged Alpha Epsilon Pi while attending the University of Pennsylvania, where he graduated with a degree in marketing and finance in 2010. He then took a job at Google while planning his rap career. He made good use of his undergrad degree and job experience in his chosen path, as his music and persona come off like a well-executed pitch meeting. Superficial pop production belies rapped and sung songs full of cliché platitudes about life and girls. His career is a snapshot of internet-bubble culture, one that lives, breathes, and feeds on itself, regardless of history, context, or taste. Allen's success is based on his direct marketing to fans through email and social media; he asks fans to message him which songs they'd like to hear at each upcoming tour stop. It is literally an experience paid for and controlled by the consumer, and what could be more internet than that?

The most egregious of the frat rappers is, without a doubt, Rhode Island native Mike Stud, a former college baseball relief pitcher at Duke University who started recording tracks in GarageBand and putting them online as a joke after he got injured. Stud's 2013 debut *Relief* was ordinary, typical frat rap fare, full of boasts and meat-market come-ons. He has since evolved into an Auto-Tuned fake Drake with a flow as satisfying as a flat Michelob Ultra. He may be a copycat, but he did have an audience large enough that Esquire

TV gave him a reality show, *This Is Mike Stud*, which aired eight episodes back in 2016. The show captured Stud and his team's penchant for binge drinking, womanizing, and playing shows to entirely white audiences. Nowhere in interviews or the many video documents he posts on social media has Stud ever referenced black artists as an influence, aside from wearing an Outkast shirt. His take on his place in hip-hop is that he put a track up online and since people liked it, he figured that meant he was a rapper now. Thanks to the internet and the crowds of white kids who want to see white performers doing black music without a care for racial implications, someone like Stud has been able to market himself directly to his audience outside the major label system by booking tours through regions where the music is connecting. In the past, there used to be a proving ground for artists in clubs, theaters, and venues known for showcasing hip-hop talent, but today white rappers, if they're just popular enough, can mount a national tour without ever coming in contact with audiences that would frown upon (or much worse) their take on hip-hop.

There is a comedic branch of frat rap that takes a satirical/serious approach to the music, thereby circumventing the racial issue in another fashion. Artists like the Lonely Island, three childhood friends who have worked together as a professional comedy troupe since 2001, including a stint at *SNL* as writers and on-air talent, have been lampooning rap and pop to hilarious effect since their breakthrough digital sketch "Lazy Sunday" aired in 2005. Andy Samberg, Akiva Schaffer, and Jorma Taccone make music that, like the best *SNL* skits, is at once hilarious and pointed cultural satire. Take, for example, "Spring Break Anthem" from their 2013 release, *The Wack Album*, which juxtaposes the misogynist, animalistic behavior of spring break culture with the civilized desires of same-sex couples that want nothing more than the right to marriage and a traditional life. Their point is that one is accepted as normal by straight culture, whereas the other is seen as immoral and perverse. In each chorus, a punch-list of testosterone-fueled frat-boy antics to be achieved on spring break is ended with the directive "Marry a man!" to hysterical effect.

At the other end of the spectrum, the advertising industry birthed another white rap product in Lil Dicky, a Philadelphia native who not-so-humorously touts white privilege and latent racism as an artist trope—because you know he's kidding, right? There is self-deprecating comedy in his persona and music, and in interviews he brims with the skin-crawling awkward self-awareness of a desperate stand-up comedian, which makes him generally unpleasant to consume anyway. None of that can excuse his blatantly repugnant stance that being a white guy with a higher education (he's very proud of his 3.03 GPA from University of Richmond), who left that life to struggle as a rapper, is something to be celebrated.[9] As Drew Millard pointed out on *Noisey*: "Though it's easy to write Dicky off as an annoying curio, his message—that upper-middle-class white dudes are underrepresented in society—is a relatable one, namely among the upper-middle-class white

9. Drew Millard, "Lil Dicky Isn't a White Supremacist, He's Just an Asshole," *Noisey*, October 17, 2014.

dudes who have been flocking to his shows." It's hard to believe that a rapper who was included in *XXL* magazine's 2016 freshman class cover story (a long-standing harbinger of successful careers to come) shares the same point of view as those who would be found at a Make America Great Again rally, but those are our times. It's one thing to make fun of yourself as the oddball, the white guy in a black medium, but it's quite another to equate such a privileged white man's burden with the struggle of street life. Having it all and "risking it" is very different than coming from nothing at all because the first scenario comes with a built-in backup plan. Lil Dicky put his résumé on the front of his only album, 2015's *Professional Rapper*, for comedic effect, to illustrate what he was leaving behind to pursue music, but his insistence that this was akin to an outlaw stance if he chose to return to the workforce is idiotic. If he's that dedicated to his craft, he should get a face tattoo like every SoundCloud rapper worth their streams would tell him. He did, after all, tell *Noisey*, "I'm bringing back real hip-hop . . . I wouldn't say it's comedy, I'd say it's rap music. I think it's misguided if you think it's comedy, I think I'm a rapper who's funny."[10]

There is only one artist associated with the frat rap school who is worthy of consideration, and that is the late Mac Miller, who died of heart failure after a lethal overdose of fentanyl, alcohol, and cocaine in September 2018 at age twenty-six. Miller was born in Pittsburgh, Pennsylvania, his mother a Jewish photographer and his father a Christian architect.

---

10. Millard, "Lil Dicky Isn't a White Supremacist."

He was a self-taught musician who could play piano, guitar, drums, and bass before he was a teenager. He started rapping in his early teens, and in high school pursued it like it was his job until, soon enough, it was. After releasing well-received mixtapes as a fifteen- and sixteen-year-old, he was signed by local Philly independent label Rostrum in 2010, sold out a national tour, and saw his first full-length album, *Blue Slide Park*, debut at number one on the *Billboard* 200 in November 2011 when he was just nineteen. The record was the first independent debut to take the top spot on the charts since *Dogg Food* by Tha Dogg Pound in 1995.

Miller has plenty of frat rap party anthems like "Up All Night" and "Frick Park Market" in his repertoire, but even at his most shallow, his musical choices and skilled flow are not. In "Party on Fifth Ave.," Miller sampled the loop from 1987's "The 900 Number" by the 45 King, which sampled a baritone saxophone from Marva Whitney's "Unwind Yourself" from 1968. The same loop was also used on DJ Kool's worldwide hit "Let Me Clear My Throat" in 1996. Considering that he was four years old when that song came out, choosing such a sample, and discussing it reverently in the audio commentary that accompanied the re-release of his album, means that Miller had a sense of hip-hop and his place in it. As his career progressed, he developed a sound of his own, one well beyond the party anthems that made him famous. Driven by his natural abilities and interests as a musician and producer, Miller's music became more introspective and honest, as he spoke openly of his struggles with depression and substance abuse. Miller had a horrorcore-inspired alias named

Delusional Thomas and produced for a variety of artists from SZA to Vince Staples to Lil B under the name Larry Fisherman. He even released an EP as Larry Lovestein and the Velvet Revival, which is a collection of moody and engaging jazz arrangements that sees Miller crooning about love. And he did most of this before the age most people graduate from college.

By the time Mac Miller released his third, fourth, and fifth albums, GO:OD AM (2013), *The Divine Feminine* (2016), and *Swimming* (2018), he had become a bona fide star, aware of his place as a white rapper in the new hip-hop landscape. As he told Brian Hiatt in *Rolling Stone*, "I just see myself as somebody who makes music that happens to be white. In America, race has a huge thing to do with what your experience is. I just try and make music that's for everybody . . . I'm not directing what I'm talking about to one race in particular. That doesn't, like, move who's involved in the discussion . . . I just make music, and I happen to be white. And whoever gives me an ear is more than welcome to be in the conversation."[11] Miller may have been introduced to the world along with the wave of white rappers who sold directly to white college audiences on iTunes circa 2010, but he never wanted that. "I remember touring and doing shows and I was the first rap show ever in all these colleges. Six thousand kids and I'm the first hip hop show because I'm white-college friendly. That was always a demon for me. It was hard to sit here and

---

11. Brian Hiatt, "Mac Miller: The 2016 Rolling Stone Interview," *Rolling Stone*, September 7, 2018, https://www.rollingstone.com/music/music-news/mac-miller-2016-interview-ariana-grande-kendrick-lamar-720847/.

know that because I was a white dude, I was able to sell easier and be more marketable. That wasn't tight to me. I wanted to go through the same shit that everyone else did."[12]

Miller had respect for authenticity, much like a school of white alternative rappers who have maintained their integrity, guarding the inner sanctum of independent hip-hop and playing to a devoted following since the mid-1990s. Alternative hip-hop is a lyrically inclined, musically authentic scene, rooted in the intelligent old school stylings of a Tribe Called Quest, De La Soul, the Pharcyde, the Jungle Brothers, Digable Planets, Arrested Development, Goodie Mob, and Outkast. The music doesn't conform to the stereotypical rap subgenres of gangsta, hardcore, party, or pop rap. It is united by boom-bap beats, loping instrumental loops, and flowing lyrical stories taking precedence over flash and boast aesthetics.

The pillars of this scene are acts like Minneapolis's Atmosphere (Slug, Spawn, and Ant) and their iconic label and hip-hop collective Rhymesayers, as well as El-P and his now defunct but influential Manhattan label Definitive Jux. Another unique group that falls into this category is Eyedea and Abilities, fronted by Eyedea, a skilled freestyle MC from Minneapolis who died in 2010 of an accidental opiate overdose. The group fused rock and electronic music into its tracks, and Eyedea's philosophical and socially conscious point of view embodies the essence of the scene. He also walked the talk: after winning HBO's Blaze Battle in 2000, Eyedea won

12. Matthew Trammel, "What Is the Place for White Rappers Today?" *The Fader*, October 6, 2015, https://www.thefader.com/2015/10/06/white-rappers-mac-miller-vince-staples-interview.

a significant cash prize but could have won more if he opted to sign a contract with Diddy's Bad Boy Records. He declined and instead signed with Rhymesayers. Other notable artists in this school are Sage Francis, RJ-D2, Aesop Rock, Evidence, and Vinnie Paz. These groups are all different, with styles that reflect a wide spectrum of influences, but all are united by a purity of purpose to uphold the soul of hip-hop culture. As hip-hop evolved into forms divergent from its origins, these artists maintained their integrity by insisting on creative and financial independence from mainstream record labels. In so doing, they have carried the torch for a dedicated and sizable audience of all ages from all walks of life.

The most notable recent character of this type to achieve success is Action Bronson, an Albanian Jewish rapper from Queens who began life as a chef and who gained notoriety through an online cooking show called *Action in the Kitchen*. After breaking his leg, he took his musical aspirations more seriously, and after two well-received independent releases, *Dr. Lecter* and *Well Done*, Bronson was signed by Eminem's manager, Paul Rosenberg, in 2012. Bronson was featured in *XXL*'s 2013 freshman class, had a very popular show on Viceland TV called *Fuck, That's Delicious*, and has gone on to release three well-received albums, the latest being 2018's *White Bronco*. Bronson's use of food metaphors and obscure allusions to sports teams and athletes has garnered him a large and diverse following.

The racial issue of being a white performer in hip-hop has played out in an interesting and troubling manner in the pop music world, where artists have either avoided the issue by any means necessary, made it so much their own that it has taken center stage, or allowed it to derail their success. That is what happened to Iggy Azalea, an Australian rapper and pop singer who came under fire for her cultural appropriation and the blatantly offensive comments she casually tweeted about people of color before she was famous. Azalea moved to the United States from Australia in 2006 to pursue a career in music, landing in Los Angeles and eventually Atlanta, Georgia, where she picked up a southern accent that she utilizes in her rapping. She was the perfect pop product: a blonde, sexy Barbie type who sang and also rapped like she'd grown up in Atlanta. Her debut album, 2014's *The New Classic*, received mixed reviews, but her single "Fancy" reached the top of the *Billboard* Hot 100. The same week, Ariana Grande's "Problem" featuring Azalea reached number two, a technicality that granted Azalea the unwarranted achievement of being the only act besides the Beatles to have their first two entries in the top one hundred land at number one and number two simultaneously.

Azalea went on to great commercial success but was stubbornly defensive on issues of race, culture, and her place in hip-hop. She took an imperialist conqueror's stance that since hip-hop influenced her, she had the right to treat it as her own, regardless of the music's history or cultural context. Worst of all for her, she insisted on responding to her critics, famous and not, without filter, on Twitter and Instagram. Though she was vouched for by Atlanta rapper T.I., who signed Azalea to his Grand Hustle label, the Australian lost said sponsorship after treating hip-hop legends like Snoop Dogg and Q-Tip as if they were annoying upper-class bullies and she were an incoming freshman. Azalea's public feuding started over a perceived slight from Nicki Minaj during Nicki's acceptance of her BET Award in 2014. Minaj mentioned that she writes all her own raps, which Azalea inferred as a nod to the accusation that she employed ghostwriters—an issue that Minaj had never weighed in on.

She had a long, drawn-out, and very telling feud with the intelligent and outspoken Bronx rapper Azealia Banks, who was justifiably upset to see hip-hop being increasingly whitewashed at the highest levels of consumer consumption. In an on-air interview with Hot 97, Banks said regarding Azalea's nomination and Macklemore's three wins over Kendrick Lamar in 2013: "When they give these Grammys out, all it says to white kids is 'You're amazing, you're great, you can do anything you put your mind to.' And all it says to black kids is, 'You don't have shit, you don't own shit, not even the shit you created for yourself.' And it makes me upset."[13] Iggy responded to Banks in a series of rude, insensitive tweets, including this one: "you created your own unfortunate situation by being a bigot and don't have the mental capacity to realize yet. Probably never will."[14]

In a move that cost her the relationship with T.I., Azalea got into a Twitter feud with Q-Tip, who strove to open a dialogue with her about why black hip-hop artists find her

13. Reni Eddo-Lodge, "Azealia Banks vs. Iggy Azalea," *Telegraph*, December 23, 2014, https://www.telegraph.co.uk/women/womens-life/11308082/Azealia-Banks-Vs-Iggy-Azalea-White-people-shouldnt-steal-hip-hop.html.
14. Eddo-Lodge, "Azealia Banks vs. Iggy Azalea."

statements offensive. He considered that she is foreign and thoughtfully gave her an extended history lesson on the socioeconomic origins of hip-hop culture that she found patronizing. "I'm not going to play hip-hop squares with a stranger to somehow prove I deserve to be a fan or deserve to be influenced by hip-hop."[15] Azalea has released a few failed singles and an EP in the years since but has canceled two national tours due to support acts dropping out and poor ticket sales and has all but disappeared from music for the past five years. As of November 2018, Azalea was released from her contract with Island Records and claims to have received a $2.7 million deal as part of an undisclosed partnership that would allow her to own her own master recordings and be entirely independent.

At the other end of the spectrum from Azalea's callous appropriation is Macklemore, the Seattle rapper who achieved tremendous commercial success with his DJ/production partner Ryan Lewis, including four Grammys for their major label debut, 2012's *The Heist*. From the start of his career as an independent artist, Macklemore was aware and apologetic of his role as a white rapper, understanding that the color of his skin gave him an advantage. He was influenced mostly by East Coast underground rappers like Aceyalone, Hieroglyphics, Taleb Kweli, and Freestyle Fellowship. For the majority of his career, which stretches back to the early 2000s, Macklemore has made social justice, race, and LGBT rights a recurring theme in his music. If anything, his pop breakthrough,

---

15. James Hendicott, James, "TI and Iggy Azalea Are No Longer Working Together," *NME*, September 17, 2015, https://www.nme.com/news/music/nme-428-1224391.

aside from the song "Same Love," was a departure from the norm—a departure that shut out a far more skilled rapper, Kendrick Lamar, in every single Grammy category the two acts were both nominated for. The fact that Lamar's record was a more meaningful and timely record in every way added insult to injury in an industry and a country that has seen the racial importance of hip-hop further wiped away with each passing year. It was bad enough that, at the 2014 Grammys, the rap awards were still being handed out at a nontelevised ceremony.

To his credit, Macklemore apologized to Lamar by text message, then took a screenshot of it and posted it to his Instagram account. "You got robbed," he wrote. "I wanted you to win. You should have. It's weird and sucks that I robbed you. I was gonna say that during the speech. Then the music started playing during my speech, and I froze. Anyway, you know what it is. Congrats on this year and your music. Appreciate you as an artist and as a friend. Much love." He went further in his caption, stating that Kendrick deserved the best rap album, which most critics, though clearly not those on the Grammy committee, agreed was true.

This apology campaign continued into Macklemore and Lewis's 2016 follow-up, *This Unruly Mess I've Made*, which included a nearly nine-minute opus about white privilege ("White Privilege II") and cameos by a number of early hip-hop pioneers, including Melle Mel, Kool Moe Dee, and Grandmaster Kaz. The album was given very mixed reviews for its ponderous soul-searching and did quite poorly on a commercial level, dropping from a number four debut to number thirty-one in its second week on the *Billboard* 200. It has failed to sell platinum in the United States as of this writing, compared to *The Heist*'s 1.5 million copies sold. It would appear that overly ambitious self-awareness isn't popular when it comes to white privilege, and Macklemore seems to have gotten the memo. After *Mess* underperformed on every level, he parted ways with Lewis, his collaborator of twelve years, for *Gemini*, an album full of collaborations that he characterized as "not extremely politically motivated or heavily subject or concept oriented . . . I wanted it to be fun."[16]

In the pop world, at the highest levels of consumerism, knowledge isn't always welcome, and in the case of Macklemore, neither is a history lesson. This is why the acts that completely avoid the racial issue at all costs seem to be skipping over the surface of these complicated waters without a care in the world. Case in point, Danielle Bregoli, the Floridian teen who became an internet meme sensation in 2016 after she and her mother appeared on an episode of *Dr. Phil* titled "I Want to Give Up My Car-Stealing, Knife-Wielding, Twerking 13-Year-Old Daughter Who Tried to Frame Me for a Crime." Among Bregoli's underage misdemeanors, she stole a crew member's car during the shooting of the episode and challenged the entire bemused studio audience to "cash me ousside, how bout dat?" Bregoli and the phrase went viral, and she soon found herself signed to a management deal by Adam

16. Christopher R. Weingarten, "Macklemore Talks 'Gemini,' His Upcoming Career Reset Without Ryan Lewis," *Rolling Stone*, September 14, 2017, https://www.rollingstone.com/music/music-features/macklemore-talks-gemini-his-upcoming-career-reset-without-ryan-lewis-124464/.

Kluger, head of an agency that places products in music videos and in recordings, which this most certainly was. He secured her a multimillion-dollar record deal with Atlantic as well as a lucrative endorsement deal from Copycat Beauty, a company that makes knock-off makeup, and saw her become the youngest female rapper to debut on the *Billboard* Hot 100.

Bregoli, who raps under the alias Bhad Bhabie (pronounced "bad baby"), is the perfect spokesperson for Copycat, because she raps in a fake black accent that disappears when she speaks, one which she claims she got "from the streets." Her rapcent, if you will, is interesting because it speaks to what Bregoli, at fifteen, thinks a bad bitch, from-the-hood rapper should be. Her persona is an elevated play on the delinquent antics that made her famous, and in this context they work, though her style and music are at best a capable mimicry that comes off like what it truly is: her manager's most lucrative product placement. Her success is a clear indication that racial privilege, when it comes to white rappers, has grown worse since Eminem's rise to fame. It's an undeniable fact that if a teenager of color behaved the way Bregoli did on national television, she wouldn't land nearly $2 million in record and endorsement deals with a headlining national tour to boot—she'd end up in juvenile detention.

Another rapper who takes his own word for his place in hip-hop is Oakland's G-Eazy, a guy who touts his brief association with Bay Area independent hip-hop circles as sufficient time served to warrant his right to hip-hop pop stardom. After working as a producer while attending Loyola University in New Orleans, Eazy returned home and gained some recognition for his involvement with the East Bay scene that birthed artists like Lil B and the Cataracts. He then began releasing mixtapes and gained notoriety at festivals like the Vans Warped Tour circa 2012, as did many of the aforementioned frat rappers. G-Eazy may be the most well-accessorized of all of them, because unlike Mike Stud, who pretends that black hip-hop doesn't exist, G-Eazy, across his five studio albums, presents himself as someone who is very much "for the culture." Rather than overthinking his role and constantly discussing it like Macklemore, Eazy assumes his word as bond for his authenticity and never hesitates to celebrate the bourgeois spoils of rap success to which he feels entitled. Where Macklemore is self-conscious, G-Eazy is self-absorbed, lifting from rappers like Drake and Kendrick Lamar and pulling from rap styles of the recent past while delivering a product that sounds static and laborious. It's no surprise that G-Eazy's biggest successes have come from dropping verses for white pop singers like Britney Spears.

By contrast, twenty-three-year-old Post Malone takes a different approach to dealing with his role as a white man using rap to succeed in pop music: he simply denies that he's rapping. A Syracuse, New York, native raised on emo rock, hip-hop, metal, and country, Malone blends a number of genres into a sedated pastiche of generic pop tracks fronted by laconic half-sung, half-rapped lyrics drenched in Auto-Tune. To date, his debut single "White Iverson" is certified quadruple platinum in the United States, and his number one album, *Beerbongs and Bentleys*, has broken a number of streaming records, while his 2016 album *Stoney* broke the thirty-four-year-old record for consecutive weeks on the *Billboard* Top R&B and Hip-Hop charts that was previously held by Michael Jackson's *Thriller*. Malone has waffled on his identity as a hip-hop artist at various stages in his career. When he was approached to be a part of *XXL*'s freshman class of 2016, the rapper turned it down. According to Vanessa Staten, the magazine's editor in chief, "We were told by his camp that he wasn't paying attention to hip-hop so much. He was going in more of a rock/pop/country direction."[17] Malone later responded at length on Instagram, claiming he was too tired to take the six-hour flight to New York for the magazine's photo shoot, among other things.

> Dear Vanessa, XXL, Internet, etc.—My love of music shouldn't be questioned. I shouldn't be chastised for expressing myself in whichever way I see fit. That being said, I have never once said, "I'm not going to make hip hop anymore" . . . I have a hip hop album coming out in August. Everyone has a right to do whatever the fuck they want to do. I want to continue making hip hop. I want to continue writing songs on my guitar . . . I am in this for the pure purpose of creating what I want, because it's who I am. No ulterior motives . . . If you don't like me, politely fuck off.[18]

In the years since, Malone, like Iggy Azalea before him, has been quick to bemoan the hardships of the white rapper, which is precisely why he doesn't choose to see himself

---

17. Danny Schwartz, "Post Malone Going in 'Rock/Pop/Country Direction,'" *HotNew HipHop*, June 13, 2016, https://www.hotnewhiphop.com/post-malone-going-in-rock-pop-country-direction-news.22223.html.

18. Claire Lobenfeld, "Post Malone: My Love of Music Should Never Be Questioned," *Fact*, June 16, 2016, https://www.factmag.com/2016/06/16/post-malone-my-love-of-music-should-never-be-questioned/.

as one. "I definitely feel like there's a struggle being a white rapper," he told Bijan Stephen in GQ. "But I don't want to be a rapper. I just want to be a person that makes music. I make music that I like and that I think kicks ass, that I think the people who fuck with me as a person and as an artist will like."[19] Malone's greatest concern is keeping his image free and clear of a complicated issue that, should he get involved, might hurt his ability to successfully do what he wants, when he wants, how he wants.

White performers in hip-hop have multiplied and mutated drastically since Eminem blew the doors open. Changes in technology have forever altered the music and touring industries, enabling artists to find their audiences entirely outside the culture that taught them the ropes. This has allowed, in many instances, an entirely white hip-hop universe to arise and exist completely apart from black hip-hop. The results have been interesting at best, offensive at worst, and in all cases, odd and unsettling to true fans of the music and culture. The most unfortunate aspect of this development has been the timing. In the past few years, leading black hip-hop artists have been more outspoken and political about race and society than ever before. It has been a shame to see this enlightened age in popular hip-hop undermined by the least racially sensitive and most deliberately unaware era of white hip-hop that we have ever seen. Hip-hop has become the most popular genre of music consumed in America, and in music, as in sports where they are the outcast, white people

19. Bijan Stephen, "Don't Call Post Malone a Rapper," GQ, January 25, 2018, https://www.gq.com/story/dont-call-post-malone-a-rapper.

root for white people. Perhaps it's the American instinct to applaud the underdog, or just a case of consumers wanting to see their own faces reflected in the artists they follow. Whatever it is, one thing is certain, whether they're willing to admit it or not, white rappers still have a tremendous advantage over their counterparts of color when it comes to mounting a successful career. Because whether they're wack or not, it's easier than ever for white rappers to find eager white people to rap to.

Chapter 5

Going through Changes

In June 2010, *Recovery* was released, and it was clear from the opening track that Eminem had regained his voice and a sense of clarity, serving up an album of lyrics more honest than any he had written in years. He did away with the accents, he mostly did away with Slim Shady, adopting a no less intense but dramatically more confessional tone as he mined material that emotionally, and to some degree musically, echoed the most candid moments of the *8 Mile* soundtrack and the psychotic go-for-broke intensity of *The Marshall Mathers LP*. *Recovery* is widely considered one of Eminem's best albums and for good reason: it was easy to get excited about, because after a hiatus followed by a concept album-and-a-half that confused most and satisfied only the few who understood the exorcism, here was an album that gave the people what they wanted.

"To watch somebody so great fall from grace to the point of almost dying, then come back and say, 'Okay, I'm going to talk about how fucked up I was as a person when I was on drugs,' that was something," says Mr. Porter. "Not only did he do that with *Relapse* but when he realized that the album didn't connect with people the way he wanted, he went back, figured out what didn't connect, and changed it. The accents, he did away with those and refined his work and turned around and made *Recovery*, one of the absolute best albums he has ever made."

Eminem had made a career of airing his dirty laundry, and *Recovery* was the moment he came clean about hitting bottom, his real name, no gimmicks. On *Relapse*, he'd painted a picture of his addiction (the cover was literally a collage of his face made of pills), a visceral portrait of his demons. It was loopy and disturbing, a metaphorical and allegorical investigation of his darkest impulses and the addiction that nearly ended his life. It was an artistic exploration, and considering how short of a time he had been sober, a brave or, depending on your perspective, foolhardy one, as it can be risky to publicize recovery when freshly sober. As he'd always done, Mathers took his addiction to task the way a seasoned battle rapper would an opponent, using metaphor, wit, and rhyme to chop it down. But the album was not a literal, straightforward discussion of what he'd been through, and in this way it did not benefit from the degree of autobiography draped in outlandish costume that Eminem has employed so successfully in his music.

"He has said publicly that *Relapse* was him relearning how to rap, but I don't see it quite the same," says Mr. Porter. "The skill was there, because he will always have that gift. It was the content that he had to figure out. His rapping on *Relapse* was better than ninety percent of what came out that year. So he wasn't relearning how to rap, he was relearning how to be relatable. He was learning how to reinstate himself in society, the way someone does after they get out of jail or rehab. He was relearning how to relate to people after being in a bubble for so long. He woke up out of his bubble like, 'Hey, look, I can still rap!' They didn't accept it, so he had to figure out how to get them back into him. But that rap skill ain't never left. It's like telling Mike Tyson he can't box no more. Mike Tyson might not compete, but he'll still whup your ass."

On *Recovery*, Eminem righted that wrong and launched a new era, one in which he was determined to properly clean out his closet, with as little artifice as possible. The album opens with "Cold Wind Blows," a song about Eminem's return to dominate the rap game, at once looking forward while nodding to the past with production by Just Blaze that would be at home among any of Dre's beats from *The Eminem Show* or *Relapse*. This seems appropriate because the song finds Shady/Eminem up to his old boasts, lampooning flash-in-the-pan pop stars, threatening loose women, and employing Mathers's gift with language to offensive ends, because, you see, he's as cold as the wind when it snows and it's twenty below zero.

> *If you don't like it, you can kiss my ass in a lint thong*
> *Now sing along, slut this, slut that, learn the words to the song*
> *"Oh, bitches don't like that," homie, I'll be nicer to women*
> *When Aquaman drowns and the Human Torch starts swimmin'.*

More than ever, on *Recovery* Eminem is preoccupied with proving himself as a rapper and justifying his place in hip-hop history. He's always had a chip on his shoulder, even on *Relapse*, but there the conflict was internal, a struggle to uproot his own darkness in an effort to prove that he was stronger than his destructive impulses. Here, the focus is different. As usual, Eminem is most inspired when he has opponents to destroy, and on *Recovery*, when he's not bearing his soul, he lets fly at the state of music literally and allegorically as he comments on all that has transpired during his five years away.

In "On Fire," Eminem once again takes aim at pop stars, in this case 2008's *American Idol* winner David Cook and Brooke Hogan, daughter of the wrestling legend Hulk Hogan, who tried to mount a pop music/reality TV career with two albums and two reality shows in 2006 and 2009. "We were in the middle of creating *Relapse 2*," Mr. Porter recalls. "That was the plan; it was a whole album by then, and I swear, one day I gave him 'On Fire,' which I made when we was recording in Hawaii, and I told him to just rap how he used to, just saying his bars in his low tone, no screaming, no nothing. He did it, and that was the moment things shifted and that is where *Recovery* started. We came home, and the next set of songs I heard blew me away. That's when I realized that he wasn't a rapper anymore. He was way bigger than that now; he was a complete artist."

In "On Fire," Eminem mentions another irksome development in music that arose during his absence: the abuse of Auto-Tune, the audio processor used to alter pitch in vocal and instrumental recording and performances. Originally intended to disguise or correct off-key inaccuracies, the software (used in the studio) and the hardware (used in live performance) allow vocals to be perfectly tuned despite being off-pitch, by shifting them to the nearest true, correct semitone. Auto-Tune can also be used as an effect to distort the human voice when the pitch is raised or lowered significantly. The resulting effect causes the voice to leap from note to note stepwise like a synthesizer, lending it an artificial, robotic quality.[1]

Antares Auto-Tune was created by Andy Hildebrand, an electrical engineer and former classical flute virtuoso who studied linear estimation theory and signal processing. Hildebrand worked for Exxon in the late 1970s, where he was employed to help analyze seismic monitoring data in order to pinpoint oil drilling locations along the Alaska pipeline. Hildebrand created highly complex algorithms to solve Exxon's problems, then quit the company to start one of his own, utilizing his findings to pioneer an integrated hardware/software work station that could process thousands of lines of data and quickly create three-dimensional seismic maps. After retiring wealthy in 1989 and then benefitting further when the company he founded was bought by Halliburton for a reported $525 million, Hildebrand came out of retirement to profit from overturning another industry—music. Looking for a problem to solve, and inspired by a friend's wife who said, "Why don't you make a box that will let me sing in tune?" he took on what sound engineers considered the Holy Grail: creating a software program that could pitch correct vocals without requiring a North American Aerospace

---

1. A step is the difference in pitch between two consecutive notes of a musical scale.

Defense Command (NORAD)–grade computer to operate it. Utilizing the same principles and superhumanly complicated math that allowed software to sketch maps from massive data sets, Hildebrand applied the same technology to pitch correction, and, voila, Auto-Tune was born.[2]

He developed the software over the course of a few months in 1996, on a specially equipped Macintosh, and in 1997 debuted it at the National Association of Music Merchants (NAMM) Show.[3] The reception was overwhelming. At the time, recording engineers were forced to create pitch-perfect vocal tracks by splicing the best bits of numerous vocal takes into a seamless whole. This was time-consuming, tedious work for the producers and artists. It was also costly, as sound engineers had to do this manually, note by note, track by track. For a major pop artist expected to deliver perfection, the cost for correcting an entire record could stretch into six figures and require weeks of work.

That changed overnight when Auto-Tune was released to the recording industry. Instantly, the studios that integrated it into their hardware or software setup were able to complete projects faster. Before then, the standard practice was to capture at least a dozen or more performances of a song.

---

2. Zachary Crockett, "The Mathematical Genius of Auto-Tune," *Priceonomics*, December 14, 2015, https://priceonomics.com/the-inventor-of-auto-tune/.

3. The NAMM Show is a trade-only conference held annually in January in Anaheim, California. The organization has been in existence since 1901, and the show is one of the two largest music product trade shows in the world, the other being the Musikmesse in Frankfurt. Product exhibits are the main business of the show, allowing dealers and distributors to see new products, negotiate deals, and plan their yearly buys.

Suddenly, producers using Auto-Tune could manufacture a suitable vocal after the artist recorded just one pass. A new age and a new industry standard was born within months: studios with Auto-Tune were able to take in more clients at lowered costs, and those without it couldn't compete. For the first year of its existence, Auto-Tune remained a dirty little trade secret, with producers using it subtly to fix off-key notes, none of them eager to reveal the use of the program to the public. But all that changed in October 1998, when Cher released "Believe," a Euro-dance ballad with a soaring chorus featuring a robotically pitch-shifted vocal line, an effect that was not intended or expressly described in the manual. The software includes a setting that goes from zero to ten, which allows the user to control how quickly the pitch of the incoming signal is adjusted. The zero setting, which no one thought to use at first, causes the software to adjust the pitch at the very moment it receives the signal. Most producers were adjusting the setting carefully, making minor corrections to a vocal so as to retain the natural quality of the voice. When assigned to zero, however, the pitch shift is intentional, the result unnatural, revealing the digital manipulation. Producers Mark Taylor and Brian Rawling took advantage of this and started a stylistic trend that has yet to die.

While working on the Cher track, the pair did it as an experiment that they were at first afraid to play for Cher, worried that she would disapprove. Quite to the contrary, she loved it so much that when her record company heard the song and asked that the effect be removed, she replied, "Over my dead body."[4] Cher's "Believe" sold eleven million copies, landed her a spot in the *Guinness Book of World Records* as the oldest female solo artist to top the *Billboard* Hot 100, and won her a Grammy for Best Dance Recording that year. The success of the track and the vocal effect that no one had ever heard before naturally brought attention to its creators, who at first lied about the ingredients of their secret sauce. In one interview, Taylor claimed, in great detail, he had used a complicated sequence of equipment (a DigiTech Talker FX pedal plus a tone from a Nord Rack as a carrier signal, all sequenced through the digital audio workstation Cubase) to get "a vocoder effect" in what seemed like a deliberate effort to lead attention away from the team's (mis)use of Auto-Tune.[5] His explanation of achieving the quality of the rest of her vocals was equally convoluted. Eventually the truth came out, and once it did, recorded music was never the same. Soon enough, Atares Auto-Tune was marketed as simply "The Cher Effect," and it instantaneously became ubiquitous in genres as diverse as country, reggae, and Bollywood.

In hip-hop and R&B, there is only one name to know when it comes to the proliferation of the saturated Auto-Tune sound, and that is T-Pain (born Faheem Rasheed Najm). Though the software was definitely used on rap records before him, no one found a proper place for "The Cher Effect" in

---

4. Neil Strauss, "Cher Resurrected, Again, by a Hit; The Long, Hard but Serendipitous Road to 'Believe,'" *New York Times*, March 11, 1999, https://www.nytimes.com/1999/03/11/arts/cher-resurrected-again-by-a-hit-the-long-hard-but-serendipitous-road-to-believe.html.

5. Sue Sillitoe, "Recording Cher's 'Believe,'" *Sound on Sound*, February 1999, https://www.soundonsound.com/techniques/recording-cher-believe.

the genre until the Tallahassee rapper bent it to his will in the late 2000s. After being signed by American Senegalese singer-songwriter-producer Akon to his Konvict Muzik label, T-Pain pivoted to singing. His natural singing voice is very good, but he didn't believe it would be enough to differentiate him from the pack. He needed a gimmick.

"I used to watch TV a lot, of course. You know, Americans," he said during an interview on NPR's *All Things Considered*. "So there was this commercial on the channel I would watch. And it was one of those collaborative CDs, like a various artists CD, and it was this Jennifer Lopez song, 'If You Had My Love,' but it was a Darkchild remix. And that was the first time I heard Auto-Tune. Well, she only used it for, like, a second. Ever since I heard that song—and I kept hearing it and hearing it—on this commercial, I was like, 'Man, I gotta find this thing.' And I had to go find it; then I heard Teddy Riley use it on 'Let Me Go Deep' with Blackstreet. And I was like, well, I gotta find it now because I want to remix this song but I can't do it without that effect."[6]

He finally got a free version from a hacker friend who found it online, and he fiddled with it until he learned its parameters and, using it, developed a sonic style that resonated with him. His signature sound uses Auto-Tune masterfully, bending his laidback delivery into clipped bionic bits of longing and yearning that stand out alongside his less processed singing. It comes off as more than just an off-kilter setting in a

6. Monika Evstatieva, "T-Pain Rises Above the Haters," *All Things Considered*, NPR, November 13, 2014, https://www.npr.org/2014/11/13/363759981/t-pain-rises-above-the-haters.

piece of recording software; T-Pain's music gives the impression that he is playing Auto-Tune, his voice another instrument in his sonic collection. The result is easy on the ears—a combination of deep bass and crisp drum kit sounds with T-Pain's straightforward, relatable lyrics and penchant for hummable melodies. There is no doubt that T-Pain had the talent to make it as a traditional R&B artist, but he reached the heights that he did thanks to his use of Auto-Tune. The combination of traditional elements with a celebration of deliberately manipulated reality—in his case, taking his more than capable, completely pleasant singing voice and changing it into something computerized and detached—was utterly of the moment. It reflected the internet- and technology-obsessed culture of the early 2000s and, unfortunately, directed the world toward an era in music in which the opposite of T-Pain's formula has become the norm. Auto-Tune's legacy is that those without the once required skills of musical performance can mask their inabilities, as the public has become content to consume the medium, not the message. The medium is the end game, and thanks to technology, menial skills and proper marketing can get you there. For some time now, in hip-hop, R&B, and pop particularly, the sound created by digital machinations combined with an easy-to-remember repeated chorus (typically featuring "oohs" and "ohs"), rather than substantial lyrics and musical talent, has dictated what connects with the public.

T-Pain was well ahead of his time: from 2005 through 2010, his sound made hits for everyone he worked with. During those years, three of his albums went gold, and in a move that was savvy in terms of business but spread the Auto-Tune effect quicker than a zombie plague, he produced and appeared on more than fifty chart-topping singles, including Flo Rida's "Low," which went platinum six times over. Late in 2007, over the course of two weeks, T-Pain was featured on four different songs in the top ten on the *Billboard* Hot 100. Artists he worked with, most notably Lil Wayne and Kayne West, went on to adopt his technique to such great success that T-Pain demanded that those who worked with him and used Auto-Tune in his style give him a royalty (Diddy actually did).[7]

On *808s & Heartbreak*, West used Auto-Tune like an Instagram filter to colorize the themes of mourning and loss that drive the album, lending the result a disembodied and detached cadence. West had ended an engagement and long-term relationship with Alexis Phifer and had lost his mother, Donda, the year before, all of which infuse the album with a mood of despair and dejection. T-Pain was brought into the studio to coach West on how to best apply Auto-Tune to his music and is listed as a writer on "RoboCop." The album was the most West had ever used Auto-Tune in the studio to that point, and he loved it so much that he's stuck with it in one way or another ever since. Though he changed directions again after *808s*, West's most experimental record has had a lasting effect on hip-hop, ushering in an era of introspective, emo rap and replacing braggadocio with raw emotion, isolation, and explorations of more sensitive subject matter.

---

7. Shaheem Reid, "T-Pain Says It's Time for 'Everybody Else' to Stop Using Auto-Tune," *MTV News*, November 19, 2008.

The album's commercial and critical success encouraged established artists like Jay-Z to make more left-of-center records and essentially created the blueprint for Drake's entire career. It also opened the door to the big time for left-field artists like the Weeknd, Frank Ocean, Childish Gambino, and Kid Cudi.

For his part, Lil Wayne has made T-Pain's style of Auto-Tune such an integral facet of his music that younger fans ignorant of T-Pain think that Weezy more or less invented the use of Auto-Tune in hip-hop.[8] Wayne and T-Pain were friends and collaborators from the start, guesting on each other's records as early as 2007, even creating a collaborative group called T-Wayne that released a free mixtape in 2017, with another on the way in 2019. T-Pain may have brought Auto-Tune to Lil Wayne, but the stylistic combination of Wayne's narcotically laid-back delivery and T-Pain's digital depersonalization was a pairing as sweet and intoxicating as his ever-present Styrofoam cup of purple drank.[9] It allowed Wayne to grow

---

8. Lucas, "How Lil Wayne Influenced the Hip Hop We Know Today," Lilweezy.net, July 27, 2016, https://lilweezy.net/how-lil-wayne-has-influenced-the-hip-hop -we-know-today/.

9. Purple drank—also known as lean, sizzurp, syrup, drank, jelly, Texas Tea, and dirty Sprite—is a combination of prescription-strength cough syrup containing codeine and promethazine mixed with soft drinks like Sprite, Mountain Dew, or Grape Fanta, often with a Jolly Rancher candy added for extra sweetness. The cough syrup is added in doses grossly above what is medically recommended, imparting to the user a euphoric, dissociative high that comes with impaired motor skills, lethargy, and drowsiness. This dangerous recreational drug was popularized in the southern United States, most notably Houston, Texas, in the 1990s and when combined with alcohol and other drugs can be lethal since the promethazine is a respiratory depressant that, in large doses, can cause the user to stop breathing. It has caused a number of deaths in hip-hop, most notably Pimp C

stylistically, experiment with new flows, and add an additional layer of otherworldly oddity to his already unusual voice. An entire generation of rappers—Young Thug, Lil Uzi Vert, and Future among them—have taken from Wayne in one way or another, from his flow, to his tendency toward strange and funny phrases, his dyed dreadlocks, his use of Auto-Tune, and his taste for face tattoos. But, no one does it like Wayne: on his allegedly final album, 2019's *Tha Carter V*, with nothing but a simple acoustic guitar line, a bass drum, and an intimate vocal awash in Auto-Tune, the plaintive "Mess" creates a mood as moving as when he first worked with the effect ten years ago.

For his part, T-Pain, the king of Auto-Tune, actually became a partner at Antares Audio Technologies, spreading awareness of the technology and partnering with Andy Hildebrand on an iPhone app called I Am T-Pain that allowed the user to speak into their phone and create T-Pain songs. It was downloaded two million times and sold for three dollars each, earning them a few million dollars apiece. This fast friendship ended in a lawsuit after T-Pain founded a company, trademarked his name, and turned to a competing audio company to create his own pitch correction brand. They sold "The T-Pain Effect," and a number of products bearing his name, including a software engine and a toy microphone that shouted, "Hey this ya boy, T-Pain!"[10] Antares and T-Pain settled out of court for an undisclosed amount.

---

and A$AP Yams. Lil Wayne is a huge fan of the stuff and was hospitalized after suffering a series of seizures associated with prolonged codeine abuse.

10. Crockett, "The Mathematical Genius."

T-Pain's processed signature sound reached complete saturation and began to slowly fall from favor around 2010, though its legacy was just ramping up. A slew of younger rappers took to the style as wielded by Lil Wayne and Kayne, using it obviously and often, ushering in the age of the mumble rapper. It is no longer an aid to fix a performance. It has become the performance, allowing subpar vocalists to sell false ability to the uninformed. It is used in some way on nearly every record released for public consumption today and has encouraged a shiny, happy homogeny in pop music. The uniform perfection of Auto-Tuned vocals in pop has made hit singles hard to differentiate from one another, as all are engineered to have perfect pitch and be in perfect time and tune. It takes listening to about three songs on any Top 40 station these days to prove this point. As one journalist in *Time* put it, Auto-Tune is "Photoshop for the human voice."[11] Another article in *Time* included Auto-Tune in its list of the fifty worst inventions.[12]

All this exploded during Eminem's five years in self-created purgatory, but none of it escaped him. As he raps on "Cold Wind Blow,"

> But I swear, you try to diss me, I'll slaughter you
> I put that on everything, like everyone does with Auto-Tune
> The last thing you want to do is have me spit out a rhyme
> And say, "I was writing this and I thought of you."

11. Josh Tyrangiel, "Auto-Tune: Why Pop Music Sounds Perfect," *Time*, February 5, 2009.

12. Dan Fletcher, "The Fifty Worst Inventions: Auto-Tune," *Time*, May 27, 2010, http://content.time.com/time/specials/packages/article/0,28804,1991915_199 1909_1991903,00.html.

"I think that T-Pain discovered something that was pretty ingenious," Mathers says. "I think the way he did it was interesting. It was new; I mean I had never heard it used that way until he did it. But then it just got carried away. You know what I mean; everybody is doing it. You even hear some singers doing it who can actually sing. Not that T-Pain can't sing, but he did it for a reason. You hear, like, real singers doing it on purpose and you're just like, 'What the fuck?' Why are they doing that?"

Eminem has only ever overly processed his vocals for comedic effect because he is more than capable of bending his voice to his will, and unless otherwise noted, singing all the parts on his albums. He also simply doesn't understand the appeal of the Auto-Tuned delivery to evoke emotion where there is none, which remains the prevailing fashion in hip-hop. When the packaging outshines the content, what are you left with?

"It's a trend that has really taken over. I hope like all trends it will come and go, because, I mean, there are some songs that I hear using Auto-Tune and they're okay, they're decent songs, but would they be without it?" he asks. "Is that what people like about them? I don't know how long this trend is going to last, but I will say that T-Pain should keep it as his thing forever because it was his thing first. That dude is creative as fuck with what he does with it. And he's got writing skills—his melodies, all that shit, the dude is talented as fuck."

On *Recovery*, Eminem also makes a point of acknowledging the artists who have done great things in his absence, most notably Kanye West and Lil Wayne, artists whose work would still shine without the Auto-Tune effect. On "Talkin' 2 Myself," he admits that watching from the sidelines, incapacitated by his drug abuse and the time it took to get clean, he was angry watching those two rappers enter the most creative and celebrated period of their careers. He admits to being jealous of Wayne in particular and almost writing diss tracks about each of them but concludes that he'd have had his ass handed to him.

"Lil Wayne seemed like he just got good out of nowhere," Mathers says. "When he first came out, it was like, 'All right, this guy is cool,' you know what I mean? You hear what he's saying and he's got an interesting voice and he's got an interesting flow. Lyrically, he started elevating as he got older, because you have to remember, he was really young when he first got in the game. I was hearing things he was doing and was like, 'Damn.' He is one of the guys who has kept me being a fan of rap."

It is true—Wayne (born Dwayne Michael Carter) was discovered and signed to Cash Money Records at eleven years old in 1993, first rising to national prominence with his label mates B.G., Juvenile, and Turk as Hot Boys, whose 1999 single "Bling Bling" made them nationally known. Wayne's first solo album, *Tha Block Is Hot*, sold platinum, but it wasn't until his fourth album, *Tha Carter*, in 2004 that he grew into his own as a major creative force in hip-hop. Much the way 50 Cent did, Wayne followed a pattern of releasing mixtapes alongside his more produced commercial releases, satisfying rap purists and more mainstream fans alike, all the while piling up a continuous stream of top ten hit singles as well as successful collaborations.

He and Eminem collaborated on Wayne's seventh album, *Rebirth*, a rock-themed record that debuted at number two on the US *Billboard* 200, and though it was generally panned by critics, it nonetheless produced four charting singles and sold gold in the States. The general consensus was that the record was Wayne's idea of what rock music is, and as such is neither rock nor rap, just a confused, ill-conceived hybrid of the two. Wayne has often called himself a Martian, and this album may be undeniable truth that he is, because it sounds like an alien tried to make an album after listening, from space, to two very different radio stations. The best songs are the ones that don't slam an Auto-Tuned Weezy against the mixed bag of rock styles (pop punk, nu metal, thrash, grunge) he tries on for size. The critics that did have positive words for the album universally called out one track as the collection's highlight and the only moment the rock concept worked. That song was recorded on Eminem's home court, Effigy Studios in Detroit, and was released in December 2009, four months before Em released "Not Afraid," the first single off *Recovery*. "Drop the World" went four times platinum. The song is an angsty dirge that slowly gains steam, as Wayne and Em, both at a world-weary moment in their lives, lyrically destroy their haters and promise to pick up the world and drop it on its fuckin' head.

The pair reunited on *Recovery* for the standout single "No Love," which sold more than a million digital downloads and reached number twenty-three on the *Billboard* Hot 100. It was the third single from the album, released in October 2010, and it remained on the charts for twenty weeks. The song is a tour de force, two of the greatest MCs in rap going back to back, with Wayne playing opening act for what is one of Em's best verses on this record or any other. Their disparate styles are perfect foils. Wayne's slow, nasal, deliberate, intricate flow is the lit fuse that burns through the first verse, getting ever closer to Eminem's powder keg bars, with sparks flying as Eminem sings the first chorus and explodes into an unbroken twenty-five lines linked by dizzying interwoven, rapid-fire rhyme schemes.

> *When I'm not even in my harshest*
> *You can still get roasted, 'cause Marsh is not mellow*
> *'Til I'm topplin' from the top, I'm not gonna stop*
> *I'm standin' on my Monopoly board*
> *That means I'm on top of my game*
> *And it don't stop 'til my hip don't hop anymore*

"No Love" is an incendiary five-minute showcase of the two rappers' skills. Considering where they were in their lives, with Wayne about to go to prison for a year and Em striving to regain the commercial and critical dominance he effortlessly enjoyed on his first three albums, the song is a snapshot of the talent that put both of them at the top in the first place.[13] Lil Wayne's verse is one of his best, both defiant

---

13. Wayne was arrested in July 2007 in New York City after a show at the Beacon Theater and charged with criminal possession of a weapon and marijuana. After several court postponements, he pled guilty and was handed a one-year sentence in March 2010 that he served in Rikers Island. He was released after eight months

and humbled, the portrait of a man who isn't backing down but is looking for answers or an alternative to the only life he's known:

Married to the game, but she broke her vows
That's why my bars are full of broken bottles
And my nightstands are full of open Bibles

Another notably creative element of "No Love" is producer Just Blaze's repurposing of Trinidadian German singer Haddaway's early 1990s' club hit "What Is Love?" best known as the theme song for Chris Kattan and Will Ferrell's *Night at the Roxbury* characters. Where the slick and danceable original portrays a plaintive jilted lover begging for mercy, this new take flips the script, making a tune for the brokenhearted into an anthem of strength and contempt. "I like to take unconventional source material and just make it into something you can actually rock to," producer Just Blaze (born Justin Smith) said. "I came up with the beat but I didn't take it seriously. I kind of just did a quick skeleton and it sat for a while. There was another record that me and Em were working on. We actually had a sample clearance issue with it so we had to dead it. I can't get into what it sampled. The day we got the confirmation that we absolutely couldn't use it, we were all sitting in the studio, like, 'Where do we go now?'"[14]

---

but was also sentenced to thirty-six months of probation as a result of an arrest in January 2008 in Arizona during which a police K-9 Unit recovered 3.7 ounces of marijuana, 1 ounce of cocaine, 1.4 ounces of Ecstasy, and $22,000 in cash. Wayne was charged with a number of possession-with-intent-to-sell felonies.

14. Ahmed "Incilin" Insanul, "Just Blaze Talks Best Baseline Memories & Making Eminem's 'No Love,'" *Complex*, October 4, 2010, https://www.complex.com/music/2010/10/just-blaze-talks-best-baseline-memories-making-eminems-no-love.

The track they were working on was very personal to Marshall, and all involved were disappointed that it could never be released. "We didn't know what to do after that," Blaze recalls. "I remember that I had the idea with the Haddaway sample in my computer so I threw on the headphones, touched it up and played it for him. At first he didn't get it one hundred percent. I think he wasn't sure what I was going for because it's such a comic sample. But once I broke down the idea to him, another angle: 'I don't need you no more, don't want to see you no more, you get no love.' Then it clicked. He did his vocals two days later and was like, 'Yo, I want to get Wayne on it.' I jumped on a plane and went down to Miami. I kicked it with Wayne about the record, he did his vocals in one night. Came back up to New York, I added more to the hook. And that was it."[15]

Though *Relapse* was technically his return to hip-hop after a five-year hiatus, *Recovery* was Eminem's true reentry. Though it wasn't intended as such, *Relapse* and the new material included on *Refill* constituted the album he had to make, the one just for him, much like Kanye had done with *808s & Heartbreak*. *Recovery* was the album he *wanted* to make, the one for the fans, for the public, for his legacy, and for hip-hop.

"From what I'd been hearing on the radio, hip-hop was starting to get into a bad place, just real watered down lyrically in terms of content," he says. "Hip-hop had started to stray a little bit. Content, subject matter, everything, but at

---

15. Insanul, "Just Blaze Talks Best."

the same time there had been artists keeping it going. Lil Wayne and Kanye, and also T.I., who has also elevated his game while I was away. Other people had been doing things but not like those three dudes. I've done some sessions with T.I. and spent time just vibing and writing when he was in town a couple of times. He was dope; I'd hear rhyme patterns and shit he was doing and wish I'd thought of them! When he sits down and puts pen to paper, it's almost scary what he can do. Because usually in the studio he does a couple of lines and works them out in his head and then does two more or whatever. At the level he's at, it's incredible to watch."

Most of *Recovery* is concerned with Eminem's quest to prove himself and reclaim his place as the best rapper in hip-hop, which signals a paradigm shift from the Mr. I Just Don't Give A Fuck of yore. He has always, as all rappers do, boasted about his skills and constantly proved his dexterity, but the undertone was always that he was doing it for himself first, his fans second. Up until this point, he had recorded songs celebrating his skills, acknowledging his fame, and bemoaning the pressure and expectations of said fame, as well as the dehumanizing process of being commodified. All those tunes have a different texture than the songs on this album. For the first time, it is as if Eminem is courting the public, reminding them that they think he's great. Between the boasts, there is a touch of insecurity, no doubt due to approaching his art form and his audience, for the very first time, entirely devoid of the filter of drugs and alcohol. "There was a time when I didn't think I could do anything sober," he told syndicated radio host

Big Boy on *Big Boy's Neighborhood* in 2010. "Talk to people, have a conversation, go to the studio, record, watch movies. I couldn't do anything without being high."[16]

There is also a tinge of betrayal when he speaks about hip-hop, a theme that began on *Recovery* and has grown louder with every subsequent album. On the surface, "Seduction" seems to be a Shady-style boast about stealing the girlfriend of an unnamed MC right before his eyes, inspiring gossip-inclined fans to theorize about the unnamed rapper's identity.[17] Upon closer inspection, the girl in the song is hip-hop itself, portrayed as a fickle woman who wants to be with the most skilled MC, and given the verbal gymnastics routine that Em lays down on the track, it's clear that the girl in question is leaving with him. Moving from well-crafted sections to looser freestyle-type rhymes dropped without a beat for a backdrop and ending with a clip of staccato machine gun verbiage, it's a lyrical workout.

---

16. "Eminem on Big Boy's Neighbourhood (2010)," interview by Big Boy, video, 9:50, June 23, 2010, https://www.youtube.com/watch?v=vkjfytGr4zY.

17. Since we are talking about a battle rapper with a long list of public beefs that have played out in his songs, the online speculation about every figure that Eminem in some way attacks in his lyrics is plentiful and robust. Much of it is ludicrously tenuous yet simultaneously interesting for the truly creative connections made by these lyrical conspiracists. Their numbers speak to just how much rap fans love to see Eminem square off and how many meanings they know he's capable of weaving into a line. In the case of "Seduction," the minority consensus was that the song was one of many shots fired at Nick Cannon, Mariah Carey's husband. Eminem took Carey to task over the fact that she publicly denied their romantic relationship back in 2002, after which they baited each other on various songs until 2009.

Ice Cube, Dr. Dre, and Eminem during Eminem in Concert at the House of Blues (Los Angeles, CA; February 26, 2006). Credit: Kevin Mazur / WireImage c/o Getty Images Entertainment.

Eminem and Deshaun Holton, a.k.a. Proof of D12, during the Forty-Fifth Annual Grammy Awards, held at Madison Square Garden (New York, NY; February 23, 2003). Credit: Michael Caulfield / WireImage c/o Getty Images Entertainment.

Eminem, Proof, and Bruce Springsteen, backstage at the Forty-Fifth
Annual Grammy Awards, held at Madison Square Garden (New York, NY;
February 23, 2003). Credit: Kevin Mazur / WireImage c/o Getty Images
Entertainment.

Fans of rapper Proof gather around a makeshift memorial at the CCC bar
(red building) on Eight Mile Road, where Proof was shot and killed in
the early morning hours of April 11, 2006 (Detroit, MI; April 11, 2006).
Credit: Bill Pugliano / Getty Images Entertainment.

Eminem appears onstage during BET's 106 & Park (New York, NY; December 4, 2006). Credit: Scott Gries / Getty Images Entertainment.

50 Cent, Eminem and LL Cool J attend the *Eminem: The Way I Am* book release party at Nort/ Recon (New York, NY; October 15, 2008). Credit: Kevin Mazur / WireImage c/o Getty Images Entertainment.

Eminem and Rihanna perform on stage at the 2010 MTV Video Music Awards held at Nokia Theatre (Los Angeles, CA; September 12, 2010). Credit: Kevin Mazur / WireImage c/o Getty Images Entertainment.

Eminem and Jay-Z perform their Home & Home concert at Yankee Stadium (New York, NY; September 13, 2010). Credit: Kevin Mazur / Wire Image c/o Getty Images Entertainment.

Lil Wayne and Eminem performs onstage at the Fifty-Second Annual Grammy Awards, held at Staples Center (Los Angeles, CA; January 31, 2010). Credit: Kevin Mazur / WireImage c/o Getty Images Entertainment.

Rihanna and Eminem perform onstage during the Fifty-Third Annual Grammy Awards, held at Staples Center (Los Angeles, CA; February 13, 2011). Credit: Lester Cohen / WireImage c/o Getty Images Entertainment.

Rihanna and Eminem perform on the V Stage on day two of the V Festival at Hylands Park (Chelmsford, UK; August 21, 2011). Credit: Samir Hussein / WireImage c/o Getty Images Entertainment.

Eminem, Earl Sweatshirt, Taco Bennett, and Tyler, the Creator, attend the YouTube Music Awards (New York, NY; November 3, 2013). Credit: Jeff Kravitz / FilmMagic, Inc. for YouTube c/o Getty Images Entertainment.

Eminem performs onstage at the 2014 MTV Movie Awards at Nokia Theatre (Los Angeles, CA; April 13, 2014). Credit: Christopher Polk / Getty Images for MTV.

Eminem attends the *Southpaw* New York premiere (New York, NY; July 20, 2015). Credit: Dimitrios Kambouris / Getty Images Entertainment.

Eminem performs on What Stage during day three of the 2018 Bonnaroo Music and Arts Festival (Manchester, TN; June 9, 2018). Credit: Jeff Kravitz / FilmMagic, Inc. for Bonnaroo Music and Arts Festival / Getty Images Entertainment.

The song "25 to Life" is a clearer exposition on Eminem's feelings about hip-hop, the closest he comes on this album to the raw emotion of *The Marshall Mathers LP*. Once again, hip-hop is a fickle woman, which, given Eminem's lifelong issues with the females in his life, is a fitting metaphor. The song runs through the twenty-five years he has devoted to rap: his fascination began when he was around twelve, and at the time of recording *Recovery*, he was thirty-seven. There is another parallel: when the *Slim Shady EP* was released in 1997, Eminem was twenty-five. Eminem's delivery throughout *Recovery* is mostly fierce, his voice the controlled, enraged shout he wields so well, and here it is in full effect. He lays into the "selfish bitch" he married, the one who has imprisoned him, chewed him up and spit him out without appreciating him or making him feel worthy. In two long verses that flow over, above and at times completely apart from the beat—perhaps on purpose—he declares that he is finished with hip-hop, serving it divorce papers and leaving it behind.

> *But when you spoke of people*
> *Who meant the most to you, you left me off your list*
> *Fuck you, hip hop! I'm leavin' you*
> *My life sentence is served bitch.*

The song ends with Eminem taking command of his life, a theme for any addict living in recovery, and it dovetails with many other songs here that assert his dominance and control over his life, his art, and the crown he vows to regain. This process of caging his demons began on *Relapse*, as a metaphoric murdering of Slim Shady's deepest, darkest impulses.

On *Recovery*, the quest for supremacy is still the thematic center, but here it isn't a quest for dominance over the boogeyman by becoming him and killing him from the inside; it's an effort to grasp and hold the things that Marshall Mathers sees he's lost and wants to regain—another play on the album's title. "For people that have a long history of trauma from early on in their lives, they have a really hard time getting that they don't have to fight to survive," says trauma and substance abuse counselor Dr. Tina Galordi. "They have a hard time getting that it's safe, it's okay, they're not gonna die if they stop fighting. Once someone gets sober, that has to be acknowledged and moved through."

Recovery is a new beginning for Marshall Mathers in another significant way. It is the first time that none of the singles from an Eminem album were in any way playful, satirical, or cartoonish. It is the first time that all of them were serious, straightforward, and as cinematic as Eminem's solo songs on the *8 Mile* soundtrack. In fact, if there are two musical touchstones that have come to define Eminem's singles in this new era, they are "Sing for the Moment" and "Lose Yourself." Take *Recovery*'s first single, "Not Afraid," a rousing, straightforward anthem about overcoming addiction and having the courage to return to music. The dramatic style, complete with a choir backing Eminem on the chorus, is more mainstream and direct than anything in his catalog. Considering the subject matter and where he was in his cycle of sobriety, these are not weaknesses—they are strengths. "Not Afraid" is a stirring hymn to getting clean, intended to give back to anyone going through the same struggles. It is as motivating and emotive as the pulsing introduction to "Lose Yourself," a song that has been empowering game faces in all manner of competitive activity since 2002. "Not Afraid" is the bookend companion to "Lose Yourself," equally ardent and compelling and all the stronger for its uplifting theme of emancipation. By 2010, Marshall Mathers was able to speak about his struggles and was deep enough into his sobriety that he was ready to begin giving back—a crucial make-or-break aspect of living with addiction.

"Coming off of everything, I literally was up twenty-four hours a day for three weeks straight. And I mean, not even nodding off for a fucking minute," he recalls. "Like I was literally just up, looking at the TV. I had to regain motor skills, I had to regain talking skills, it's been a learning process. I'm growing. I just couldn't believe that anybody could ever be naturally happy or naturally functioning or be just enjoying life in general without being on something. So I would say to anybody that it does get better. It just . . . it does."[18]

The megahit single that followed "Not Afraid" was "Love the Way You Lie," which is similarly cinematic. To date, it is Eminem's best-selling record, sitting atop the *Billboard* Hot 100 for seven weeks in 2010, moving six million copies in the United States and one million in the United Kingdom. The song is Eminem's most thoughtful, mature, and clear-eyed look at dysfunctional relationships and the terrible cycle of domestic violence. The track originated from a demo by British hip-hop/pop wunderkind Alex Da Kid (born Alexander

---

18. *How to Make Money Selling Drugs.*

Grant), who has produced a number of hits across multiple genres including "I Need a Doctor" for Dr. Dre, "Massive Attack" for Nicki Minaj, "Airplanes" for B.o.B., and "Radioactive" for Imagine Dragons. Working with a then-unknown singer-songwriter named Skyler Grey (born Holly Hafermann), they wrote a song about an abusive relationship that was a metaphor for Grey's continued devotion to and rejection by the music industry. The hook caught Eminem's ear, and in his mind he unequivocally heard Rihanna singing it. "It's one of those tracks that I felt like only she could pull off," he said.[19] The Barbadian singer, who has been public about her abusive relationship with rapper Chris Brown, took to the song immediately.[20] "It's really beautiful, and it really stands out," she said. "It's a really unique record."[21]

For both artists, and for the massive number of people moved by their heartfelt performances, the music resonated. It was honest, reflecting issues each musician had faced in their lives, so the emotion conveyed by both was tangible. Eminem's lucid lyrical gifts captured an abuser's possessive jealousy, rage, and self-loathing all too well. Punctuated by

---

19. "Eminem Talks Rihanna, Pink, and Lil Wayne Collaborations," *Rap-Up*, June 1, 2010, transcribed from an interview on Skyrock FM, Paris, https://www.rap-up .com/2010/06/01/eminem-talks-rihanna-pink-and-lil-wayne-collaborations/.

20. Much like Eminem and his ex-wife, Kimberly Scott, Rihanna and Chris Brown had been on-again, off-again since 2006, when they were still teenagers. Their drama came to a head in 2009 after an incident in which Brown battered Rihanna in a car and was charged with felony assault, an incident that was still quite recent when she recorded her vocals for "Love the Way You Lie."

21. James Dinh, "Rihanna Tells Story Behind Eminem Duet, 'Love the Way You Lie,'" *MTV News*, June 21, 2010, http://www.mtv.com/news/1641998/rihanna-tells -story-behind-eminem-duet-love-the-way-you-lie/.

Rihanna's wounded monotone, her voice devoid of its characteristic vibrato, sounding more vulnerable and truthful than the unflappable singer ever has, the song took its rightful place at the top of countless year-end, best-of lists. The accompanying video, directed by longtime Eminem collaborator Joseph Khan, starring actors Megan Fox and Dominic Monaghan, broke a YouTube record at the time, logging 6.6 million views in one day.

Recovery is a turning point in Eminem's career, a seismic shift when it comes to his studio albums. For the most part, it marks the end of Slim Shady as we know him: there are no satirical pop-culture-obsessed singles or party anthems. Shady is confined to just a few songs—"Cold Wind Blow," "So Bad," and "Untitled." Dr. Dre, who produced every track but one on *Relapse*, appears even less frequently than Shady, lending his skills to but one track on the initial album release, "So Bad," and just one more, "Ridaz" (another Slim Shady number), on the iTunes deluxe edition. *Recovery* is entirely Eminem and Marshall Mathers: the alias that personifies the non-Shady rapper and Marshall himself, the side that allows his true nature and bits from his real life to come through in the music. But unlike in *The Marshall Mathers LP*, here these two are governed, as Mathers purposely reveals very little of what is actually going on in Marshall's real life. He had learned the hard way that the downside of putting it all out there for the world to hear was that it compounded the delirium of fame. Mathers recognized this trope of his as one of the factors that contributed to his cycle of addiction, and he was eager to be rid of it. Besides, his daughters were older, and though they had all the creature comforts that his ample fortune could buy, he wanted to afford them as normal a life as he possibly could, one that he would never know. "I'm going to try to keep my family life personal from now on," he told me in 2009. "I just want to let the kids be kids, and I don't want to comment on them too much anymore because I've definitely done that."

"Harrison Ford once said that being famous is like walking down the street with a skunk on your head," says Dr. Donna Rockwell, who specializes in the psychological effects of fame. "I feel for people like Eminem because it's hard enough to live a life, but to have to live it in front of everybody is something else. To make mistakes in front of everybody, to have your heartaches in front of everybody. It's not easy, and it takes tremendous courage and bravery to keep walking down the street with that skunk on your head."

Perhaps as a part of the regime he followed to stay sober or perhaps simply for the sake of newfound creative inspiration, during the making of *Recovery*, Eminem switched up his production game, not only by working less with Dre but by parting ways (for the most part) with producers and engineers he had been relying on for years. He cleaned house and began to make music differently, enlisting a variety of producers, some of whom he'd never worked with before.

Overall, no matter who worked on the track, it was clear that Eminem's new musical direction was more serious than it had ever been. Considering the scatological references and juvenile one-upmanship throughout the record, it's inaccurate to say that he had matured exactly; it's more on point to say that he had grown older and wiser and more introspective. From *Recovery* forward, as he has entered his forties, Eminem's music has maintained a predominately serious tone with the occasional flippant nod to Shady, who has never again been given the pop star treatment showcased in "My Name Is," "The Real Slim Shady," "Without Me," and other songs. Eminem/Shady/Marshall Mathers do all have one thing in common besides residing in the mind of the greatest wordsmith rap has ever known: each one reflects a man who is an outsider, an anomaly, a singular voice in hip-hop. Free and clear and on the other side of the mountain that almost killed him, the lone wolf has become ever more isolated, his music ever more polarizing, and his place in hip-hop ever more rarefied and debated.

Chapter 6

See You in Hell

No matter how you slice it, 2010 was Eminem's year: ten Grammy nominations, 3.42 million copies of *Recovery* sold, making it the top-selling album of the year and his sixth to debut at number one, with two number one singles in "Not Afraid" and "Love the Way You Lie."[1] He was on every year-end list in both hip-hop and mainstream music and voted Hottest MC in the Game by MTV despite strong releases by peers like Jay-Z, Kayne, and Drake. *Recovery* wasn't just a reminder of how great a rapper, songwriter, and creator Eminem is; it also debuted an entirely new style of release from him.

Eminem's presobriety (*Relapse* included) Shady-heavy albums produced with Dr. Dre had begun to follow a format of upbeat, sing-song, deliberately catchy singles that took aim at pop culture figures and events current at the time of

---

1. Eminem was nominated more than any other performer at the Fifty-Third Annual Grammy Awards but walked away with only two wins—Best Rap Album and Best Rap Solo Performance for "Not Afraid." *Recovery* was Eminem's second year-ending bestseller: *The Eminem Show* earned that accolade with 7.61 million copies in 2002.

their recording. To continue the jester-like theme of defying expectations, the albums were far from the same. The singles were the odd kids out, with the remainder of the album cuts being much more intense, often introspective, menacing, and dark. It was always a fantastic feat to see Em turn dysfunction and aggression into singles so undeniably catchy and hilarious that the world couldn't keep from singing along to his most demented, fantastical couplets. That formula changed forever with *Recovery*. The singles were now straightforward songwriter affairs, tackling hefty subject matter and designed to reach the top of the pop charts in a more traditional manner. The goal was no longer to subvert the status quo but to enrich it.

To get there, he changed his work habits and his collaborators, opting to leave his home studio alone for the entire creation of *Recovery*. "I still have the studio at my house, but it reminds me of when I was in a really dark place," he says. "As soon as all the pills were flushed out of my system and I started seeing things clearer, going downstairs in my basement and recording creeped me out a bit."[2] Working with a variety of producers from Just Blaze to Boi-1da to Alex Da Kid and Jim Jonsin, most of whom he'd never worked with before, allowed Em to create a sound that was more varied and current. The resulting album was such a huge win because it had the lyricism to satisfy hardcore rap and Eminem fans as well as two bona fide pop powerhouse songs to hook younger fans.

---

2. Monica Herrera, "Eminem: The *Billboard* Cover Story," *Billboard*, June 25, 2010, https://www.billboard.com/articles/news/957616/eminem-the-billboard-cover -story.

Previously, Em's singles seemed to be aimed at people his age and younger—disenfranchised kids who identified with his angst and saluted his proud middle-finger wave to the mainstream pop world. Now, without sacrificing his credibility or performance identity, he had changed the message and, in so doing, hit a much more universal target.

The evolution inherent in *Recovery* speaks to another evolution in Eminem, because it is the first time that he took criticism to heart. Though he won a Best Rap Album Grammy for *Relapse* and saw it enter the charts at number one (it was also the best-selling rap release of the year and has sold over three million copies), he seemed to take the mixed reviews from critics and fans to heart. He had more than enough material recorded during the *Relapse* era to release a follow-up, but he didn't. Instead, he put out the few songs he felt were worthy on *Refill* and went back to the drawing board to rethink his entire sound and strategy. These were the choices of a very different man than Marshall Mathers circa 2002. "We all have a voice inside of us that I refer to as the 'inner critic,'" says Dr. Tina Galordi. "When you are using and the inner critic is really loud, you take substances to quiet it down. When you get rid of the substances and the inner critic gets really loud again, you have to fight it to be able to produce. As a result, you are going to be way more sensitive to criticism from the outside world if you are still battling fiercely with the inner critic. When someone in that stage hears criticism from the outside world, it increases it drastically in the inner world."

Eminem's overly critical view of himself and his music drove the perfectionism that resulted in *Recovery*. "I must have gone through 200–300 beats. I probably picked a hundred of them and made songs to all of them and then nailed it down. I wanted to put the best of the best on this record."[3]

As a sober artist, Eminem had to take every aspect of his art and creative process one step at a time, including touring of any duration. A change that was greater for him than performing sober, however, was performing without Proof, who had, on stage as he had in life, been beside Em since the start of his career. It was a tremendous decision to make, one that carried as much weight for Marshall as it did for the only person capable of filling those shoes, Denaun "Mr. Porter" Porter. "I didn't want to do it at first," he recalls. "When Marshall said it, I felt the weight of it on me, which is something he probably doesn't even understand, because choosing that role, you give up a lot of yourself. I was working to have an identity and was having one successfully as a producer. I never put out a solo album because I didn't want it to be in the shadow of D12. Me and Proof went back so far with him as his closest friends, though, that it made sense and of course I was going to do it, but in all honesty it was one of the hardest things I've ever had to do."

Porter had backed up Em before, here and there when Proof was sick or couldn't make a show, so he wasn't starting from scratch. Still, nothing could have prepared him for the emotional impact of standing in his fallen friend's footsteps for the first time, in their hometown, on May 19, 2009, at a free show at the Motor City Casino to celebrate the release

---

3. Herrera, "Eminem: The *Billboard* Cover Story."

of *Relapse*. "I broke down backstage afterwards," he says. "It was the most emotional experience I've ever gone through as a performer, period. But who the fuck else gonna do it? I had to, and it was an honor that day as it is every time I take the stage with Marshall. That was a weird night for me too because D12 was there and I thought they'd be more supportive, but they weren't. I didn't get no 'hey, that had to be hard,' no pats on the back. I guess it was weird for them, seeing me up there."

Porter wasn't expecting to be tapped to fill that role in Em's show; in fact, considering that he was in the throes of handling a few severe health issues, he was surprised to have been called upon at all. "I wasn't in my best skin; I wasn't happy with myself, with the way I looked, and, to be honest, I wasn't ready," he says. "If I'd have known he was ready to get back on stage that quick, I'd have at least hit the gym! I was up there that first time at 260 fucking pounds, just huge, in the worst physical shape I've ever been in. And I was already insecure. But I love Marshall so much for trusting me with such a thing, especially with me in that state." Porter has since gotten healthy, and he and Em have become a seamless team in concert. He has taken Paul Rosenberg's advice to have fun, be cool, and not worry about it and has truly come into his own as support MC. "The first couple years were crazy because I was literally tracing Proof's footsteps, all his cues, coming from the back when he would, ducking behind Em like he would. I'd be up there knowing I was doing what he used to do. I felt him up there, with us, and I still do, every night. It's very tough to be up there sometimes. It's like trying to cast your own shadow next to the Empire State Building, but, man, I tell you, I wouldn't trade it for anything. I get to travel and perform all over the world with family that I've known my whole life."

With the live show locked in, Em's team booked a series of European festival dates in the summer of 2010 and just four dates in the fall in support of *Recovery*. "I'll do these shows and see how I feel afterward, then set up a couple more," Em said. "I've had to relearn to do shows sober, because there were so many years that I didn't know how to do it. Alcohol, Valium—all these things were crutches for me so that I didn't have to feel anything when I went onstage. Everything right now is a step at a time, a day at a time."[4]

He might have been wary, but it didn't keep him from making history. Dubbed the Home and Home Tour, he and Jay-Z coheadlined four dates in their respective hometowns. Initially planned as just two concerts—one in Detroit and one in New York—an additional date was added to each tour stop after the first two sold out in a matter of hours. The tour was announced by Jay-Z and Eminem during a ball game between the Detroit Tigers and the New York Yankees since the shows would be taking place in each team's respective home stadium. The resulting performances were long walks through each artist's deep catalog of hits, featuring an array of collaborators, from Dr. Dre, 50 Cent, D12, G-Unit, Trick Trick, and others for Em's sets and Beyoncé, Kanye, Chris Martin of Coldplay, Drake, Nicki Minaj, Memphis Bleek, and more

---

4. Herrera, "Eminem: The *Billboard* Cover Story."

for Jay's sets. The four-date tour made an estimated $15–$20 million.[5] Those who saw them, fans and reviewers alike, were left breathless after more than four hours of top-notch hip-hop. "I was fortunate enough—yes, fortunate enough—to attend the duo's first of two dates at Yankee Stadium and my experience can be summed up in one word: Wow," wrote Alex Young in *Consequence of Sound*.[6]

The show was, as Jay-Z said during his Yankee Stadium set, "a historic night. There will never be another night like this." He was right; it was a tour-de-force retrospective of two artists with different styles and different backgrounds who had traveled far and were still at the top of their game. It was an epic exploration of the music, complete with fitting tributes to fallen figures like Proof and the Notorious B.I.G. Jay-Z even called hip-hop pioneer DJ Kool Herc up to the stage from the audience to pay tribute to his contribution to the culture that had been born right where they were standing.[7] "We wouldn't be here without you," Jay-Z said above the roar of a deafening crowd. "Whether you love or admire or respect them from a distance, Jay-Z and Eminem were remarkably, at times exhaustingly serious artists sweating out their lives

5. Staff, "The 2010 HipHopDX Year End Awards," *HipHopDX*, December 13, 2010.

6. Alex Young, "Jay-Z, Eminem, Kanye and Friends Dazzle Yankee Stadium," *Consequence of Sound*, September 14, 2010, https://consequenceofsound.net/2010/09/jay-z-eminem-kanye-and-friends-dazzle-yankee-stadium-913/.

7. Kool Herc, born Clive Campbell, is the Bronx-raised Jamaican American DJ who is credited with isolating the drum breaks in hard funk records. He used the two turntables and a mixer setup common among disco DJs of the 1970s to mix between the same section of two copies of a record to extend the break. Essentially, he created the sonic backbone of rap music and hip-hop culture.

in vivid detail on a Jumbotron canvas," Charles Aaron wrote in Spin. "The next generation of stars, many of whom were in attendance, inevitably will struggle not to seem pixilated and daunted by comparison."[8]

The concert was, in scope, intent, production, and perform-ance, a serious affair, the likes of which had never been seen in hip-hop. "It was an amazing night, worthy of comparison to the Rolling Stones or Springsteen," wrote Mick Stingley in the Hollywood Reporter, "though after four hours, one can see why these things don't happen every day."[9] It was an opportunity that perfectly reflected Eminem's new sound and persona. He had reinvented himself, how he worked and how he sounded, and though beloved hits like "My Name Is," "The Real Slim Shady," and "Without Me" made it into his set, Eminem seemed most energized performing newer material and anthems old and new like "Cleanin' Out My Closet," "Sing for the Moment," "Like Toy Soldiers," and of course "Not Afraid" and "Love the Way You Lie." For the first time in too long, Mathers seemed to know exactly who he was and where he wanted to go.

Eminem entered 2011 celebrating a rare pedigree. In April, two of his albums were certified diamond by the RIAA, sig-nifying sales in excess of ten million copies apiece—the only rapper to hold that distinction at the time. The albums were

8. Charles Aaron, "Jay-Z and Eminem in NYC: 'Illest' Show Ever," Spin, September 14, 2010, https://www.spin.com/2010/09/jay-z-and-eminem-nyc-illest-show-ever/.

9. Mick Stingley, "Jay-Z and Eminem, Concert Review," Hollywood Reporter, Oc-tober 14, 2010, https://www.hollywoodreporter.com/review/jay-z-and-eminem-concert-30015.

The Marshall Mathers LP and *The Eminem Show*. He would later receive two more diamond certifications for the singles "Not Afraid" and "Love the Way You Lie." In the earliest months of 2011, Eminem was named the top-selling artist of the first decade of the new millennium, selling thirty-two million copies of his albums between 2000 and 2010.[10]

For all the times he had announced that he was back, this time there was no doubt. His next project would see an even greater return to his roots than anything he'd done. It was, quite literally, more than a decade in the making. Bad Meets Evil was the short-lived group he formed at the behest of Proof with fellow Detroit lyricist Royce da 5'9" (born Ryan Montgomery) back in 1998, just before Shadymania took the world, and Marshall Mathers, by storm. They released one single, "Nuttin' to Do," with the B side "Scary Movies," on Game Recordings. CD versions of the single included an additional Royce track, "I'm the King." Recorded at the height of his Slim Shadiest, the material bears all the markings of what underground fans fell in love with: irreverent, offensive imagery, top-notch rhyme schemes, gangsta rap–inspired beats, and off-kilter, unexpected vocabulary. In Royce, Eminem had a true lyrical partner.

From the start, the duo organically fed off each other, and quite possibly there are none in hip-hop who have stitched together narrative lines as complicated as these two. They

10. Roy Trakin, "Eminem First to Receive Two RIAA Digital Single Diamond Awards," *Billboard*, June 10, 2014, https://www.billboard.com/articles/news /6114162/eminem-first-to-receive-two-riaa-digital-single-diamond-awards.

have a similar approach not only to storytelling but to rhyme itself, and when they are on a track together, the creative one-upmanship is mutually cathartic and inspirational. They met in 1997 at the Palladium in Detroit when Royce was opening for Usher, and with Proof's encouragement, they started working together. They recorded the track "Bad Meets Evil," which was featured on *The Slim Shady LP* and from which they took their moniker, but their first release was the aforementioned single, "Nuttin' to Do." The B side, "Scary Movies," was eventually featured on the soundtrack to the parody film *Scary Movie* in 2000.

One of the duo's great early collaborations was the song "Renegade," which was recorded and intended for Royce's first studio album, *Rock City*, released in 2002. Most hip-hop fans know the more popular version of that song: the one featuring Jay-Z and Eminem from Jay's 2001 classic, *The Blueprint*.[11] At the time, Eminem and Royce had completed "Renegade" as well as "Rock City," intended as the title cut on Royce's debut. However, Interscope Records would only allow Royce to feature their new boy wonder on one track of his album. Royce chose "Rock City" and put "Renegade" aside. When Jay-Z called Eminem, since Em knew "Renegade" would not be released, he asked Royce for permission to give the song to Jay. When Royce agreed, his vocals were removed, Eminem changed one line (in which he called Royce the king of Detroit), and after Jay-Z laid down his

---

11. Released September 11, 2001, the same day as the terrorist attacks on New York City.

verses, the only track that Eminem and Jay-Z have ever collaborated on came to be.[12]

"Renegade" has further historical significance in the history of hip-hop. As is wont to occur in a genre based on competition, much ado has been made among fans over who outdid who on that song. Beauty lies in the ear of the beholder, of course, but comparing these two rappers here or anywhere is more a case of apples and oranges. On "Renegade," Jay-Z tells the story of his upbringing as a drug dealer and an outlaw and getting out of the game before it claimed him, and he does so in a poetic style, utilizing emotive imagery. By contrast, Eminem's verses focus on being targeted by society for his outspoken, outlandish, and offensive lyrics. His verse is more complex linguistically, with dexterous use made of internal rhyme schemes. In general, Eminem is a more straight-ahead rapper who drops lines that are easy to grasp because their meanings are crystal clear. He would rather hit you over the head with his intended message but do so in a manner more linguistically complicated than the average listener realizes. Eminem utilizes double entendre and certainly has done so more as he's grown older, but he has never shown a preference toward phrases with obscure meanings. He says exactly what he means in a complicated, multilayered fashion, whereas Jay-Z is more likely to evoke a mood, using coded references to his life's events. In general, Eminem's rhyme play sounds better to the ear, catching the listener with the physical act

---

12. Yoh Phillips, "Eminem Handed 'Renegade' to Jay-Z After It Got Cut from Royce da 5'9"'s Album," *DJBooth*, April 19, 2016, https://djbooth.net/features/2016-04-19-eminem-jay-z-renegade-history.

of his percussive use and abuse of language. By contrast, Jay conveys a story through the melodious implementation of cinematic language and description. On "Renegade," Em's delivery is his acrobatic greatest, impossible to ignore for its verbal athleticism, while Jay's is his beloved signature style—coasting, boasting, and bulletproof.

Wherever you stand on the issue, remember that Eminem wrote his verses before he knew that they would be placed next to Jay's, on a Jay-Z song no less, not to mention as the only rapper featured on the entirety of *The Blueprint*. Clearly Em was confident in the quality of his output on the track, because no one would want to give anything less than their career best on a stage of such significance at the start of their big-league rap career. The track is legendary, even more so because this cast-aside Royce song ended up at the center of one of the most interesting moments in the most creative and celebrated hip-hop beef in history: Jay-Z versus Nas. Eminem's verses on "Renegade" are one of Nas's many points of focus on the incredible Jay-Z diss track "Ether" from his 2001 album *Stillmatic*. "Ether" is the reason the Em versus Jay "Renegade" debate exists at all. Among a host of insults slung at Jay, ranging from stealing other rappers' styles and ideas to having an affair with Foxy Brown to being ugly, Nas spits, "And Eminem murdered you on your own shit."[13] "Ether" is considered one of the wildest, most unhinged diss tracks in the history of hip-hop and a crucial turning point in the long-running feud between the two that energized and boosted both rappers'

---

13. Foxy Brown later confirmed this a few years later on her track "Let Em Know."

careers. The song has become the bar by which all other diss tracks are judged and has been sampled and referenced by artists from Game to Joe Budden to Joey Bada$$. Eminem even sampled it in the Xzibit song "My Name," which was a diss song to Jermaine Dupri, and today, in hip-hop and urban slang, to "ether" someone means to completely destroy your opponent in a highly humiliating fashion. The Em and Jay version is a classic, but the original version of "Renegade" featuring Royce, which was later released on mixtapes, is no slouch either. It is an interesting case study as to how two rappers can take a beat and a narrative in two very different directions.

Thanks to Eminem, Dr. Dre heard "Renegade," as well as "Bad Meets Evil," which he decided to include on *The Slim Shady LP*. After Royce flew to LA to recut his vocals for the album version of the song, Dre expressed interest in signing him to his label, Aftermath. Royce was even tapped to do some ghostwriting that was featured in "The Message" on Dr. Dre's *2001*. This was a dream come true for an up-and-coming rapper, but the dream ended when Royce's manager, Akino Childrey, did an interview where he publicly revealed that Royce had ghostwritten for Dre and dissed Dre's rap skills: "I've seen Em sit Dre down like a pupil and coach him on rhymes." Dre told Royce that if they were to work together, he would have to fire his manager, and when Royce refused, their working relationship ended.[14] Royce then signed to Tommy Boy Records for a reported $1 million, which was significantly

14. Royce is still managed by Akino Childrey.

greater than the quarter million being offered by Aftermath. That offer, however, came with unlimited access to beats by the Doctor—a decision that the rapper regrets having made to this day.

At the very beginning of his major-label career, Royce was Eminem's hype man, stepping in when Marshall and Proof (as well as Marshall and the others in D12) were experiencing the type of periodic falling out that occurs between lifelong best friends, particularly in their hard-partying twenties. They eventually reconciled, and when they did, Mathers began to focus on promoting D12's career. This caused friction between him and Royce, as it put pending projects the pair were planning on hold. Royce protested by resigning as Eminem's hype man halfway through his dates on the Vans Warped Tour, marking the moment that Proof assumed that role for Em until the day he died. It also was the start of an estrangement between Royce and the Shady camp that continued for years and nearly turned lethally violent. The he-said–he-said of it all is more complex than any of those involved care to relive or officially comment on for this book, but a few key events are worth mentioning for the sake of posterity.

The beef resulted in a series of diss tracks, and the very public rivalry, which obviously spelled the end of Bad Meets Evil, carried on for several years. On the Royce side, his musical output focused on five of the six members of the group. Royce struck first with "Shit on You," recorded over an instrumental version of the D12 song of the same name and aimed at D12 member Bizarre. He then released "Malcolm X," after which D12 responded with "Smack Down," which was recorded over the instrumental version of 50 Cent's "Back Down." In addition, Proof recorded a track about Royce called "Many Men," which was recorded over 50's song "Many Men (Wish Death)," as well as another track recorded with ICP affiliates the Purple Gang called "Beef Is Ova." In response, Royce released a third diss track, "Death Day," recorded over 50 Cent's "In Da Club" instrumental.

The antagonism came to a head in the summer of 2003 when Proof and Royce got into an altercation outside a Detroit club. Friends of both rappers joined the tussle, resulting in Royce drawing a gun and Proof and Royce being arrested. The two spent the night in adjacent cells and talked out their differences, thereby ending the feud.[15] The death of Proof brought Eminem and Royce back together in 2006, but it wasn't until 2008, when Em was freshly sober, that they started talking regularly again. "We haven't really spoken in depth about anything creative," Royce said at the time. "That session hasn't happened yet. He told me he had some of the best shit recorded right now that he's ever done in his life. I ain't even got a chance to get with him to hear it yet. He ain't heard what I got and I ain't heard what he got. That's kind of like what our friendship is, it's always been real competitive. It's always been that we motivate each other. And I think we at a point in our careers where we both need that . . . I felt like I never had a beef with him. It was more of a falling out

---

15. Royce and D12 buried the hatchet so thoroughly that Royce was featured on the 2008 D12 project *Return of the Dozen*, and their subsequent tour of Europe and Canada, as well as on *The Devil's Night Mixtape* in 2015.

between two brothers. It was just two brothers not speaking to each other for a minute. But now we speaking again. So sky's the limit on what's gonna happen from here."[16]

The pair had both been through tough times: after three DUIs, coupled with three instances of driving with a suspended license, a Detroit judge sentenced Royce to a year in jail in 2006. Royce emerged with a renewed vigor and immediately jumped back into music. He wrote "Tell Me" for Diddy's album *Press Play*, began a working relationship with the legendary DJ Premier, and released a trilogy of mixtapes (*The Bar Exam*, *The Bar Exam 2*, and *Street Hop*) that cemented his long-overdue reputation as one of rap's great lyricists. He also teamed up with rapper Joe Budden, Crooked I, and Joell Ortiz to form the underground supergroup Slaughterhouse, which was eventually signed to Shady Records by Eminem and Paul Rosenberg in 2011. It was at this point that Eminem and Royce began collaborating again, and after more than a decade, Bad Meets Evil was resurrected.

"It felt like the continuation of a conversation, and even though it started many years before, there were no hiccups at all," Royce says. "Everything felt natural and organic, and if there's one thing that I've learned as an artist in the past twenty years, it's that the things that feel the most natural and don't feel forced, the things that happen when they're supposed to, those are the things that usually work out the best for me. This album was one of those things. We didn't go

16. Paul Arnold, "Breaking: Eminem and Royce da 5'9" Squash Beef," *HipHopDX*, March 12, 2008, https://hiphopdx.com/news/id.6542/title.breaking-eminem-and -royce-da-59-squash-beef.

in with any type of caveat in mind, not trying to make any type of record. We just went in, recorded, had fun with it, and it worked for us."

Hell: The Sequel was worth waiting for, because it is everything the duo's auspicious beginnings promised: complex rhyme schemes, rapping at the speed of sound, and songs with alternating verses that become increasingly tighter until the pair are going line for line, finishing each other's thoughts. There is no duo in rap that comes close to this degree of lyrical integration and heightened technicality. The EP was recorded over just six months in 2010, and two of the songs, "Living Proof" and "Echo," were leaked in November of that year.

The entire project was executive produced by Mr. Porter, who was as much a fan as he was a guide and collaborator. "Me and Royce started going in on it at my studio, and when Em joined us, he told me, 'You kickin' ass, man,'" he says. "It wasn't hard; watching the two of them going back and forth in the room was incredible. I didn't know what I was going to get every time, so for me it was a pleasure. Some days I'd put a piece of music together just to see what they'd do with it. Every blue moon a producer gets lucky, and I was privileged and blessed to get an opportunity like that. It was like watching Muhammad Ali and Mike Tyson sparring. My first executive production credit was with two of the best in the world! To me, they are the best rappers out there, and they both make incredible songs. If Royce had a bigger platform people would realize that. Motherfuckers don't put him in their Top 5 lists, which is just crazy, but fuck a list anyway!"

The finished nine-track EP was released in June 2011, debuting at number one on the *Billboard* Hot 100. It sold 171,000 copies in its first week and was certified gold in August. For the most part, the EP received positive reviews because there is no denying the stylistic chemistry between Eminem and Royce. On the EP's first single, "Fast Lane," the pair are in top form, showing off the horrorcore-laced boasts and second-to-none verbal proficiency they are known for. The hook, sung by Sly Jordan, is delivered in classic G-funk style, à la the late great Nate Dogg.

The song "Taken from Me" sees both rappers lamenting those in their lives who take advantage. In Royce's case, he calls out his older brother and their problematic relationship.[17]

> I ain't tryin' to say something I'd regret
> So I'mma just stop chasin' the pain
> And let you deal with the fact that we don't get along
> 'Cause I got a big face in the game.

Em's verses confront his relationship with those who steal or leak his music as well as fans who are critical of the changes in his content and delivery in recent years.

> You might not think it's that big of a deal
> To steal from me, but music's all I got
> Aside from my daughters, not to sound like a martyr.

Hell: The Sequel was Eminem's gift to the hardcore fans, because it provided an opportunity for him to become Slim Shady once more, with an equally gifted accomplice riding

---

17. Royce would go into further detail about his brother on the track "Protecting Ryan" in his autobiographical masterpiece, 2018's *Book of Ryan*.

shotgun. It was a safe place for Shady following his exorcism on *Relapse*. Enough time had passed and enough reinvention had been accomplished that Em was able to put on his old costume for this reunion with an old friend. Whereas *Relapse* was a painful dive into Slim Shady's serial killer pathology, on this outing, Em/Shady seemed genuinely happy to be exploring his old stomping ground, no doubt energized by the tangible creative electricity of his partner in rhyme. While just about any other rapper alive would fall flat alongside Eminem unhinged, Royce, never a sidekick, always an equal, holds his own. Even on songs like "Reunion," with the type of nightmarish nursery rhyme melody that typically accompanies Shady's darkest exploits and sickest lyrical moments, Royce's storyline is equally compelling and twisted. The song tells the tale of a hapless girl who makes the mistake of thinking that Marshall/Shady is much nicer than he seems on record, while Royce describes a vicious fight between his wife and his mistress in a club. The language here and throughout the album is as unflinching, misogynist, and violent as the deepest depths Shady has ever plumbed, and as a result some saw the EP as a "step back for both rappers."[18] It was, of course: it was the culmination of a relationship that was cut short thirteen years earlier. A. T. Horton put it best: "Eminem and Royce da 5'9" are perfectly capable of standing on their own, but it's clear that even after all these years, they inspire something special

---

18. Alex Young, "Bad Meets Evil, 'Hell: The Sequel,'" *Consequence of Sound*, June 15, 2001, https://consequenceofsound.net/2011/06/album-review-bad-meets-evil-ihell-the-sequel/.

in each other. They may have gone through hell separately, but it's hip-hop heaven when they're together."[19]

The only moment on *Hell: The Sequel* that does not add up is the single that went double platinum and kept the EP on the charts, "Lighters," featuring a chorus sung by Bruno Mars. His yearning, sensitive performance ("This one's for you and me / Livin' out our dreams / We are right where we should be") over a simple piano line, combined with Royce and Eminem's uplifting, positive verses are quite the contrast to the lighthearted song about drug abuse, "I'm On Everything (ft. Mike Epps)," and low-down Bad Meets Evil fare like "The Reunion" and "Above the Law (ft. Claret Jai)." "Lighters" would have been right at home on *Recovery*, but perhaps that was the point—to include something that would hook fans of Eminem's more pop material into listening to the entire record—at which point they would be pummeled by hardcore horror rap and some of the most well-crafted verses in hip-hop that year. "We figured we'd have one song for other people to listen to," Royce said. "People who don't like listening to straight-up, raw, rappitty-rap lyrics. One joint to show versatility."[20]

Though *Hell: The Sequel* covered the hell that each rapper had gone through—Royce's incarceration and the troubled

19. A. T. Horton, "Bad Meets Evil (Eminem & Royce Da 5'9")—*Hell: The Sequel*," *HipHopDX*, June 13, 2011, https://hiphopdx.com/reviews/id.1698/title.bad -meets-evil-eminem-royce-da-59-hell-the-sequel.

20. Luke Fox, "Royce Da 5'9" Talks Bad Meets Evil, Explains How the Bruno Mars- equipped 'Lighters' Got Lit," *Exclaim*, June 20, 2011, http://exclaim.ca/music /article/royce_da_59_talks_bad_meets_evil_explains_how_bruno_mars-equipped _lighters_got_lit.

family issues he was just beginning to discuss in his music, and Mathers's struggles with sobriety, fame, and his place in hip-hop—the battle was far from won for Royce. He had yet to quit drinking despite its increasingly tragic effects on his life and his health. He tried to get it in check to no avail over the next few years, quitting his poison of choice, tequila, for wine, but nothing curbed his addictive appetite. It took the threat of losing his wife and children, a situation exacerbated by the emergence of a sex tape of Royce with another woman, to set him straight. In a moment of clarity and not wanting to continue his dysfunctional patterns, he reached out to Marshall for help and entered a hospital soon after.

"When we recorded the album, I would work with Em in the daytime until about 7:00 or 8:00 p.m.; then as soon as we were done I'd go straight to the store and get my alcohol for the day, then continue on to another studio where I'd record my night sessions and get twisted," Royce recalls. "I'd never drink in front of him, but some days I'd need to go to the store and get little shooter bottles and drink one real quick when he wasn't looking. I could always write sober as long as I knew I had a drink coming later."

As he is for Royce in the studio, Marshall Mathers was the push Royce needed to start the process of eradicating alcohol from his life. "Everything he does inspires me, his whole journey. When we got back to being cool, just to see the level at which he was recording and all of the work he was putting in was eye-opening to me. I feel like Marshall was put in my life to inspire me and to set things straight when I needed it. When he has put his hand on me and touched my life were when I got my first record deal and when he helped me get sober. Those are milestones." Like Em, it took Royce quite some time to relearn the creative process once he got sober. "It took me about a year to learn how to use my brain and have it click on all cylinders," Royce says. "One of the first things I had to learn was patience. That was the biggest lesson. If something isn't working you've got to sit there and wait it out; there's no taking shortcuts. At first I'd go to the studio, sit there for four or five hours, get frustrated, and leave. When I was drinking, I'd never leave without being able to write something, so I panicked. I thought I had lost it. This went on for a whole year. But once you learn extreme patience, you eliminate the existence of writer's block. Once you understand that what you are trying to express is in your mind and you know it's coming at some point, then there is no writer's block."

A truly Zen-like approach was the only way through for Royce. "I spent hours, long days in the studio until I had no concept of time," he says. "There was no other way. I had to be there to do it. I shut everything else down and gave it all to the art. If you really want to make something that is gonna last, that is what you need to do. Marshall would tell me not to worry, just wait and it will come. And it did."

As for the future of Bad Meets Evil, all signs point to further collaboration, particularly considering the amazing production work Mr. Porter did on Royce's album *Book of Ryan* (2018), featuring "Caterpillar," a stand-out track featuring

Em. "I'm always ready to drop whatever I'm doing and jump right in when he's ready," Royce says with a chuckle, "but he goes through different creative and mental processes, you know what I'm saying? So whenever he's ready and he gives me a call, I'm ready."

Eminem spent the next months working on Slaughterhouse's *Welcome to: Our House*, which would be the most successful and final album by the hip-hop supergroup. He also began writing and recording the material for his next album. In May 2012, he did a few radio interviews and revealed on Detroit's 95.5 that he had begun work on it, but it wasn't until August when he revealed on his Sirius station, Shade 45, that he was devoting himself entirely to writing and recording his next album and that Dr. Dre would play a larger role than he had on *Recovery*. Eminem laid low for the next six months, and no news was released until February 2013, when Paul Rosenberg announced what was ahead for Shady Records. "We fully expect to be releasing a new Eminem album in 2013," he said. "He's been working on it for some time. It's safe to say that it will be post–Memorial Day at some point, but we're not exactly sure when." The album was released quite a bit later, in November 2013, leaving an eager public to speculate as details began to leak over the next months. The world wondered where this album would fall along the spectrum of styles and content and if it would live up to Royce's estimation of what he heard at a very early stage. "Marshall is in the studio right now, laying the most awesome lyrics in the world," he said. "I'm not so sure how the world is going to respond from some of the things I've heard from him."[21] The world responded with monumental enthusiasm, celebrating a return to form that critics and fans weren't sure they'd ever see from Eminem again.

21. Rob Markman, "Eminem and No I.D. Collaborating for the First Time," *MTV News*, September 10, 2012, http://www.mtv.com/news/2499157/eminem-no -id-recording-together/.

Chapter 7

Rap God

Every artist who hits a creative peak faces the unavoidable reality that peaks aren't flat. They can be spacious, and artists can devise ways to stretch them into plateaus, but even in cartoons, the longest plateaus slope down at the end. The question remains: How to scale those creative heights again? Some attempt an ascent every outing, the best attaining that peerless view for at least a passing moment each go. Others seek inspiration elsewhere, turning sharply from their previous path. Some find new peaks altogether. Others never do. Regardless, it is inevitable that artists who remain relevant will have their subsequent work compared to their past glories, just as it is inevitable that fans of their original best will yearn for that artist to transport them back to the moment they first heard it.

It is a tricky business, a risky enterprise, one that walks a tightrope with no net between two chasms: banking on nostalgia and destroying a legacy. Consider how infrequently sequels equal or exceed the quality of the original: for every

Godfather II and *Empire Strikes Back* there are countless *Jaws 2*s and *Hangover* films. The worst sequels, like bad reboots, recycle the best moments of the original, striving for the same result but often imparting no more than a queasy sense of déjà vu.[1] The best sequels pick up where the first left off and then some: they add a new chapter that both gives depth to the original and tells a new story in its own right. The best sequels are companions, not copycats.

With *The Marshall Mathers LP2*, Eminem accomplished the near-impossible task of creating a bookend to a masterpiece. *The Marshall Mathers LP* is one of the most justifiably celebrated albums of the millennium and was created at the absolute apex of his career. It is a storytelling tour de force—unflinching, honest, and cinematic in its scope. At the time, no figure was more simultaneously polarizing and reflective of what it meant to be coming of age in America (and the world) to a huge cross section of the population. To those his barbed and violent rhymes victimized and offended—predominantly gays and women—he was a living boogeyman. To those whose pain, confusion, and angst he drafted into a Technicolor slasher cinema verité of his life, he was a hero. And to those who worshipped the masterful wordplay at the heart of rap music, he was an innovator the likes of which they'd never heard. He was a lightning bolt that struck earth, leaving a scorched crater in his wake.

---

1. All signs point to Hollywood eventually just remaking the same film over and over. At last count, there are three Spidermans, five Batmans, five Hulks, and three Hollywood Godzillas.

It was a brave decision to set foot on such ground again. "Calling it *The Marshall Mathers LP2*, obviously I knew that there might be certain expectations," he said. "I wouldn't want to call it that just for the sake of calling it that. I had to make sure that I had the right songs—and just when you think you've got it, you listen and you're like, 'Fuck, man! I feel like it needs this or that' to paint the whole picture . . . To me, it's more about the vibe, and it's more about the nostalgia."[2]

It is a testament to Eminem's creative impulse and never-say-die worldview that after enduring the first bad reviews of his career for *Encore* and *Relapse*, at the darkest point in his life, he settled on a sound and formula with *Recovery* that worked critically and commercially. He essentially created his own genre—the rap power ballad—the roots of which harken back to "Cleanin' Out My Closet" and "Lose Yourself," but in terms of pop crossover appeal, this style of Eminem song truly came into its own on *Recovery*. Most artists regaining their confidence and their hold on the public's attention might err on the side of safety and stay in that lane on their next album, but Em did not. In fact, "The Monster," again featuring Rihanna, is the only song on *TMMLP2* that seems out of place. It sold triple platinum and went to number one in the United States and eleven other countries, and though it does fit in with the themes explored on the rest of the album, stylistically it might as well have been imported from

2. Brian Hiatt, "Eminem Exclusive: Slim Shady on His New LP," *Rolling Stone*, October 23, 2013, https://www.rollingstone.com/music/music-news/eminem-exclusive-slim-shady-on-his-new-lp-78117/.

Recovery, which is something that cannot be said about any of the other twenty-one tracks.

Eminem at his finest embodies unbridled rhyme, obsessive-compulsive wordplay, a fiend's appetite for vocabulary. Those lucky enough to have been around him in his early days (myself among them) all have stories about Em rhyming constantly, rapping in a stream of consciousness flow about whatever he laid his eyes on, mimicking people's speaking voices, adopting (yes, to great comedic effect) accents, and generally just having a ball. It was as if rap and rhyme were oozing from him in abundance, and he had no choice but to give it release. He learned to harness and hone this gift as he evolved beyond his roots as a battle rapper into a more nuanced and masterful storyteller. There was a hyperactive glee to his output in those early days that carried over, a brilliant light that fame, drama, and substances slowly dimmed and nearly extinguished.

For the first time in years, on *TMMLP2*, Marshall Mathers sounded like he'd found a Mountain Dew–filled fountain of youth within him and rediscovered a love for the past. He'd had to relearn how to write as his mind cleared from the drug haze, and on this album, it felt like everything had finally fallen into place. Though *Relapse* and *Recovery* were chock-full of distilled, intricate rhymes, none of them was ever as swaggeringly fun as those on *TMMLP2*. Even when spewing homophobic and misogynist hate or exorcising deep-seated childhood trauma, the pure enthusiasm of his delivery on the record conveys a lust for life that had long been absent.

This is, of course, precisely the quality that conservative religious, women's, and LGBT rights groups have always found most dangerous about Eminem's music. He is a great elocutionist, and like a rap Sinatra, his words are as easy to hear as his lyrics (aside from his extensive double and triple entendres) are to understand. When confronted with his most deliberately offensive verses, many of them delivered in a psychotic isn't-this-fun lilt, it's also easy to understand why his attitude is taken for unapologetic zeal. Though he's long made a case for those moments being tongue-in-cheek and not reflective of his beliefs in real life, Eminem has never once eased off the hate-filled language and shocking imagery.[3] *The Marshall Mathers LP* signified the height of his status as a societal blight, one in which his concerts and television appearances were picketed. If anything, this album echoes but doesn't duplicate the harsh language of its predecessor. Homophobic and misogynist imagery have always been part and parcel of Eminem's canon, a feature amplified by his battle-rap instinct to take every image and metaphor to its absolute limit where it cannot be bested.

His words are intended to shock and awe, but to some degree they are inspired by true events. Marshall Mathers's complicated feelings toward women are simply part of his makeup, a side effect of complicated, traumatic, contentious, and abusive relationships with his mother and the mother of his daughter. *The Marshall Mathers LP* explored those relationships through the lens of visceral, graphic murder

---

3. In an interview with Anderson Cooper on *60 Minutes* in 2010, Mathers claimed that he doesn't allow profanity or cursing in his house or around his daughters.

fantasies, as it also delved into how the desperation of poverty, neglect, a broken home, and an inability to fit in effected the young man who became Eminem.

On *The Marshall Mathers LP2*, the rapper looks back at these issues and the first album with thirteen years of life and MC experience on his side. It is a reexploration of that moment in time, the influences, musical and otherwise, that got him there, and how he felt about all of it as a sober-thinking man of forty-one. Considering the generally somber tone of *Recovery* and Eminem's tendency, post-*Encore*, to rap, larynx clenched, the way he did on "The Way I Am," there was every chance that this trip down memory lane could have been an adrenaline-soaked rage reunion. Far from it, the album is the most musical, entertaining, and diverse collection he'd put together since *The Eminem Show*.

The opening song, "Bad Guy," is a direct link to the first album, brilliantly picking up where "Stan" left off. It opens ominously with the sound of slasher film synth strings over the noise of someone sifting dirt. The first verses lead the listener to believe that the song is another Eminem murder ballad, likely aimed at Kim, his mother, or another lucky lady in his life.

> Can I hold grudges? Mind saying, "Let it go, fuck this."
> Heart's saying, "I will, once I bury this bitch alive
> Hide the shovel and then drive off in the sunset."

For all intents and purposes, this is business as usual in Eminem's musical universe and an indicator that this sequel may be just another reboot after all. There is a hint in the second verse that things might not be what they seem ("You left our family in shambles / And you expect me to just get over him, pretend he never existed?"), as he employs a slightly different vocal delivery (representing a character who has yet to be identified), but it isn't until the third verse that Eminem ties the past and the present together, revealing that the narrator is Stan's little brother, Matthew Mitchell, now all grown up and seeking revenge on Eminem for causing Stan's suicide.

> *Last album now, 'cause after this you'll be officially done*
> *Eminem killed by M and M, Matthew Mitchell*
> *Bitch, I even have your initials.*

The song then witnesses Matthew kidnapping Marshall, putting him in the trunk of his car like he did to Kim and Stan did to his pregnant girlfriend, with a plan to bury Mathers alive in the grave the listener now realizes he was digging at the start of the song. But after speeding (doing ninety on the freeway—another "Stan" reference) and attracting the attention of the police, Matthew decides to drive the car off a bridge into the water, letting Eminem drown the way his brother and brother's girlfriend did.

The most interesting and exciting part of the song, however, is the fourth verse, when the car hits the water, the kick drum and music fall away, and a narrator's voice takes on something greater, a type of supernatural embodiment of Marshall Mathers's karma coming to collect its debt for all the wrongs he's done in his lyrics.

> *I'm the bullies you hate that you became*
> *With every faggot you slaughtered*

Coming back on you every woman you insult, batter
But the double-standards you have when it comes to your daughters.

A funereal dirge—driven by cinematic keys and a military-style snare lifted from Lou Donaldson's oft-sampled "Ode to Billie Joe"[4]—picks up as the list of consequences of Mathers's lyrical crimes continues, embodied by ringing ears, vocal cord polyps, and denial that his career is ending. The voice grows fainter as he portrays Eminem as a tragic artist tortured by his own drawings, trying to capture lightning in a bottle twice, until:

Blacker and darker than anything imaginable
Here goes a wild stab in the dark
As we pick up where the last Mathers left off.

If Eminem was at all worried about falling short of the heights he had attained in his best storytelling songs, he checked that box in the first track, because "Bad Guy" is as strong as his most epic poems. "The way I was thinking when I wrote the song was, what if this nightmare just happened: I decided to do this album and everything started coming back on me," he said. "Matthew came back, Stan's little brother, he came back to kill me, just all this shit started happening."[5]

---

4. Elements of this 1967 track from the saxophonist's album *Mr. Shing-a-Ling* have appeared through the years in more than a hundred hip-hop tracks by a diverse collection of artists, among them a Tribe Called Quest, Lauryn Hill, Cypress Hill, Kool Keith, Kanye West, J Dilla, Das EFX, and Onyx.
5. Nadeska Alexis, "Did You Find the Secret Buried in *The Marshall Mathers LP2*? Eminem Opens the Closet," *MTV News*, November 12, 2013, http://www.mtv .com/news/1717299/eminem-marshall-mathers-lp-2-bad-guy-stan-connection/.

"Bad Guy" is a masterful opener, tying the past to the present, continuing a saga of obsessive fandom so well crafted on *The Marshall Mathers LP* that the word "stan" has been added to the English language as a noun and verb.[6] That would be enough, but it also presents a predominant theme of the record that unfolds more like a rock opera than anything ever attempted in the history of hip-hop: a rapper's Dickensian revisitation of the past in order to understand the choices and consequences that led the protagonist to the present.[7]

After Marshall drifts to the bottom of Lake Michigan, murdered by the legacy of his evil rhymes, the direct DNA link to the first record continues in the next track with the skit "Parking Lot." "Criminal," the final song on *The Marshall Mathers LP*, begins with Eminem criticizing anyone who thinks that

---

6. "Stan" was added to the *Oxford English Dictionary* in 2017. The official entry is as follows: "stan, informal, noun: An overzealous or obsessive fan of a particular celebrity. verb: Be an overzealous or obsessive fan of a particular celebrity. Origin: Early 21st century; probably with allusion to the 2000 song 'Stan,' by the American rapper Eminem, about an obsessed fan. sample sentence, n: he has millions of stans who are obsessed with him and call him a rap god. sample sentence, v: He's the only gay man not stanning for Beyoncé." *Oxford English Dictionary*, s.v. "stan," accessed July 2019, https://www.lexico.com/en/definition/stan.

7. There have been a few examples of "hip hopera" over the years, among them *Carmen: A Hip Hopera*, a 2001 musical film interpretation of the 1875 opera *Carmen* produced by MTV, featuring Mekhi Phifer, Mos Def, Rah Digga, Wyclef Jean, Jermaine Dupri, and Beyoncé Knowles in her first acting role. There have been hip-hop productions of *Romeo and Juliet*, and of course there is the Broadway smash *Hamilton*. In terms of albums as conceptual pieces akin to rock operas like *Tommy* (1969) by the Who, *The Wall* (1979) by Pink Floyd, and *American Idiot* (2004) by Green Day, there are few: *Trapped in the Closet* (2005–2012) by R. Kelly, *The Incredible True Story* (2015) by Logic, *A Grand Don't Come for Free* (2004) by UK rappers the Streets, and *A Prince Among Thieves* (1999) by Prince Paul.

what he says on his records is what he does and believes in real life before Shady gleefully aims his razor-sharp wit at gays, Bible-thumpers, his mother, and his upbringing before signing off and ending the record. In the middle of the song, however, he robs a bank and shoots the teller, a mother of two, even after she cooperates and begs for her life. Shady has once again made his point with lead-heavy severity: he's whatever people say he is. They think he's a criminal in real life, so he might as well be one on the record too. On *TMMLP2*, "Parking Lot" begins with Shady shooting the teller and taking off with the money, only to find that his partner has left him, and the getaway car won't start. The police come, he runs through some backyards, shooting a dog along the way, and is then cornered by the authorities in a parking lot. Rather than turn himself in, Shady, without hesitation, takes his own life. Two songs in, and both Eminem and Slim Shady are symbolically dead, leaving Marshall Mathers alone with his thoughts for the rest of the record.[8]

The next song, "Rhyme or Reason," is one of the three incredible tracks produced by the visionary Rick Rubin, who established the sound of popular hip-hop as we know it back in 1984 as cofounder of Def Jam Records and producer of classic albums by Run-DMC, LL Cool J, the Beastie Boys, and more. Rubin has gone on to produce landmark records and win eight Grammys (out of eighteen nominations) across every genre

---

8. On the final song, "Evil Twin," Shady arises from the dead, but the song is concerned with pointing out that Shady lives within Eminem and that for the first time he's confident enough to say that there is no difference between them; they are the same.

from rock to pop to country. Countless artists have credited his Zen-like approach in the studio as the catalyst that pushed them to create some of the most vital, and often transitional, work of their careers. Eminem refers to him as Yoda for his encouraging nature and overall wisdom. "Working with him is the most relaxed atmosphere. He's not afraid to try anything," Mathers said. "The weird thing about it is nine times out of ten, we would know instantly if something didn't work and feel right, you know. He's almost like a coach."[9]

One of Rick Rubin's signatures when it comes to hip-hop production is blending hard rock guitar riffs with heavy breaks. From "Rock the Bells" to "Fight for Your Right to Party" to Jay-Z's "99 Problems," nobody does it better. "Rhyme or Reason," like all the Rubin tracks on *TMMLP2*, features hefty classic rock samples skillfully reinterpreted. In this case, it's the mono version of the Zombies' organ-heavy come-on "Time of the Season" from 1968. Flipping the script from the first album, where Debbie Mathers gets eviscerated on the songs "Kill You" and "Marshall Mathers" with lyrics that make "Cleanin' Out My Closet" seem tasteful, Em goes after his father, who at twenty-two married Debbie, who was just fifteen. Marshall arrived two years later, and his father left for California—and for good—eighteen months after that.

In the past, Mathers has denounced his father fleet-ingly, calling him a faggot ("Cleanin' Out My Closet") and

---

9. Brian Hiatt, "Eminem Q&A Exclusive: The Making of 'The Marshall Mathers LP2,'" *Rolling Stone*, November 1, 2013, https://www.rollingstone.com/music/music-news/eminem-qa-exclusive-the-making-of-the-marshall-mathers-lp-2-54874/.

neglectful ("The Way I Am"), but here he puts the elder Marshall Mathers center stage, blaming him for the developmental dysfunction that fueled his rage and his rhymes. In two of the verses, he talks about and to his father as himself, then he lets Shady have at him.

So yeah, Dad, let's walk
Let's have us a father and son talk
But I bet we wouldn't probably get one block
Without me knocking your block off, this is all your fault.

Essentially, his conclusion is that his father's absence made him into the twisted controversy courter that he is, and therefore it's his father's fault that hip-hop has become, to some, the devil's music. The song is absolutely bonkers, the reworked hook and bridge too catchy to forget—quintessential Slim Shady.

Eminem does the heretofore unimaginable elsewhere on the record: he forgives his mother, penning one of the most touching songs of his career, "Headlights." The song features a hymnal piano progression and beautifully plaintive vocals by Nate Ruess of the indie rock band fun., reinterpreted from his band's song "Jumping the Shark." It is an apology to Debbie Mathers for the blame her son has laid at her feet over the years, coupled with his tangible regret that she has not been involved in his children's lives as they have grown. Em goes on to give her credit for raising him as a single parent and mentions the overwhelming sadness he felt the last time they saw each other, as they went their separate ways and her car's headlights drove off into the night.

I saw your headlights as I looked back
And I'm mad I didn't get the chance to
Thank you for being my mom and my dad.

Eminem has often used sentimental scenarios as extended setups for surprise endings and punch lines, lyrically setting the table before yanking the cloth away. He does so here stylistically but not to impish effect. Instead, he employs his smoldering rage cadence, building through the verses to a presumed pinnacle, but on "Headlights" that moment never comes, leaving the listener with the most emotionally poignant and honest piece of music Marshall Mathers has ever released. It is the work of an artist who has matured and, for the first time, is not afraid to lay complicated and vulnerable feelings on the line without hiding behind righteous anger. Instead of basking in his hurt as he has over the entirety of his career, here he sees both sides of the most important developmental relationship in his life and tells his mother, without irony, that he loves her. "I put it out there and that is probably all I'm going to say about that," he said of the song to Sway Calloway during an interview on his Sirius radio station, Shade 45. "Everything that I needed to say and get off my chest, I said it . . . It is a really personal record and for me to go there was something that I just wanted to get off my chest. What I said on the record is what I had to say."[10]

On *TMMLP2*, in the song "Stronger Than I Was," he also discusses his beyond-complicated roller-coaster relationship

10. "Eminem Shade45 Sirius Town Hall November 2013," interview by Sway Calloway, video, 51:41, November 5, 2013, https://www.youtube.com/watch?v=AOP9Db-GtFY.

with Kimberly Scott, his ex-wife twice. It isn't an apology, and it isn't a malediction; it's more of a Rorschach sketch of their relationship, with splayed feelings and stylized memories forming shapes and patterns to be interpreted by the listener.[11] One message comes through clearly: Eminem has turned a corner and will not allow himself to repeat the cycle of their emotionally (and allegedly physically) abusive bond, one born out of childhood trauma and patterns they could not overcome as partners.

> And I thank you, 'cause you made me
> A better person than I was
> But I hate you, 'cause you drained me
> I gave you all, you gave me none.

"Stronger Than I Was" is a brave and realistic look at the second-longest relationship Marshall Mathers has had in his life. It isn't the polar opposite of the tone and content of "Kim" from the first album, but once again, it is evidence of someone who has soul-searched and grown. It is Eminem making an effort to get past the one-dimensional solace of blind rage in order to take control of his life and create healthy and permanent change.

This theme continues across the record, another fascinating foil to the first *Marshall Mathers LP*. In "Brainless," he turns trauma lemons into lemonade by spinning one of his mother's favorite insults into a strength. "If you had a brain, you'd be dangerous," he remembers her saying, to which he responds, "Guess it pays to be brainless." The song is a classic

---

11. Eminem references their anniversary as "November 31," a nonexistent date.

Slim Shady as avenging angel tale, every bit as sing-song as "Brain Damage," with Eminem recalling bullies and failures but ultimately relishing the fact that he was right when he used to say, "Momma, I'ma grow one day to be famous, and I'ma be a pain in the anus."

On "Asshole," he again puts his career in context through a wiser man's perspective:

Came to the world at a time when it was in need of a villain
An asshole, that role I think I succeeded fulfillin'
But I don't think I ever stopped
To think that I was speaking to children.

The lyrical content of the rest of the song is a prototypical example of Eminem's skill in full effect. It is filled with ludicrously well-crafted double entendre rhymes, images, and, since he's looking back with open eyes, some honesty slipped between the one-liners. Case in point:

It's apparent I shouldn't have been a parent
I'll never grow up, so to hell with your parents
And motherfuckin' Father Time
It ain't never gonna stop a pessimist
Who transformed to an optimist in his prime.

These lines capture the entire mood of *TMMLP2*, an album made by an artist who is unapologetically confident, aware of his past, his present, his future, and his legacy. If nothing else, it's a historical moment to hear Eminem call himself an optimist in rhyme.

Another new take on an old gripe is "So Far," again produced by Rick Rubin. It is another playfully misbehaved tour de force that re-creates the unhinged exuberance of *The Slim*

Shady LP and the blond miscreant who seized the world's attention back in 1999. More than a decade later, still on top, Mathers was more interested in exploring the weight of fame and all that comes with it, like the permanent loss of privacy and the unsettling displacement of one's sense of self. He'd done so on *Relapse* and *Recovery* and as early as *Encore*, where his tone veered between spoiled brat and enraged lunatic. He had never given fame the lighthearted slapstick comedy treatment befitting his natural sense of humor the way he does here. "So Far" is a series of fuck-my-life moments, starting with an emergency pit stop in a McDonald's bathroom that gets interrupted by an autograph seeker pushing a napkin under the stall. In the past, he would have raged against this inhuman degree of entitlement by a stranger, but instead he's hilariously vintage Shady.

> On second thought, I'd be glad then.
> "Thanks, dawg! Name's Todd, a big fan."
> I wiped my ass with it
> Crumbled it up in a wad and threw it back and
> Told him: "Todd, you're the shit." When's all of this crap end?

The song also sees him proudly referencing his white trash roots with references to Hamburger Helper, corn and mashed potatoes, NASCAR, Welch's, and Jed Clampett, while boasting that his meager beginnings and remaining in Detroit have kept him humble and grounded. The sample that anchors the song, from Joe Walsh's "Life's Been Good" (1978), an iconic tongue-in-cheek tale of rock-star excess, is another tribute to Mathers's upbringing and the classic rock he listened to until his uncle Ronnie exposed him to hip-hop. As one of the biggest music stars in the world, the jokes here are even funnier than the way he celebrated his loser status on "My Name Is." It's also a welcome twist on the sometimes too-serious bellyaching about fame that came before.

Mathers undertakes an even more refreshing, remarkable, and enlightened (for him) exploration of the past in the form of genuinely celebratory reminiscences of the music that inspired him. No doubt influenced by having Rubin as his executive producer, many nostalgic looks back pay tribute while still sounding fresh and vital.

The album's first single, "Berzerk," is an incredible homage to both Rubin and old-school hip-hop that samples the Beastie Boys' "Fight for Your Right" (1986) and Billy Squire's "The Stroke" (1981) as well as Naughty by Nature's "Feel Me Flow" (1995). Complete with a music video featuring a massive boom box that recalls the cover of the Rubin-produced *Radio* (1985) by LL Cool J, Eminem calls out inspirations past and present from MC Ren to Public Enemy, Future to Kendrick Lamar, and Kangol hats to Birdman. "If you listen to what's going on in hip-hop, this is not what this is," Rubin said about the song. "Em wanted to do something as kind of a throwback to some of the early records that we were making in the old days and it more reflects that energy of the early days of hip-hop."[12]

"Love Game (featuring Kendrick Lamar)" is the final Rubin-produced track on the album, and it deftly combines the producer's knack for mixing rock and rap with two of

---

12. "Eminem: Berzerk Explained: Behind the Scenes 1," Eminem Music, video, 2:03, October 3, 2013, https://www.youtube.com/watch?v=5KsabeJ1UEk.

the best MCs alive. Built on a sample from "Game of Love" by Wayne Fontana and the Mindbenders (1965), a track that was also sampled by De La Soul on "My Brother's a Base-head" (1991), "Love Game" is a clever she-done-me-wrong song that humorously details roller-coaster relationships. Furthermore, Eminem pays lyrical and musical tribute to one of the greatest songs in hip-hop history, "Scenario," from A Tribe Called Quest's legendary album *The Low-End Theory* (1991). "Scenario" is the song that put Brooklyn rapper Busta Rhymes, a major Em influence, on the map, and here he not only name-checks him but re-creates his flow over a quick sample of the song.[13]

> *Think I might be about to bust her, bust her*
> *The thought's scary, yo, though and it hurts—brace!*
> *Hope it ain't "Here we go, yo!"*
> *'Cause my head already goes to worst-case*
> *Scenario, though in the first place,*
> *But you confirmed my low-end theory though.*

It is an amazing and seemingly effortless tribute to his past favorites that no other rapper would be able to pull off with such aplomb in the midst of telling a story about catching a cheating fiancée. Eminem not only pronounces the words

---

13. Eminem and Busta Rhymes (born Trevor Tahiem Smith Jr.) are the same age and have worked together several times, most notably on the epic "Calm Down" in 2013. Busta claims that the first time he heard *The Slim Shady EP* in 1998, he bobbed his head so hard that he cracked a window on Wyclef Jean's tour bus during the Smokin' Grooves Tour. (Kyle Eustice, "Busta Rhymes on Grooming Hip Hop's Next Generation & What He Did 1st Time Hearing Eminem," *HipHopDX*, September 26, 2018, https://hiphopdx.com/news/id.48586/title.busta-rhymes-on -grooming-hip-hops-next-generation-what-he-did-1st-time-hearing-eminem).

"bust her" like "Busta," and the line that ends with "brace" in a style representative of Busta's first group, Leaders of the New School, but he also references the song "Scenario" and the album on which it first appeared.

There is only one rapper aside from Eminem featured on *The Marshall Mathers LP2* and that is Kendrick Lamar, who in 2013 had signed to Interscope/Aftermath Records and was about to become one of the biggest rappers in the game. It is a good thing too, because Lamar is one of the only rappers alive clever and skilled enough to share a track with Eminem and not seem like he's from a lesser league. Lamar's verse is equally as hilarious and wordy as Em's, delivered in a style that nods to Shady. A purist to the end, Eminem tested Lamar when he first came to the studio to see if he was as good of a lyricist as people said. "The thing with Em, that's crazy to me, he kicks everybody out the studio," he said about that visit on *The Bump Show* on Australian radio. "It's not even him. He gives you your space. I took it as him kicking everybody out to see if that's really you writing them raps, to see if that's your writing."[14]

With these four songs—"Berzerk," "Love Game," "Rhyme or Reason," and "So Far"—Rubin and Em found a way to bring the playful brattiness of Slim Shady's legacy of sing-song singles into a new age. They paid tribute to the past, and when he did complain about the present, it was in a more clear-eyed and balanced manner than ever before. It was a mature take on the fun to be had in being immature.

---

14. "Kendrick Lamar and J. Cole Talk about Eminem (2014)," Southpawer Extra, video, 4:08, January 22, 2016, https://www.youtube.com/watch?v=5OIcQcnVj-U.

Another song that takes a look at Marshall Mathers's origins in a different light is "Legacy," a song in which the typically complicated rhyme master chose to utilize one single rhyme pattern throughout the entire song. Rather than celebrate his ability to court controversy and spit barbed lines that inspire hate, he admits that he's happy his brain is wired differently from the norm and gives a more honest idea of how his thought process works.

There is, however, no other song on the album (or anywhere else) that cements Eminem's skill as a syllable manipulator than "Rap God." Released as the third single from the album, it debuted at number seven on the *Billboard* Hot 100. It went on to sell more than three million copies globally. Clocking in at more than six minutes, the song contains 1,560 words and holds the Guinness World Record for a hit single (a song to chart in the top fifteen) with the most words.[15]

It is a singular showcase of Eminem's varied rhyme styles, all of them linked together seamlessly. In a genre fueled by braggadocio and competition, to claim immortality and superhuman powers is quite the boast indeed. It's something of a phenomenon to actually be able to back it up. "I rap to be competitive, and everybody, every time they make a song, wants to be able to say 'I'm still here, don't forget about me.' But my thing is, sometimes I get bored

---

15. Two years later, UK drum and bass rapper Harry Shotta released a song called "Animal" that has 1,771 words, but it failed to chart in the top fifteen. Since "Rap God," many underground rappers have released songs expressly aimed at squeezing more words in or rapping faster than Eminem did on the track. Of course, neither the number of words nor the speed at which he rapped were ever Eminem's goals when writing the song.

with rap and what I mean is, I always want to be able to try to discover new flows and new patterns and new ways to work words and shit like that. So that particular song is just me kinda tinkering around with different styles," he said. "The way that the beat was structured, there are calmer parts and then it gets amped again and energetic. I wanted to make sure that the rhyme matched with what the beat was doing. And you know, in about a minute and a half it was done."[16]

Taken as a whole, *The Marshall Mathers LP2* is rooted in Eminem's trademark style but breaks new ground. It is musically varied and approaches the complex subject matter of his life and childhood with newfound insight. After admitting his addiction and getting it under some control, it makes sense that he would also strive to gain a new sense of control over his art.

Considering the most popular hip-hop albums of 2013, from Kanye West to Jay-Z to Drake, to J. Cole, Chance the Rapper, Run the Jewels, and Earl Sweatshirt, *TMMLP2* makes no concession to the sounds of the times. Eminem never has. This album, in every way, solidifies the argument that Eminem occupies his own sonic island—and is popular enough that he can live there on his own. Even his worst albums have sold platinum and debuted at number one, and even when reviewers have criticized his work, none can deny his technical ability and whip-smart manipulation of English.

---

16. "Eminem's 'Rap God' Lyrics Took Six Minutes to Write," *MTV News*, November 5, 2013, http://www.mtv.com/video-clips/mmkidq/eminem-s-rap-god-lyrics-took-6-minutes-to-write.

This album was no different. Globally, with 3.8 million copies sold, it was the second-best-selling album of the year behind One Direction's *Midnight Memories*. In America, it sold nearly 800,000 copies in the first week and 1.72 million copies by the end of the year, making it, once again, the second-best-selling album after Justin Timberlake's *The 20/20 Experience*. In the United Kingdom (as in the United States), *TMMLP2* became Eminem's seventh consecutive album to debut at number one, making him the first American act to do so and tying him with the Beatles for the greatest number of chart-topping albums in a row in the United Kingdom. His popularity had endured.

Since *Encore*, however, Eminem had begun to be criticized by factions of the music press who had previously been fans. Some had praised his return to form in the years following his sobriety, most notably on *Recovery*, but there began to be a change in tone in many reviews once he proved he could craft anthemic ballads capable of dominating the charts across multiple genres. Despite the fact that he looked at his life and past with a more level-headed perspective than ever, some critics complained about what he had to say. "His last few albums have sounded tired and even apologetic, as he battled drug addiction and creative inertia," wrote Greg Kot in the *Chicago Tribune*.[17] "Though he was hardly at peace, he didn't seem to loathe himself or the world," Sasha Frere-Jones wrote in his review, recalling Eminem circa *The Slim Shady LP*.

17. Greg Kot, "Eminem, 'The Marshall Mathers LP2' Review," *Chicago Tribune*, November 3, 2013, https://www.chicagotribune.com/chi-eminem-marshall-mathers -lp2-review-20131103-column.html.

"Now we are left with his second, damaged iteration—a man who is never not mad at himself or someone else. It's hard to feel good about a talented person who returns haunted and paranoid."[18]

The most critical reviews accused him of retreading an era of former glory because he'd run out of ideas and of "growing older but not up," unlike his contemporaries, Jay-Z and Kanye West.[19] In 2013, those fellow elder statesmen were lauded by most critics for doing something different— Jay with the rigid and repetitive *Magna Carta Holy Grail* and West with the musically experimental *Yeezus*. The comparison is unjust because neither West's nor Jay's album holds a candle to *TMMLP2* as a hip-hop record. Jay-Z's effort has its moments (his very sincere and concerned takes on fatherhood and philanthropy) but falls well short of its grand aspirations, and West's album, clocking in at barely forty minutes, is musically interesting but often lyrically bereft. If that is what an "over forty" record is supposed to be in hip-hop, these two outings make aging seem awful: one like a fancy but dull dinner party and the other an old guy trying to show the kids what edgy is. By contrast, even if someone wants to call Eminem's tributes to hip-hop's glory days "dated," his one-hour-and-forty-two-minute look into

---

18. Sasha Frere-Jones, "Shady and the Lady," *New Yorker*, November 25, 2013, https://www.newyorker.com/magazine/2013/11/25/shady-and-the-lady.

19. Jon Caramanica, "Eminem Grows Older, but Not Up," *New York Times*, November 5, 2013, https://www.nytimes.com/2013/11/06/arts/music/eminem-grows-older-but-not-up.html.

his past with open eyes is a sonic therapy session, this one with a real therapist, after graduating with a degree from Anger Management U (okay, maybe he still has some credits to fulfill). For a man with a lifetime of dysfunctional family drama and a decade of addiction just three years in his rearview, to still be angry is normal, and to be speaking about it more openly and trying to understand it is healthy. The musical diversity on the album isn't a sign that Eminem has never settled on a musical aesthetic as much as it is an indication that he can create comfortably within a number of them.

Eminem had long been a popular, populist artist of the highest order, and those have never been the types of acts music critics fawn over, no matter how much they mean to the global population. There are, of course, things to not like about Eminem's music—his continued use of homophobic and sexist slurs, his dated cultural references (if that kind of thing bothers you)—but some of the critiques of this record felt like they were being made for the sake of making them. There were even some who faulted Eminem for turning his family drama into lyrics for too many years running, then turned around and criticized him for not doing the same with his present-day life. "After the drug phase documented on *Relapse* and the overcoming of it captured on *Recovery*—his last two albums—Eminem may well be done putting himself in the spotlight. He still lives in his hometown, Detroit. His daughter was just crowned homecoming queen. He undoubtedly has new wounds—we just may never get to hear about them."[20] There is no greater sign of maturity than learning from the past, understanding your mistakes—and not repeating them.

What Eminem pledged to do with himself instead, on this record and looking forward, was to dedicate himself to the constantly evolving flow of wordplay that keeps rap fresh. Of course, the most celebrated of critics, the self-proclaimed "dean of American rock critics," got it. "But here his musicality runs free as his practiced articulation reminds us what flow used to mean, delivering lyrics honed until every line offers up an internal rhyme or stealth homophone or surprise pun or trick enjambment," wrote Robert Christgau. "Also, he holds his Slim Shady side in check here—offensive cracks remain undeveloped, with the 'I'm a sucker for love you a sucker for dick' stanza delivered by none other than guest paragon Kendrick Lamar. You don't like it, you don't like the art form, simple as that."[21]

The Marshall Mathers LP2 was the end of an era or, rather, an earlier era's fitting end. Eminem and many others have said that his first three major label studio albums were a period of time and should be seen as such. I would add this album to complete the cycle, with *Encore*, *Relapse*, and *Recovery* taken as a second phase. It's uncanny that in the days after Eminem released *TMMLP2*, the house he grew up in (for the most

20. Caramanica, "Eminem Grows Older."
21. Robert Christgau, "Eminem: *The Marshall Mathers LP2*," *Robert Christgau, Dean of American Rock Critics* (blog), n.d., https://www.robertchristgau.com/get_album.php?id=17377.

part), at 19946 Dresden Street, which was immortalized on the cover of both *Marshall Mathers LPs*, suffered a fire. It had been up for auction through the Michigan Land Bank for months, and at the time a Tennessee woman named Shelly Hazlett and her husband were in the process of bidding on it to turn it into an Eminem museum. "A lot of people think it's insane," Shelly Hazlett said. "Most rappers rap about stupid stuff, but Eminem is real. He raps about his life. I want to do my part to help put Detroit back on the map."[22]

After the fire, which destroyed the interior and much of the roof, the city condemned the building and it was torn down.[23] The place where so much good and bad in Marshall's life had taken place—where he had been photographed for the first album cover, where he had met Proof, where he had lived through so much trauma that he turned into art—was gone. Eminem mentioned that he drove by the house often during the writing of *The Marshall Mathers LP2* and was well aware that it was up for auction but clearly liked to keep his memories of the place as just that. He had taken numerous lyrical snapshots, so it was gone but not forgotten. And not quite gone either: Eminem and his manager purchased the rubble from the demolition company and kept it in storage for three years until they came up with a fitting tribute. In

22. Eric Lacy, "Bid Placed on Eminem's 'Marshall Mathers LP2' Detroit Home; Museum Plans Revealed," *MLive*, November 4, 2013, https://www.mlive.com/entertainment/detroit/2013/11/eminems_childhood_detroit_home.html.
23. Kate Abbey-Lambertz, "Eminem's Childhood Home in Detroit Burns After Woman Tried to Purchase It," *Huffington Post*, November 8, 2013, https://www.huffpost.com/entry/eminem-childhood-home-detroit-fire-burns_n_4240795.

2016, without warning, Eminem put seven hundred bricks from the house up for sale on his website, each signed by him, and offered along with a cassette copy of *The Marshall Mathers LP* as well as dog tags made from wood recovered from the home—literally giving the public a chance to own a piece of Marshall Mathers's life story.

Chapter 8

Do You Believe?

Eminem did not release his next studio album for another four years, and the music that he released in the interim didn't indicate the stylistic direction that album would eventually take. It is a well-established fact that Eminem is a bit of a Howard Hughes, a visionary who prefers to shut himself away from the world when he doesn't have anything to share, thankfully devoid of the agoraphobia, germaphobia, and paranoia. Eminem prefers to keep his tours short, as the schedule and displacement are triggers for his substance abuse, and when he's in writing mode, he doesn't share many details until the album is done. "When some people get sober, they must choose to become reclusive," says substance and trauma expert Dr. Tina Galordi. "The outside world is very stimulating, and if they have surviving trauma, addiction, or both, it is easy for them to get triggered. They need a place where they can really drop their guard, where they find a sense of safety. It takes quite a long time for an individual to increase their level of tolerance so that they can be uncomfortable in the world without being overwhelmed. The challenge is to rebuild a life in which they can track themselves and know when things are starting to get too much. Some people need to be isolated to do this. The challenge then, of course, is that they don't feel too much isolation because one of the most important pieces of healing in addiction is connection. You simply must have connection."

Eminem took his Rapture Tour to festivals in Europe in 2013 and did a brief tour of Australia and New Zealand, plus two sold-out dates at Wembley Stadium in London in support of *The Marshall Mathers LP2*. The Wembley shows were truly historic on several levels. They marked the first time a rapper had headlined the ninety-thousand-capacity arena, plus they were the first shows Eminem had played in London since 2001. They weren't planned; they came about after the rapper was banned from performing at the Hyde Park festival by the Royal Parks for having lyrics that were too offensive, since they would be heard by neighboring residents, which violated the British constitution. "I heard that I wasn't going to be approved to play in Hyde Park and it made me even more excited to play London this summer," Eminem said. "The easiest way to get me to do something is to tell me I can't do it. Thanks to the Royal Parks for making it all possible . . . for Wembley."[1]

In addition to making history in London, there were a few appearances at American summer festivals like Lollapalooza

---

1. "Eminem Is Banned from Performing in Hyde Park Due to 'Offensive' Lyrics," *Daily Mail*, June 26, 2014, https://www.dailymail.co.uk/tvshowbiz/article -2670604/Eminem-banned-performing-Hyde-Park-offensive-lyrics.html.

and the Squamish Valley Music Festival in Vancouver before Eminem capped off the year with a coheadlining tour with Rihanna, dubbed the Monster Tour, which ran through the month of August, beginning in Los Angeles and ending in Detroit. It was one of the highest-grossing tours of 2014 (number six behind Billy Joel, George Strait, One Direction, and others), taking in $36 million for just six shows, compared with much longer runs by the other artists on the list. The two shows at MetLife Stadium in New Jersey, for example, grossed $12.4 million. The concerts typically began with a short set by both artists, followed by a Rihanna set, then an Eminem set during which Rihanna would join Em for "Love the Way You Lie," "Airplanes, Part II," and "Stan." Each artist then did their own brief encore before coming out together to end the night with "The Monster."

On the final nights of that tour, in Detroit, Eminem wore a gray T-shirt emblazoned with the logo "Shady XV," which was a forthcoming compilation album to commemorate fifteen years of his record label, featuring Shady artists past and present. His new contributions to the collection have one thing in common: all of them question, one way or another, whether he should continue his career. Facetious or not, they take a more somber tone to the existential middle-age crisis that informs some of the songs on *TMMLP2*. It's an interesting quirk in a genre where nearly every verse dropped by successful artists is concerned with proving or reminding the listener just how much better, richer, and more desirable the narrator is than everyone else. Then again, Eminem has always explored this terrain since the day he started writing songs "where I die at the end" ("Cum on Everybody," *The Slim Shady LP*). More than any MC besides Kool Keith, whose music cultivates his bizarre and allegedly unstable mental state without irony,[2] Eminem gets at both sides of what makes him tick—the ego and the lack of it—with honesty. As someone who has quite literally achieved nearly all there is to achieve in music of any popular genre, Eminem's self-doubt may seem unreasonable to some, but his need to continually explore it is very real. His conclusion to the soul-searching is that he's only good at one thing—rapping—and that he plans to do it until he's absolutely useless at it or has no more fans—whichever comes first. According to some critics, this isn't a good thing.

Throughout his original songs on the two-disc collection, Eminem's technical skills are on full display. On "ShadyXV," a five-minute verse that opens the record, over a sample of Billy Squier's "My Kinda Lover" (1981), he delivers another technical triumph of assonance and interlaced rhyme schemes. It is an amazing brag fest with lyrical patterns so dense that it sounds like Eminem himself is a spectator to his own flow.

> *Fuck that, I'll battle 'em all, I'll battle a mall*
> *I'll stand there and yell that at a wall*
> *'Til the mannequin dolls scatter and the inanimate objects*
> *That I'm battering all shatter and fall.*

---

2. Rumors of several hospitalizations for personality disorders and depression have followed the underground icon since the Bronx rapper first came on the scene in 1987. The only documented stay occurred in the early 1990s, when he checked in to Creedmoor Psychiatric Center in Queens for a time.

Later in the song, he addresses the critics who complain that Eminem's use of rock samples is dated, often more country rap than hip-hop.

Know you really tired of me sampling Billy Squire
But classic rock acid rap is the genre
Got Slash on guitar, splash of Bizarre, Thrasher, and Aerosmith

As usual, Eminem, a battle rapper to the end, beat any complaints to the punch, compartmentalizing the song style before anyone else could call it.

Other highlights include "Guts Over Fear," a sensitive duet with Australian singer-songwriter Sia (their second, following "Beautiful Pain" from *TMMLP2*), which was featured in the end credits for the Denzel Washington film *The Equalizer*. The song takes yet another look back at Eminem's struggle to reach the top of the hip-hop food chain but isn't particularly confident in its boasts. It is a self-conscious musing, introspective and almost apologetic: "Sometimes I feel like all I ever do is / Find different ways to word the same song," and later, "How many different times can I say the same thing / Different ways that rhyme?" Eminem further questions his role in rap, wondering if he belongs anymore, before ultimately concluding that it's too late for him to start over, because rap is the only thing he knows.

He gets further into the cost of his fame on "Fine Line," a song that features an Eminem first that is sure to confound his religious-right haters: Bible references.

And I don't like how I see myself, so I open the Bible to Isaiah
'Cause I swear to Christ there are nights when I stay up and might
Say a prayer twice just to make sure God hears.

It could be a side effect of sobriety and the appeal to a higher power that is a foundational component of the mind training recovering addicts must apply to their lives, and if so, the good book certainly deserves a place in his lyrics, but to hear Marshall Mathers sending it up is light years away from his roots and the sign of a new era for him. The song goes on to depict the pros and cons of fame, the acceptance and the isolation, the comforts and the anxieties, and how complaining about it all does nothing but continue the cycle.

> It's like I paid the price of fame twice, I hate it
> So I bitch about my life then make another song
> Vicious cycle ain't it? Then wonder why I stay famous
> I keep walkin' the line, this fish bowl gets old.

On "Right for Me," a horrorcore party romp that is five minutes of dizzying rapid-fire rhyme schemes for the old-school fans, Eminem also subtly reveals more about his state of mind as a performer who may have peaked, saying that he will be more likely to overstay his welcome than retire on top because he just can't leave rhyming alone.

> I'm up for the long duration
> I'm just looking for something to walk away with
> Some pocket change and a little integrity
> Though I'll probably be jumping across the stage
> Till I'm fuckin' Madonna's age and
> Stuck in an awkward place in life.

Shady XV is an album for die-hard fans of Shady nation, of which there are enough to have landed it at number three on the *Billboard* 200 album chart. The week the album was released also happened to be the first that employed

Billboard's new measurement system, configured to account for albums sold, singles sold, and the number of times an album was streamed within a week. According to their new formula, 1,500 streams counts for a single sale of an album, while the sale of ten copies of a single counts as an album sale. To land at number three, the compilation sold 137,560 physical albums and logged 2,804,463 streams.[3] *Shady XV* received mixed reviews, with some critics claiming that the second half's collection of vintage material only served to highlight the lackluster new material of the first half. Listening to "Twisted," Eminem's sung duet with Skylar Grey (featuring a rapped verse by Yelawolf) that explores a dysfunctional romantic relationship, they may have a point.

> Eminem's music has been unrelievedly awful now for a full decade . . . He has never been working harder, Eminem has observed in interviews; in the sense that he's released a 78-minute album and another disc of new music all in the last year, he's right. But the wearying, dispiriting, and frankly numbing output of his current career phase isn't "work." It's maniacal persistence, of the same sort that leads some douche to text a woman 38 times about the $32k he made in June. Seconds into the 2xCD label compilation *Shady XV*, which pairs 12 new songs with a disc of "greatest hits," Eminem fires up his rappity-rap sputtering chainsaw, and it never ceases for the spiritually exhausting hour that follows.[4]

But for all the gripes by the generally Em-hating *Pitchfork*, true hip-hop heads found a lot to love on the same album.

---

3. Jay Balfour, "Hip Hop Album Sales: Eminem, Rick Ross, Beyoncé," *HipHopDX*, December 3, 2014, https://hiphopdx.com/news/id.31622/title.hip-hop-album-sales-eminem-rick-ross-beyonce.
4. Jayson Greene, "Various Artists, *Shady XV*," *Pitchfork*, November 26, 2014, https://pitchfork.com/reviews/albums/20036-various-artists-shady-xv/.

Rather than each song being broken down into X number of bars per verse, each artist comes correct with an arsenal of lyrics. Em specifically is the leader and master savant. If *TMMLP2* is any indication of his changing rap style, *Shady XV* is a continuation. More often than not, his verses go on for minutes at a time as he throws down a graphic, rhyming stream of consciousness. Thematically, and brilliantly, Em takes an introspective approach to the fame he's cultivated since "My Name Is." He spits about the stress being almost too much to handle, yet he is still able to find pleasure in eating the competition alive. It's a vicious cycle that has to be wearing him thin.[5]

Eminem's next project was the film *Southpaw*, starring Jake Gyllenhaal and Forest Whitaker, for which he did the soundtrack, although he was initially intended for a much bigger role. The film, written by *Sons of Anarchy* creator and executive producer Kurt Sutter, was picked up by DreamWorks as a vehicle for Marshall Mathers to play the lead of a welterweight boxer who sees his world crash before his eyes and must fight to reclaim his past glory. Sutter had apparently been meeting with Eminem's production team for seven years about working together and had written the entire film based on Mathers's struggles with drugs and return to music.

"I know he's very selective and doesn't do a lot," Sutter said in 2010.

But he shared so much of his personal struggle in this raw and very honest album [*Recovery*], one that I connected with on a lot of levels. He is very interested in the boxing genre, and it seemed like an apt metaphor, because his own life has been a brawl. In a way, this is a

---

5. Homer Johnsen, "Eminem & Various Artists—*Shady XV*," *HipHopDX*, November 24, 2014, https://hiphopdx.com/reviews/id.2386/title.eminem-various-artists-shadyxv.

continuation of the *8 Mile* story, but rather than a literal biography, we are doing a metaphorical narrative of the second chapter of his life . . . At its core, this is a retelling of his struggles over the last five years of his life, using the boxing analogy. I love that the title refers to Marshall being a lefty, which is to boxing what a white rapper is to hip hop; dangerous, unwanted and completely unorthodox. It's a much harder road for a southpaw than a right handed boxer.[6]

Two years later, after the film had changed hands from DreamWorks to MGM, Eminem, who does in fact box for exercise, dropped out, citing his desire to focus himself on completing *The Marshall Mathers LP2*. He praised Gyllenhaal's performance, loved the film, and recorded two original songs for the soundtrack, which he executive produced and released on Shady Records in 2015. "Phenomenal" is a massive Eminem headbanger with an ominous rock drum and cymbal beat, featuring Em chanting the title in the chorus in a warped, off-kilter maniac yowl. The music provides the mood, but Eminem dictates the tempo and beat, which is rapid-fire and relentless, in double-time contrast to the ponderous backing track. The effect is rousing, perfect for a gritty boxing film.

"Kings Never Die" is a stirring, cinematic comeback anthem, featuring a hook sung by Gwen Stefani and more incendiary wordplay that mixes boxing and sports metaphors with a number of references to Eminem's life and career, from hallucinogens, to Lucifer, to Gilbert's Lodge, the restaurant

---

6. Mike Fleming Jr., "DreamWorks Teams with Eminem and Kurt Sutter for 'Southpaw,'" *Deadline*, December 13, 2010, https://deadline.com/2010/12/dreamworks-teams-with-eminem-and-kurt-sutter-for-southpaw-90458/.

where he once worked, to Gilbert Arenas, the NBA player. The wordplay in the nearly five-minute song is rich.

I went from powdered milk and Farina
To flippin' burgers on the grill for some peanuts
At Gilbert's to arenas, call me Gilbert Arenas
Still appeal to the dreamers

These two songs point to the direction that his music was taking: unequalled lyricism, with the music, and at times even the beat, taking a back seat, as well as emotive and slightly overwrought singles driven by pop-oriented hooks sung by women.

Another ritual that Eminem had incorporated into his music production cycle by then was dropping a long freestyle single in advance of an upcoming album, as he had done since *Relapse*. For someone who completely disappears from the public eye between releases, it makes sense, considering Em's continued lyrical preoccupation with being forgotten, despite his continually astounding commercial sales. The advance single this time was "Campaign Speech," a seven-and-a-half-minute freestyle released on the night of the third and final presidential debate, just nineteen days before the 2016 presidential election. With more than twenty names dropped, from Dustin Hoffman to Colin Kaepernick to Prince to (most randomly) famed mystery writer Agatha Christie, the track is a relentless tirade against Donald Trump.

The style of "Campaign Speech" is just that: Eminem presenting himself as a candidate might, complete with his origin story and career goals as a politician. It is also the tone of his delivery, more spoken slam poetry than anything else, as he bends pronunciations to accommodate an extreme flow of consciousness. The verses, each devoted to a different rhyme scheme, are punctuated by Eminem stopping. After a short pause, the next begins. Across the first four sections, he lays out a list of immoral behaviors that he indulges in before moving on to a verse where he insults Donald Trump and his supporters.

> *Nothing's wrong, the name brand is back to reclaim status*
> *Run the faucet, I'ma dunk a bunch of Trump supporters*
> *Snuck up on 'em in Ray-Bans in a gray van with a spray tan.*
> *It's a wrap, like an Ace bandage.*

"Campaign Speech" is not as anti-Trump or political as the title of the single implies. It comes off as an opportunity for Eminem to go full Shady while reminding the world that he is, hands down, the best rhyme demon alive. The timing of the release was aimed to grab attention and to make a political statement, but if anything it was an opportunity missed considering the anti-Trump vitriol to come from Eminem after the election. Forever a reality-television personality, Trump is quick to respond to anyone famous who criticizes him, but he didn't respond to Eminem, perhaps too afraid to alienate his supporters in Eminem's fan base. It should be noted that Eminem's blistering criticism of Trump continues to get a pass, while the president condemned Snoop Dogg and his "failing career" via tweet for a music video that depicted Snoop shooting a clown called "Ronald Klump." Eminem did not, however, escape the Twitter wrath of David Duke, the former Imperial Wizard of the Ku Klux Klan. Employing anti-Semitic online diction, Duke used triple parentheses to notate a person of Jewish origin: "Eminem is a puppet of (((Paul Rosenberg))) and (((Jimmy Iovine)))—For years Eminem has been poisoning the minds of our youth #rigged."[7]

Eminem struck a similar tone on "No Favors," a song from Big Sean's *I Decided*, released in February 2017. Sean (born Sean Michael Leonard Anderson), an Eminem disciple who was born in LA but raised in Detroit and was signed by Kanye West, is a skilled trap-style rapper whose music leans toward the twitchy hi-hats, murky synths, deep bass, and Auto-Tuned vocals that capture the narcotics haze of contemporary rap.

On "No Favors," Eminem's verse is decidedly misogynist, as he references Jamie Lee Curtis as part of a *Halloween* reference and pop singer Fergie and mercilessly lets fly at attention-seeking conservative pundit Ann Coulter.

And fuck Ann Coulter with a Klan poster,
With a lamp post, door handle, shutter,
A damn bolt cutter, a sandal, a can opener,
A candle, rubber, piano, a flannel, sucker
Some hand soap, butter, a banjo and a manhole cover.
Hand over the mouth and nose smother
Trample, ran over the tramp with the Land Rover,
The band, the Lambo, Hummer and Road Runner,
Go ham donut, or go Rambo, gut her, make an example of her
That's for Sandra Bland, ho and Philando.

This echoes a moment in "Campaign Speech," when Em describes attacking George Zimmerman, the man who shot

---

7. Ryan Reed, "Hear Eminem Blast Donald Trump Supporters on New LP Tease 'Campaign Speech,'" *Rolling Stone*, October 19, 2016, https://www.rollingstone .com/music/music-news/hear-eminem-blast-donald-trump-supporters-on-new -lp-tease-campaign-speech-121699/.

and killed seventeen-year-old Trayvon Martin in 2012. Here he lyrically murders (and then some) Coulter and dedicates it to both Sandra Bland, the African American woman found dead in her jail cell in Texas after a routine traffic stop, and Philando Castile, the African American man who was killed by police in Minnesota, also during a traffic stop. All three women referenced responded to Eminem. Curtis called his parenting into question, Fergie brushed it off, and Coulter claimed that the rapper was using her to get some much-needed publicity. "It's one thing and just you know, some idiot who's—by the way—no longer a kid, but now we're seeing it play out with professors at Berkley and the head of the Berkley police," she told *TMZ*. "It's just become quite normal for the left to behave in these violent ways toward women and gays."[8]

Over the next year, as he completed his work on *Revival*, Eminem's hatred of Trump became more focused. "He makes my blood boil," he said of Trump. "I can't even watch the news anymore because it makes me too stressed out. All jokes aside, all punch lines aside, I'm trying to get a message out there about him. I want our country to be great, too. I want it to be the best it can be, but it's not going to be that with him in charge."[9]

It would be a full year before Eminem dropped another freestyle, and this one, the a cappella "The Storm" unleashed at the 2017 BET Awards on October 10, was entirely focused

---

8. Gavin Evans, "Ann Coulter Calls Eminem an 'Idiot' in Response to Him Rapping About Her," *Complex*, February 4, 2017, https://www.complex.com/music/2017/02/ann-coulter-says-eminems-an-idiot-slams-the-left.

9. David Marchese, "In Conversations: Eminem," *Vulture*, December 2017, https://www.vulture.com/2017/12/eminem-in-conversation.html.

on Trump. It was clear that Eminem's anger had fermented into something stronger.

> Trump, when it comes to givin' a shit, you're as stingy as I am
> Except when it comes to havin' the balls to go against me, you hide 'em.
> 'Cause you don't got the fuckin' nuts like an empty asylum.

The litany covered Trump's racist politics, his disrespect of war heroes, and the lies he told the working class to get elected. Eminem ended it all by telling his fans that they're either his fans or Trump supporters—they can't be both. The clip of him performing the freestyle went viral, inspiring more than two million tweets in less than twenty-four hours. Still, the four-minute rant, which has been seen on BET's official YouTube channel more than forty-eight million times, failed to get a reaction from our Twitter-happy forty-fifth president. He did, however, hear from quite a few red-state fans who voiced their disapproval and did as he asked, saying they would no longer support him or listen to his music. "At the end of the day," Em said, "if I did lose half my fan base, then so be it, because I feel like I stood up for what was right and I'm on the right side of this. I don't see how somebody could be middle class, busting their ass every single day, paycheck to paycheck, who thinks that that fucking billionaire is gonna help you."[10]

It seemed that politics, Trump, racism, and injustice were going to be a major focus of the next album, which was a

10. Dan Rys, "Eminem and New Def Jam CEO Paul Rosenberg on Early 'Broke Days,' Courting Controversy and Hip-Hop's Future," Billboard, January 25, 2018, https://www.billboard.com/articles/news/magazine-feature/8095496/eminem-paul-rosenberg-interview-billboard-cover-story-2018.

thrilling prospect. Em had battled internal opponents over his last few albums, a proposition that he had taken to the limit. He had reached the end point of looking back and looking in; it seemed like participating in the outside world again was just what we—and he—needed. At the start of his career, his satirical commentary on reality TV and celebrity-obsessed culture had justly reflected our times, as had his raw portrayal of the working-class values and troubled trailer park upbringing that forged his worldview. As an older, more experienced, even keener-eyed fault-finder, his take on current events was sure to hold a deeper layer of truth. And if he was as angry as he seemed to be, the metaphors for his madness were bound to be the stuff of legend.

On October 25, 2017, Em's manager, Paul Rosenberg, tweeted a photo of Yelawolf's new album, *Trial by Fire*, promoting the record's release that week. He strategic-ally held up the CD by the window in his office, through which the viewer could see a giant billboard on the building across the street for a prescription drug called Revival. In the ad, the *e* in Revival was backward, as is the second one in Eminem's logo. It set off a rabid round of research by Eminem fans on Reddit, which led them to a website, askaboutrevival .com, for a new pharmaceutical wonder med called Revival.[11]

---

11. Reddit is a social news aggregation site, where registered users can submit links, text, and images from anywhere on the internet. Their posts are voted up or down by their fellow members and organized into user-created discussion boards called "subreddits." The submissions that get the most up votes appear at the top of the subreddit, and the most popular subreddits appear on the website's front page. At the time of this writing, the site had 542 million monthly visitors and 234 million users. It is the sixth most visited site in the United States and the twenty-first most visited site in the world.

The conversations got heated, analyzing what all the details meant, including looking up the Latin meaning of the conditions that Revival aimed to cure, the main one being atrox rithimus, which is a nonsense phrase taken from butchered Greek and Latin words that loosely mean "bad" or "bitter" and "rhymes" or "rhythms." The website was full of other jokes, from the preexisting conditions that were incompatible with Revival (pregnancy, allergies to midwestern tympanic stimulators) to the side effects it will not cause (general feeling of head trauma, softening of fingernails) and the side effects it might (blood in phlegm, highly combustible head) as well as a note-perfect fake television ad for the drug. Truth be told, clues that this was an Eminem-related promotion weren't too hard to find: the website was registered to Interscope Records, there were a slew of Eminem song references in the website's ad copy ("Seize the moment," "Revival could be music to your ears," "I won't waste my one shot"), and when fans called the phone number listed for more information, the background music was a piano playing what sounded like "I Need a Doctor," the Dr. Dre song featuring Eminem from 2011. If the caller stayed on the line long enough, a female voice came on and casually said, "We give you some serious fucking credit for sticking through this ad."

It wasn't the first viral campaign that Interscope had created with Eminem's team for a prerelease promotion. In advance of *Relapse*, the rapper posted a photo of himself on his Twitter account, standing outside what seemed to be a fictional rehab center called Popsomp Hills. Say it quickly and you'll get the joke—"pop some pills." They created a website for Popsomp Hills, a rehab in Bloomfield Hills, Michigan, run by a Swiss founder named Dr. Balzac. Tying it all together, according to the small print on the Revival site, Popsomp was listed as the manufacturer of Revival.

All this wink-wink, tongue-in-cheek satire was very Eminem, and it certainly made complete sense for the raw and irreverent look at his drug addiction explored on *Relapse*. Leading up to *Revival*, however, particularly considering the heated political tone he took on nearly every verse he spit in 2016, the drug campaign seemed off. It did accomplish its intended goal—to arouse curiosity—though that took longer than expected, as the ads were so well done that no one picked up on the joke until Rosenberg's tweet. "At first it was so quiet that we thought we went too straight with it," Dennis Dennehy, former VP at Interscope, now chief communications officer at AEG Presents and Eminem's publicist for the past twenty years, told *AdWeek*. "We did ad buys on *SNL* in a few markets. New York wouldn't let us run it because they thought it was too on the money and misleading, which in retrospect is pretty great."[12]

Revival arrived on December 15, 2017, debuting at number one, Eminem's eighth straight, making him the first act to do so in the United States. The album also debuted at number one in Australia, Canada, Finland, and the United Kingdom. In title, as in the viral campaign, it continued the drug-related

12. David Gianatasio, "How Interscope Teased Eminem's New Album with Fake Pharma Ads That Were Almost Too Good," *AdWeek*, December 15, 2017, https://www.adweek.com/creativity/how-deutsch-teased-eminems-new-album -with-fake-pharma-ads-that-were-almost-too-good/.

names of Eminem's sober output, beginning with *Relapse* and continuing with *Recovery*. The album's first single, "Walk on Water," featuring a tasteful hook sung by Beyoncé, once again tackled Eminem's legacy, his feelings of inadequacy, and his thoughts about living up to both his and the world's expectations.

> *Always in search of the verse that I haven't spit yet.*
> *Will this step just be another misstep*
> *To tarnish whatever the legacy, love or respect*
> *I've garnered? The rhyme has to be perfect, the delivery flawless,*
> *And it always feels like I'm hittin' the mark*
> *'Til I go sit in the car, listen and pick it apart,*
> *Like, "This shit is garbage!"*

Beyoncé's vocals are beautiful, the song's piano melody elegant, and Eminem's delivery sincere, but taken together, the result is tasteful to the point of dull. When he raps about album sales declining and the world no longer caring, after the landslide success of his last two albums and habitually sold-out headlining tours, the sentiment rings false. It is a setup, of course, for the twist in the outro where Em asserts his dominance by shouting, "So me and you are not alike / Bitch, I wrote 'Stan,'" but even if it's only for the sake of that punch line, it's a big ask to believe, even for the length of one five-minute song, that the state of Eminem's career is dire. After four years of waiting for a new Eminem album, following two incendiary anti-Trump freestyles, this track as a lead single was as confusing as the fake pharma campaign. It seemed that *Revival* was going to be more *Recovery*

2 than a continuation of Mathers's new sociopolitical rap revolution.

In a way, the viral ad campaign and its irrelevance to the album were spot-on because *Revival* is Eminem's least cohesive work to date. It suffers from an identity crisis: the struggle of its creator to satisfy everybody in his extremely diverse fan base, and himself, on the same album. The end result is a collection of songs that aren't bad but don't hang together as a unit. They make sense in smaller groupings, which are unconnected in mood or presumed purpose to each other. Taken as a whole, however, *Revival* has the scattered feeling of a compilation collection, devoid of the type of unified theme that, while not always perfectly executed, runs like a river through every Eminem album. In contemporary hip-hop, Marshall Mathers continually sets himself apart by approaching his full-length studio recordings like concept albums, with themes explored from every angle, because he naturally overthinks, reanalyzes, and redrafts his work until it is a tower of immaculately crafted verse. Many of the songs on *Revival* reflect this tireless work ethic, but some don't, and the larger concept certainly does not. This time, Eminem simply didn't get there.

The confusion begins with the cover, which depicts an image of a billowing American flag subtly blended with an image of Eminem, head bowed, a hand to his brow. It is immediately patriotic and poignant, as if he were taking in the 9/11 Memorial in New York, but it doesn't jive with the satire of the fake pharmaceutical campaign at all. It is even more somber than the cover of *Recovery*, not to mention that Eminem has never referenced the flag lightly, only doing so when he has something serious to say about the country, as he did in "White America." Gazing at the cover of *Revival*, one would expect it to be Eminem's version of Bruce Springsteen's *Born in the U.S.A.*, an album that seethes with the disappointment of middle-class life in Ronald Regan's America.[13] He's more than capable of it, and in some ways *Revival* is that, because it does contain the most well-thought-out and executed political songs of Eminem's career. The problem is that the rest of the album isn't that at all.

Though a general dissatisfaction with the state of society is clear throughout the record in songs like "Nowhere Fast" ("This world's screwed, it's already fucked"), there are just two songs that tackle politics and the dire state of race relations in America: "Untouchable" and "Like Home." The first was released a week before the entire album, on December 8, 2017, and a month after "Walk on Water," yet again pointing toward an album that doesn't know what it is.

"Untouchable" was completed before many of the songs on the record and explores the rash of white police violence against young black males that is all too common in today's America. The song, which is a powerful take on the subject, likely would have achieved a greater impact if it had been released before "Walk on Water." "'Untouchable' was a subject

---

13. The album's title track has been co-opted countless times by politicians for rallies and events. The chorus gives the feel of a positive patriotic anthem, but the stylistic choice is deliberate: it stands in stark contrast to verses that depict the marginalization that working-class Vietnam veterans faced upon returning home.

me and Marshall talked about a lot before we even recorded it," Mr. Porter says. "I told him I'd love for him to touch on the subject and had the song came out when we finished it, which was four months before the album was released, it would have had a different impact. Em will tell you, 'Oh, if Joyner Lucas hadn't done his song, it would have been different.' Listen, Joyner's song is really good, but it's nowhere near 'Untouchable.'"

Massachusetts rapper Joyner Lucas (born Gary Maurice Lucas Jr.) explored the issue in a heavy-handed yet nonetheless moving style in the song "I'm Not Racist." Lucas, whom Eminem praised for the track, was later tapped for a guest spot on "Lucky You" off *Kamikaze*. Lacking Eminem's dexterity, Lucas delivers the opposing points of view in the same style, choosing to make his point visually in a video (that quickly went viral) portraying an overweight white man in a MAGA hat yelling at a black youth with short dreadlocks across a table. The other man returns the favor, then the video ends with an optimistic, completely unrealistic denouement as the two men rise to hug it out. If only it were that easy. Eminem's version is closer to the truth: there is no easy answer, so we must explore both sides.

"I was in the room when Em played 'Untouchable' for Jimmy Iovine, Dre, and Rick Rubin, and they loved it," Mr. Porter says. "Personally, as someone involved with the song as a producer, that was one of the greatest moments of my life. Their take was to get it out right away. Ultimately that didn't happen, which I'm sure was part of a bigger business decision that I can't speak to and was probably the right one, but I would have liked to have seen it come out as soon as we finished it because the events he touches on in the song were making the news, like, every other day."

The ambitious and effective "Untouchable" unfolds like a sonic play, detailing both sides of a racist white cop arresting a black male during a traffic stop. A brief introduction sets the scene, before Eminem dives deep into the psyche of a white racist in power over a track that samples and interpolates the East Coast gangsta funk of Brooklyn rapper Masta Ace's "Born to Roll (Jeep Ass Niguh Remix)" (1994) as well as Cheech and Chong's riff-heavy musical comedy bit "Earache My Eye" (1974), a highlight of their classic film *Up in Smoke* (1978). Eminem establishes time and place brilliantly in the first two lines by seamlessly referencing the slogans of the two opposing sides in the Ferguson unrest that unfolded in August and November 2014: "Hands up, officer don't shoot / Then pull your pants up, promise you won't loot."[14] Over a first section driven by a rock-heavy (read: more white) beat, Eminem explores the biases of a cop drunk on white privilege, thinking he's fighting the good fight by keeping the streets free of drug dealers and minority criminals.

I keep tellin' myself, keep doin' like you're doin'
No matter how many lives you ruin

---

14. "Hands Up, Don't Shoot" became the slogan of the Black Lives Matter movement following the shooting of Michael Brown by Darren Wilson, a white police officer, in Ferguson, Missouri, in August 2014. "Pants Up, Don't Loot" was the slogan of an organization that supported Wilson. A man named Don Alexander crowdfunded over $3,000 to pay for a "Pants Up, Don't Loot" billboard in Ferguson but never followed through.

It's for the red, white and blue.
Time to go find a new one and split his head right in two,
No one's ever indicted you.

The song's chorus answers the question of "Why?": because he's a white boy. This continues into the next verse until Eminem's voice changes tone, and he says, "Feels like we're stuck in a time warp to me / As I kick these facts and get these mixed reactions." He then takes on his own point of view, referencing the mixed reactions he got to his two politically charged freestyles. He references a backspin in the beat and, as that occurs, says that he feels like America is backsliding to its 1960s pre–civil rights era degree of institutionalized racism, which makes him ashamed to be a white boy. After another chanted Cheech and Chong–infused chorus, the beat of the song changes entirely to something much more traditionally hip-hop (read: blacker), as Eminem embodies the justified rage and frustration of a black man being profiled by a white cop.

Wait, why are there black neighborhoods?
'Cause America segregated us, designated us to an area,
Separated us, Section-Eight'ed us
When we tear it up's the only time attention's paid to us.

The verse is packed with well-thought-out, viable truths that speak to the plight of all African Americans, and it ends with the most powerful lines of all.

Home of the brave is still racist 'ville,
So this whole nation feels like a plantation field
In a country that claims its foundation was based on United States
ideals

That had its natives killed, got you singin' this star-spangled spiel
To a piece of cloth that represents the "Land of the Free,"
That made people slaves to build.

"We knew he was gonna catch backlash from black people and from white people," Mr. Porter says. "But I'm one of the producers and one of the people that championed the idea because Marshall occupies a place in society where he can speak to these things. For me and my people, as a black man, on this song Em isn't talking to us. We don't need him to understand what's happening because it is happening to us and continues to happen to us. He is a person who can get through to white people and that is exactly the point of the song. He's speaking to white people, from his perspective. This song does not play off the black plight. I'm black, that's my best friend, and I spearheaded the beat that made this song possible. The entire thing was conceived as Em talking to white people. In no way co-opting the black point of view."

There is no other rapper alive who could pull off such a complicated enactment of the troubling, deeply complex reality of being an American in today's society. It is more than a case of being intelligent enough and having the verbal dexterity to disseminate the information cohesively. Eminem possesses an actor's ability to convey the pathos of an imagined character and a comedian's ability to impersonate someone other than himself. "Untouchable" utilizes all his communicative gifts, not to mention his ability to bend the narrative to varied backing tracks to elevate the storytelling further. In terms of achieving its intended goal, this song nails it.

"Em knew that he was going to lose fans over 'Untouchable,' but he didn't give a fuck," Mr. Porter continues. "There's no another artist out there besides Jay-Z who can take that stand, doing something they believe in even if they lose part of their audience. We live in touchy times, and this is a touchy generation. People like to critique everything from their position rather than looking at the perspective that it was created from to understand the message. 'Untouchable' was intended to be what Em can say about this issue to other white people. At his level, he can do that better than anybody else. He came from the hood more than a lot of people who say they came from the hood, you know what I'm sayin? He's from *my* hood; he grew up around the corner from me. And I know what that hood is like. I got shot in that hood."

While "Untouchable" makes a visceral sonic movie out of a toxic condition that continues to plague American society, Em spends the entirety of his two verses on "Like Home," featuring a chorus sung by Alicia Keys and a bridge that recalls her turn on Jay-Z's "Empire State of Mind," going at Donald Trump in a more measured, methodical manner. Rather than focusing on the easy part—the abundant clownish characteristics of the forty-fifth president—Mathers focuses on the disrespect Trump has shown our country and the catastrophic damage he is doing to the fabric of the nation. The song is a rallying cry for Americans to forget their differences and come together, to find common ground in shared disgust for

Trump's disrespect for his office, his supporters, and the citizens of the United States.

> *Everybody on your feet, this is where terrorism and heroism meet,*
> *Square off in the street. This chump barely even sleeps*
> *All he does is watch Fox News like a parrot and repeats.*

The song is earnest and calculated for maximum impact, with production designed for placement on mainstream radio, from Top 40 to Adult Contemporary. The king of controversy doesn't curse once over the song's four minutes, and it is refreshing to see that his language is no less powerful for it. The song feels crafted for crossover acceptance at every conceivable radio station; it's so up the middle that Keys's melodious voice is stripped of its naturally soulful tones. She sounds dipped in treble, Auto-Tuned into neutrality, dosed with a digital twang reminiscent of Nashville pop country. Despite these radio-friendly components, "Like Home" was inexplicably not released as a single.

Eminem was criticized for getting political on *Revival*. Some pointed out that he was coming to the conversation late and that if he had cared so deeply he should have spoken up sooner. "In 2017, listening to an Eminem rant against police brutality or a racist president can feel like watching *60 Minutes* after spending the week on Twitter; a slow recounting of last week's news."[15] Other critics remembered that for all his bravado, Marshall Mathers is a deep thinker, one who pores over what he is going to say for months or years before

---

15. Matthew Ismael Ruiz, "Eminem: *Revival*," *Pitchfork*, December 19, 2017, https://pitchfork.com/reviews/albums/eminem-revival/.

he says it and that, given the size of his stage, his speaking out at all should be commended. "All Americans are affected by the state of this country. We are all walking through this racial labyrinth. The issue of racism will not be solved by Eminem, but his actions do show he is among us. Not even the most distant stars can ignore what is and isn't being shown on the nightly news . . . We are in the age of Trump and the myth of post-racial America is dead. Rappers are just supplying the soundtrack. I pray all this talk takes us somewhere promising, but I don't expect paradise behind the exit door."[16]

More unanimous criticism was inspired by the fact that for all Eminem's socially conscious leanings, there are many examples of gleeful misogyny and even moments where Eminem draws parallels between himself and Donald Trump on *Revival*. On "Remind Me," a disappointing reunion with Rick Rubin that samples Joan Jett and the Blackhearts' "I Love Rock and Roll" (1982) amid a slew of corny come-ons, Eminem asks his equally dysfunctional romantic interest to "excuse the locker room talk," referencing Trump's defense of his "grab them by the pussy" remark during the 2016 presidential election. "Heat" is another rap-rock throwback produced by Rubin that skillfully pulls together samples of Run-DMC's "King of Rock" (1985), the Beastie Boys' "Girls" (1987), and the riff from "Intro (Feel the Heat)" (1997), the hilariously atrocious song sung by Dirk Diggler (Mark Wahlberg) and Reed Rothchild (John C. Reilly) in the film *Boogie*

---

16. Yoh Phillips, "Eminem Left the Ivory Tower to Fight a Losing Battle," *DJBooth*, December 12, 2017, https://djbooth.net/features/2017-12-12-eminem-revival-album-losing-battle.

Nights. The song is another testosterone- and pheromone-driven romp full of double entendres and punch lines; it's the sonic equivalent of 1980s teen sex comedies like *Porky's.* There are yuck-yuck references to buns and Asperger's and zingers like, "I think you're divine, so I might swing on you." But the following section is the one that most reviews of the record took him to task for:

> *Grab you by the (meow!), hope it's not a problem, in fact*
> *About the only thing I agree with Donald on is that.*
> *So when I put this palm on your cat,*
> *Don't snap, it's supposed to get grabbed.*
> *Why you think they call it a snatch?*

Eminem's work has been characterized by controversy and dichotomy since the start, but this was understandably too much. It wasn't that he chose to include a few songs that are as sexist and misogynist as he's ever been; it was that, for the sake of a joke, he aligned himself with the figure he'd taken such great pains to publicly protest. In those few lines, he undermined the purported purpose of the entire album and called his sincerity into question. In fact, he did worse: by drawing a parallel, however fleeting, however "tongue-in-cheek" (Eminem's oft-used defense of his most offensive lyrics), he aligned himself with Trump in people's minds. He gave them a reason to wonder if he was any different from Trump and if his newly found social awareness was nothing more than calculated histrionics.

"I get the comparison with the non-political-correctness," Eminem said, "but other than that we're polar opposites. [Trump] made these people feel like he was really going to do something for them. It's just so fucking disgusting how divisive his language is, the rhetoric, the Charlottesville shit, just watching it going, 'I can't believe he's saying this.' When he was talking about John McCain, I thought he was done. You're fucking with military veterans, you're talking about a military war hero who was captured and tortured. It just didn't matter. It doesn't matter. And that's some scary shit to me."[17]

Aside from "Untouchable" and "Like Home," the majority of *Revival* strives to satisfy Eminem's core audience with a few tracks aimed at the state of hip-hop and his place in it. "Believe," produced by Eminem himself, runs through his rise to the top and asks his fans if they still believe in him. "It's hard to be in his position, man," Mr. Porter says. "I hate seeing some of the shit he goes through and that he puts himself through. The fucked-up part is that he's just being honest. With 'Believe,' I think Rick Rubin and a few others questioned him as to why he had to do that, say those things. But he did. Everybody doubts themselves at some point; we all do." The song is a rare example (at that point) of Eminem taking a swing at the trap-style music and delivery dominating current hip-hop. Over a minimal beat driven by a single hi-hat and moody synths, his cadence is laid-back but no less complex. Leading by example, with stylistic and lyrical references to Drake ("And I started from the bottom like a snowman—ground up") and Migos's signature flow ("'Nother day in the life [Uh] / Used to have to scrape to get by [Yeah]"), Eminem is illustrating that trap

---

17. Rys, "Eminem and New Def Jam CEO Paul Rosenberg."

doesn't need to be lyrically lacking.[18] Your beats can be simple, but your narrative doesn't need to be.

On the next song, "Chloraseptic," featuring Brooklyn rapper Phresher (Kashaun Rameek Rutling), Eminem goes full tilt at mumble rap, the style that propagated wildly on the audio platform SoundCloud starting in 2010. The term was coined in 2016 by Pittsburgh rapper Whiz Khalifa (born Cameron Thomaz), who said it during an interview with New York radio station Hot 97. "We call it mumble rap," he said, referring to the younger generation's style of delivery. "It ain't no disrespect to the lil' homies, they don't want to rap. It's cool for now; it's going to evolve."[19] The term came to be used to denote rappers whose lyrics are unclear or care little for lyrical quality, which typically went hand in hand with content focused on taking lots of drugs, having money, jewelry, designer clothing, and partying. Musically, these artists extensively use Auto-Tune and favor minimal, lo-fi beats and sounds. More than a few have become commercially viable bona fide success stories: Lil Uzi Vert, Lil Peep, Lil Pump, Lil Xan, Lil Yachty, Migos, 21 Savage, Future, Desiigner, XXXTentacion, Tekashi 6ix9ine, Gucci Mane, Young Thug, and more. The trend is far from over, and the musical impact

---

18. In addition to referencing the title and refrain of Drake's single "Started from the Bottom" (2013) with that line twice in "Believe," the song bears a musical resemblance. The snowman image also recalls Drake's video for his single, which features him walking alongside a white Bentley convertible in a white outfit while snow blows in his face.

19. Kathy Iandoli, "The Rise of 'Mumble Rap': Did Lyricism Take a Hit in 2016?" *Billboard*, December 21, 2016, https://www.billboard.com/articles/columns/hip-hop/7625631/rise-of-mumble-rap-lyricism-2016.

can be heard in most contemporary hip-hop and pop today, but the deaths of Lil Peep at the age of twenty-one in 2017 and XXXTentacion, at age twenty in 2018, Lil Xan's (age twenty-two) struggle with drugs and mental health, and the incarceration of Tekashi 6ix9ine (age twenty-two), who faces up to forty-seven years in prison, have rightfully called the mores of the revolution into question.

Eminem takes the entire movement to task in five minutes, again over a lo-fi-style track heavy on the hi-hat but featuring a sample of the legendary EPMD's "It's My Thing" (1988). There are references to Simon Cowell and Em wearing Skechers, all moments that a younger rapper would probably laugh off as dad jokes, such as the homophone that ends this insult:

> *This rap shit got me travelin' place to place*
> *You barely leave your house*
> *'Cause you're always stuck at your pad, it's stationary.*

Laugh as they may, no one else in the game is capable of tossing off rapid-fire insults that sound so rhythmically pleasing.

> *You're a fuckboy so next time*
> *It's gonna be heads flyin' like Dez Bryant*
> *With a TEC-9 against Rex Ryan (Yeah!)*

There are other moments on *Revival* for the diehards, most notably the horrorcore epics "Framed" and "Offended," the two tracks that Eminem said were his favorites during a pre-release radio interview on his Sirius station, Shade 45. They are both vintage Eminem. "Framed" recalls *Relapse* and tells the tale of a psychopath on a killing spree, being hunted for his murderous rhymes. The shocking imagery, a combination of cartoons and slasher films, is heavy on the gore and interwoven rhyme schemes. "The beat talks to me and tells me which way to go," Eminem said. "That came from being a student of the evolution of hip-hop. Watching it evolve, watching rappers like Trech from Naughty by Nature, Tupac, Biggie, Cool G Rap, Big Daddy Kane, to me they always said the right shit over the right beat. It was like they knew so much. 'Framed' needed some evil serial killer type shit. That beat made me think of fucked-up shit."[20]

"Offended" is another stroll down memory lane, this one seeing Mathers proudly taking credit for his most offensive lyrical moments. He takes another stab at Trump, Mitch McConnell, Bill Cosby, Kellyanne Conway, and many more. The wordplay is dazzling, made all the more disorienting by the use of the reinterpreted children's song "Nobody Likes Me (Guess I'll Go Eat Worms)." It's a tour de force of interlaced rhymes, delivered with a give-and-take intonation that teases and taunts but never lets go. It is a timeless monument to Slim Shady, a showcase of everything that the underground fell in love with when they first heard him but honed by twenty years of practice and a sober head on his shoulders. The nasal delivery may be long gone, but the fiendish pursuit of rhyme and tasteless jokes remains.

Elsewhere on *Revival*, Eminem pens what will likely be his final song about Hailie's mother, Kimberly Scott. "Bad Husband"

20. "Eminem—Shady Fireside Chat on Shade45 (Full Q&A-Session with Fans about Revival, 15.12.2017)," hosted by Alan Light, video, 45:27, December 16, 2017, https://www.youtube.com/watch?v=tl0JShVU4uY.

continues the open-eyed discussion of their relationship that he began on "Stronger Than I Was" on *TMMLP2* over quirky and pensive indie-rock-flavored production, featuring a wistful hook sung by Sam Harris of the Ithaca, New York, band X Ambassadors. The song is an open letter, full of sadness, regret, an honest look at the role both played, and an admission that they both loved each other too much, just not the right way.

> We might have loved each other too much, and maybe that's what made us do what
> We did to each other, all the screw-ups. 'Cause you always thought that you was
> More in love with me, and I was thinking I was more in love than you was.

And later, something no lifelong Eminem fan thought they'd ever hear from him in a song: an apology.

> But I'm sorry, Kim, more than you could ever comprehend
> Leavin' you was fuckin' harder than sawin' off a fuckin' body limb.

The song slants toward Eminem's more polished pop numbers, but the unpolished sentiment and heartfelt delivery carries the day, as it does on the final three songs that close out the album, which, taken together, are the best moments on *Revival*.

"In Your Head," which features a sample of the Cranberries' iconic alt-rock song "Zombie" (1993) is a somber look back at Slim Shady's legacy and how putting his life in rhyme without caring for consequences direct or collateral has taken a near-fatal toll.[21] He sees himself as a zombie,

---

21. A month after the release of *Revival*, Cranberries singer Dolores O'Riordan, age forty-six, was found dead of accidental drowning caused by alcohol intoxication in the bathtub of her London hotel room.

dead inside and empty from years of spilling his guts, as he dreams of getting in his car, driving away, and being hypnotized so he can forget his life. He laments the effects of fame, the drugs, the loss of privacy and any semblance of a stable life—something the down-to-earth Michigan homebody clearly craves. He goes on to apologize to his daughter for making her life public in his songs and tries to explain why, with so much success on his side, he's still unhappy.

> *Okay, so ladies and gentlemen, let's strip away everything*
> *And see the main reason that I*
> *Feel like a lame piece of shit, I sound cranky and bitter, complain, beef and bicker*
> *'Bout the same things, 'cause when I look at me, I don't see what they see.*
> *I feel ashamed, greedy, and lately I've been contemplating*
> *Escaping to get away and go wherever this road takes me, it's making me crazy . . .*

The song leads directly into "Castle," a solemn power ballad that continues the grave review of Eminem's life choices. The song is presented as a series of letters written to Hailie beginning in 1995, just a few weeks before her birth, through 2007, when Marshall Mathers overdosed and nearly died. "When Hailie was about to be born I would always write letters that I thought maybe one day I'd give her. Or just to have them, or whatever," he said. "That's where the concept came from: let me start from the beginning and it goes to, obviously, the addiction part. The song takes place in 2007, which leads to the overdose, which leads to Christmas and her birthday and me missing that because I was in the hospital. Me not being there for my kids on Christmas was tough."[22]

The next letters describe Mathers's struggle to get discovered, then it climaxes on the night of his overdose. It paints a picture of a man fed up with his life, his career, and the effects his choices have had on his family. It's the portrait of someone on the verge of suicide.

I'll put out this last album and then I'm done with it, one hundred percent finished,
Fed up with it, I'm hanging it up, fuck it . . .
And if things should worsen don't take this letter I wrote as a goodbye note,
But your dad's at the end of his rope.
I'm sliding down a slippery slope. Anyways sweetie, I better go.
I'm getting sleepy, love, Dad . . . shit, I don't know.

The song ends with the sound of a bottle of pills being opened and those pills being ingested before Eminem collapses and hits the floor.

This leads directly into "Arose," the dramatic final track, produced by Rick Rubin and centered on a sample from the Bette Midler song "The Rose" (1979) from the soundtrack for the film of the same name. Throughout the song, a bombastic drum beat, the methodical drone of a mechanical ventilator, and the tones of a vital signs monitor comingle with the plaintive piano and Midler's crystal-clear voice as Eminem recalls the feeling of powerlessness he experienced when he woke up in a hospital bed.

---

22. "Eminem—Shady Fireside Chat."

They got me all hooked up to some machine, I love you, Bean
Didn't want you to know I was struggling.
Feels like I'm underwater submerged like a submarine
Just heard the nurse say, my liver and kidneys aren't functioning.

He goes on to imagine what his final moments would be like, drifting between scenes the way life would flash before one's eyes. He sees his girls that Christmas without him, he sees Proof and goes to walk with him, he tells his girls to take care of their mother, he tells his little brother, Nathan, to marry the girl he's with because she's a good woman,[23] and he laments not being able to clear the air once and for all with his mother. As he begins to go under, he thinks of his daughters and searches for the strength to return. He rewinds the tape, literally taking the listener back to the end of the previous song, "Castle," so that he can flush the pills and get sober. In an even more meta-Eminem move, he drops this line at exactly four minutes into "Arose":

Consider them last four minutes as the song I'da sang to my daughters
If I'da made it to the hospital less than two hours later, but I fought it
And came back like a boomerang on 'em
Now a new day is dawnin' I'm up, Tuesday, it's morning—now I know.

Not only does the rewind come at four minutes into "Arose," but the exact time it "rewinds" to in "Castle" is also precisely four minutes into that song. These tracks are Eminem at his finest: when examining his own pain, no one

---

23. Nathan did; he's a happily married father of three.

is capable of weaving a lyrical tapestry as beautifully intricate as Marshall Mathers. "He is a true perfectionist," Mr. Porter says. "He will teach you how much of a perfectionist you think you are real quick."

The moment the *Revival* track list was revealed, critics and fans alike seemed ready to be disappointed by it, and as soon as the album wasn't received the way he hoped it would be, Eminem spoke up about it. When pressed about the overtly patriotic imagery and ramp-up to the album compared to the content, he said that the title applied to both him and America and that both needed a revival. It was this dual purpose that ultimately impaired the record, lending it a scattered identity. The songs about the problems with America were there, but there weren't enough of them. The songs about Mathers's issues were there, and they were great. But the rest of the tracks seemed to be a punch list of what he thought was expected: pop-oriented numbers featuring notable female artists, a few down-and-dirty Slim Shady numbers for the diehards, and a few about the state of hip-hop.

No one would argue that American society needs a revival, but the same can't be said for Marshall Mathers. He has overcome a crippling addiction and in 2017 was celebrating his ninth year sober. He found a way to cope with fame. He had enough of a sense of what was right to risk losing his many red-state fans by coming out against Trump. He had what seemed to be a very happy and healthy relationship with his daughter and peace and closure with her mother.

He continued to sell out stadiums and release albums that debuted at number one and went platinum no matter how many critics panned them. When it came to the idea that Eminem needed reviving, the sentiment rang a bit hollow. What he needed was inspiration.

Chapter 9

Energized Like a Nine Volt

On August 31, 2018, less than a year after the release of *Revival*, Eminem released his tenth studio album, *Kamikaze*. The album is his shortest, clocking at just under forty-six minutes, the average length of most albums released by major artists today.[1] What was most unusual about it was that Eminem had created an entirely new set of songs so quickly. Aside from his years in limbo, on drugs then fighting his way off them, he had always released music between albums—with D12, for a soundtrack, or as a guest on other artists' tracks—but since 1999, the shortest time he'd gone between studio albums was fifteen months (between *The Slim Shady LP* and *The Marshall Mathers LP*) and the longest, out of necessity,

---

1. Due to the impact of streaming services and the fact that *Billboard* now counts streams into its tally of album sales, there have been several strategies employed to maximize profit and clout. In the past few years, some artists, particularly in hip-hop, have released excessively long albums—Drake, Post Malone, and Future most notably—to increase the number of songs that will be included on streaming sites' playlists, which furthers sales. Others, like Kanye West, have swung the other way, releasing extremely short albums but more of them. The average still remains somewhere around forty to fifty minutes in hip-hop and pop.

was five years—virtually a death sentence with today's fickle audiences. Typically, there would be a new Eminem album every two to three years. He said he'd learned that from Dr. Dre, who stressed the importance of letting the public miss you for a while, but not too long, before returning. That, of course, was a different time, one in which all humans had longer attention spans and spoke to each other directly, one in which music had to be purchased at stores in packaging that could be held, and long before music, TV, film, and all manner of recorded entertainment was expected to be free, on demand, and available on any device, 24-7.

Clearly, in the fall of 2018, Eminem had something to say and was in a hurry to do it. Nothing dire had happened; no new trauma befell him in real life that required an exorcism in rhyme. Hailie was fine, his mother was getting older but they were cool, and it seemed, from the songs he'd written about her on his last two albums and what he'd said publicly, that he'd reached a comfortable degree of closure with Kim. This need to express further, after taking four years to create *Revival*, was an issue strictly his own. He was preoccupied. He wasn't after more soul-searching or self-flagellation. He hadn't forgotten an apology that couldn't wait. He did have issues to air, but they didn't involve family members or himself. He had bones to pick with a diverse group, some of them fellow rappers and journalists, some just ordinary citizens who fancied themselves as such. All of them had one thing in common: they had, in his mind, unjustly criticized his last artistic cycle, from the BET cypher through *Revival*. And this go-round, there were more of them, because for the first time in his career, Eminem didn't quite connect. He didn't make waves the way he usually did. The album sold nonetheless, but he was less celebrated and less controversial than he'd ever been in the past, and that didn't sit well with him. It's not that Eminem sees himself as some kind of divine rap ruler that no one dare speak against. He has always told people who don't like him to do the sensible thing and just not listen, and if there's anyone who believes in free and uncensored speech, it is Marshall Mathers. Without it, his career trajectory would have been a blip.

"He doubts himself, like any great artist does," Mr. Porter says, "but the shit I hate is that a lot of the criticism is unfair. He's so good at everything he does that people judge him ten times harder than they do somebody else. It's hard to gauge that when you live in a bubble. Em can't go to a bar or a barbershop or barbecue spot and get with real people who would tell him what they loved that he did and what they didn't. He doesn't get those real conversations. He's got to live in a bubble, so you've got to give him even more credit because he lives in a space where he can't maneuver the way he wants but he's still able to be relevant without dealing with society."

Eminem has always been a polarizing, divisive artist and is quite possibly the most misunderstood MC in hip-hop. From the get-go, he has labored against preconceptions, first as a white rapper, then as a rapper from Detroit who didn't sound like he was from Detroit, then as a protégé signed by a tremendously influential rap icon. In 1999, when he signed to a major label, there were some who said that Em was going to lose what the underground loved about him and, conversely, others who said that, without Dr. Dre, he essentially had no talent. Time revealed him to be a phenomenal talent with a unique perspective, but for Em, the struggle continued. He had to align himself with a new reality. He came from an underground scene, where his undeniable strengths as a rapper, from his insane lyrical skills, delightfully inappropriate humor, versatile flows, and storyteller's way with imagery were celebrated. These traits and his lyrics were seen for what they are: words meant to shock, awe, entertain, and explain a point of view. He never had to point out the line between fantasy and reality, because his fellow underground rap fans understood. His rhymes were never taken as intentions to commit felonies; they remained words, shots fired on a battlefield where no one gets hurt. As he said in "Just Don't Give a Fuck" (1999), "This is a lyrical combat, gentlemen hold your pistols." The entire point of rapping is sport; it's karate, it's competition—slaughter your opponent verbally, proving your dominance aurally. Like break dancing, rapping came about as another way, among others, to harness the intensity of a physical altercation without fighting. It was a cutting-edge cultural sport, and it still is. Just like the playoffs, the sparring benefits the spectators; it's oxygen to them, and the entire culture is enriched when the titans get into it. When a generation breeds a healthy roster of hip-hop athletes all striving to best each other artistically, the culture and everything it touches—which today is literally everything—evolves. That is the world Eminem is from.

Mainstream society didn't quite get that. Once he was a staple on radio and MTV (back when it played music, which again, aside from mail-order record clubs, was back when people had to leave their house to buy music), he was taken at his word, for his words. He was held accountable for every scheme he expressed in rhyme; they were considered acts he'd realize, given the chance. As Eminem continued to sell millions and pile up Grammys, his uphill battle continued, first against censorship, then the trauma of his upbringing and the self-medication he doubled down on to cope with the pressure of sudden fame. He became internationally known, but he was still an outsider, though now he was standing at center stage. In the past twenty years, he has achieved more than any other rapper in history[2] and opened doors for count-less artists, hip-hop and otherwise; anyone with an off-kilter life story to tell in the past two decades in pop owes him a nod. He is part of our cultural DNA, placing him in a very rarefied group of entertainers, many of whom also go by one name: Madonna, Prince, Bono, Michael Jackson, Elton John.

In his art, Eminem is justifiably arrogant and cocky, but he has never let the trappings of success define him. He wants for nothing and lives a very comfortable life, but he has never been the type to flash his wealth or devote bars to jets, cars, diamonds, or the numerous trimmings to which rappers with far less devote entire careers. Rather, he has stayed rooted in hip-hop culture, using his influence to take creative risks and

---

2. One hundred million songs sold and counting, including three diamond certified singles, fifteen Grammys (of forty-three nominations), and an Oscar.

to promote artists that he believes in, occasionally to his detriment.[3] In the same vein, he only licenses his name to clothing that he actually wears, like Nike sneakers and Rag and Bone jeans. Eminem has achieved enough for three lifetimes, and sure, everyone loves plaques and money, but at heart the guy is the same as he ever was. He's an underground MC who loves ill rhymes and unadulterated boom-bap rap.

Far lesser talents have sold out and been given a pass, yet somehow Eminem continues to be held to a higher standard. It's hard to pinpoint why. He has had so much success in his career that maybe it all blurs together in the mind of the public, his achievements dissolved into so much white noise. It could also be a side effect of his oeuvre: by making his personal life part and parcel of his career-defining albums, maybe he gave his audience an unfair sense of entitlement. Once he shifted gears and developed an arsenal of different musical styles, there were (as there always will be) factions that longed for him to only be their favorite version of Eminem. Maybe, since his early work is so brashly personal, they feel this "betrayal" more deeply than they do the stylistic departures of other

---

3. Slaughterhouse, the lyrical rap supergroup consisting of Joe Budden, Joell Ortiz, KXNG Crooked, and Royce da 5'9", comes to mind. Eminem signed them to Shady in 2011 and executive produced their critically acclaimed, commercially deficient album *Welcome to: Our House*. Due to poor sales, the label never recouped its investment in the album, and though it paid for recordings intended for a second full-length that was never released, Budden accused Eminem and manager Paul Rosenberg of withholding money. On his influential weekly podcast, Budden became one of the most vocal critics of *Revival*, calling it trash and claiming that, though he was now retired, he had rapped better than Eminem for the past ten years. He made these statements all while still signed to Shady Records.

artists. Then again, maybe this bias is just a case of someone being so superior at their craft that it inspires professional and amateur culture pundits to exploit any chink in his armor for the sake of making him more human. A review of the careers of virtuoso athletes, from Michael Jordan to Tom Brady to Tiger Woods to LeBron James, reveals journalists spending more time on the minutiae of those stars' off nights than they would any other player. It could simply be that Eminem is an institution that a younger generation (who hasn't done their homework) simply sees as authoritative, "the man," a symbol of where they want to be and feel they're being held back from. Or perhaps, by turning his life into art so well at the start of his career, there was a disconnect in the mind of the public, obscuring the fact that Marshall Mathers is an artist, ever-evolving, whose real life would only temporarily be grist for the mill. Troves of people were disappointed at first when Picasso went Cubist and Dylan went electric. The difference is, they didn't have YouTube to make reaction videos about it.

"Since the internet has become what it's become and since YouTube and all that, you've got not enough Indians and too many chiefs. Everybody on the internet, in hip-hop especially, it seems like they are either a rapper, a DJ, a writer, a producer—everybody has something to do with it," Eminem said. "I love the fact that so many people are having an easier time getting on than we had back in the day. We didn't have the platform, and I appreciate the platform. Now you've got people who are doing the same thing and they can do it better, but now you've got people who don't do anything and are just critiquing it. That's fine, people can talk crazy about me and they have a right to express themselves, but I also get to say whatever the fuck I want to about you now. I'm good with *Revival*, fuck it, because I couldn't have made this album [*Kamikaze*] without that. There is something inside me that is a little more happy when I'm angry. As bad as it feels to be there, there's a rush of it that I like. It inspires me to say something back. There are so many levels to not caring about shit."[4]

When someone is as significant a cultural figure as Eminem is, as well as a musician who is capable of rugged underground rap; conscious, positive rap; and collaboration with pop stars, everyone is bound to be disappointed by something he does. But what happened with *Revival* is that as soon as the track list was revealed, featuring seven collaborations with pop artists and one with a rapper, fans on the internet went crazy. There were endless tweets, blogs, and YouTube videos about the forthcoming album being garbage, despite the fact that no one had heard it. When the first single, "Walk on Water (featuring Beyoncé)," was released, the earnest empowering ditty did nothing to turn the tide. When the album dropped, despite its stellar debut and commercial performance, it received the most negative reviews of any album in Eminem's discography, and the notorious loudmouth simply could not keep quiet about it.

He released a remix of "Chloraseptic," featuring Atlanta rapper 2 Chainz (born Tauheed Epps), which took the

---

4. "Eminem x Sway—The Kamikaze Interview (Part 1)," interview by Sway Calloway, video, 12:07, September 11, 2018, https://www.youtube.com/watch?v=Kqh3zNhC5Kg.

negative reception to task and also undid something Mathers had worked half a year to get right when he started making *Revival*. "One of the first things I had to do when I started making [*Revival*] was I had to let off the gas," he said. "I had released a couple songs a couple years ago, 'Phenomenal' and 'Kings Never Die.' Going back to them now I realized, damn, I never took a breath. I didn't leave no space. I had to figure out how to let off the gas but not too much. In the beginning I realized that it was like that on too many of the songs. I probably recorded between forty and fifty songs for this album, and it took me about six months to feel that I had gotten the spacing right. Because I didn't want to let off the gas too much."[5]

That gesture seemed intended for his audience, as a way to make sure he was properly understood in his next collection of songs. That courtesy was promptly taken back: on the "Chloraseptic Remix (featuring 2 Chainz and Phresher)," Em floors it, then rolls open the nitro tank attached to the engine. The ominous, paranoid mood of the song is elevated by a great 2 Chainz verse and a manic one from Phresher before Eminem goes mental, rapping at the speed of light for two and a half minutes without pause.

> *Not as raw as I was? "Walk on Water" sucked?*
> *Bitch, suck my dick. Y'all saw the track list and had a fit*
> *Before you heard it, so you formed your verdict*
> *While you sat with your arms crossed,*
> *Did your little reaction videos and talked over songs*

---

5. "Eminem—Shady Fireside Chat."

He certainly has a point when it comes to reaction videos, which are a YouTube phenomenon in which self-proclaimed culture critics post videos of themselves reviewing or reacting to everything from albums to films, television shows, video games, or anything they choose. Some "reviewers" take their hobby quite seriously, using microphones on boom arms, sitting in swanky office chairs with records on the wall behind them, as if they are actually editors at a media publication. They're not; they're typically in a corner of their house, apartment, or basement. Other shows take a more organic approach: a few friends discussing a new release while they hang out listening to it in a car or sitting side by side on a couch having drinks the way buddies might do on a Friday night. Some are well versed in the history of hip-hop and are clear about their biases, and if the group is well chosen, all points of view are represented. Other talking heads, and there are many of these, spend an inordinate amount of time explaining how big of a fan they are of an artist, or why, in the case of Eminem, the fact that they are from Detroit makes them an expert, before finding fault in the music and giving advice as if they have firsthand experience of the artist and the industry. Once again, it's probably a side effect of how much of himself Eminem has put into his music or maybe they're all just taking that one shot, hoping to be noticed, but when it comes to Eminem, far too many of these YouTube savants act like they know.

"Em did not even have or care about the internet for so long, so when he called me up and said he was watching reaction videos?" Mr. Porter says, chuckling. "I've got eight computers in my house and I didn't even know what he was talking about! I was upset that he showed me too. Two seconds into the song and these people are saying, 'this is fire,' or 'this is trash,' or 'this is a classic.' That's where we live now. Everybody's a critic; everybody thinks their opinion is important, and it's not. I don't think it's going away, but it should not become the new barometer. Those people get a lot of views, and people find them entertaining because they don't know any better. Teenagers today are growing up with those videos compared to reading *The Source* or *XXL*. They do not have the same importance."

Everyone has a right to their opinion of course, and there's nothing wrong with disliking something that's not for you. But the unilateral equalizer, the internet, has encouraged people to think that if they don't like something, it's bad, as in constructed poorly and of poor quality. That simply isn't true. For example, one self-involved reviewer at an online publication of some note casually mocked Eminem's delivery on the "Chloraseptic" remix as follows: "a little bit of yelling and a lot of that clipped-cadence, every-word-must-rhyme shit he does these days."[6] It's fine to dislike Eminem's song and style (judging by his other articles, the blogger is more of an Earl Sweatshirt guy), but to brush off a delivery and lyrical complexity that almost no one is capable of as "shit he does these days" is navel-gazing ignorance. Much like that writer, the "critics" in most reaction videos confuse their personal

---

6. Clayton Purdom, "Eminem Responds to Bad Revival Reviews with Bad Remix of Bad Revival Track," *AV Club*, January 8, 2018, https://www.avclub.com/eminem -responds-to-bad-revival-reviews-with-bad-remix-o-1821882735.

preference with some kind of self-appointed professional truth.

Eminem felt like the criticism he got for making an album that sought to please every sector of his fan base (as well as educate his red-state fans) was unfair and uninformed, and the way he saw it, since everyone has a right to speak their mind about him on globally public platforms, he would use his own globally public platform to speak about them. The barrage began with the "Chloraseptic" remix in January 2018, but *Kamikaze* was the bomb that blew it all to bits.

After *Revival*'s lukewarm reception and firing that first shot, Eminem circled the wagons. He went to LA to see Dr. Dre and to figure out what he'd done wrong, as the negative opinions continued to inform his writing. "We had a couple discussions about the last album [*Revival*]. [Dre] hit me up one day and was like, 'I don't like the way motherfuckers are talking about your album,'" he recalled. "He and Jimmy had heard *Revival*. Most of the songs I had done at Rick Rubin's studio, and based off that reaction, I think Dre was a little confused too, probably not more so than me, but we had a conversation earlier in the year, and I think I only had one song at the time and I was thinking about releasing it. Then I got to Detroit and did another song. And I decided I may as well do a fucking album."[7]

At this point he closed ranks, shut down interview requests, and devoted himself to creating. He went back to basics:

---

7. "Eminem x Sway—The Kamikaze Interview (Part 2)," interview by Sway Calloway, video, 13:44, September 12, 2018, https://www.youtube.com/watch?v= wrpauWGy4tQ.

simple production, rap-heavy, hook-light compositions, each one a showcase for lyrically taking no prisoners. It would be old school and hardcore and executive produced and mixed by Dr. Dre. There would be no experiments, no pushing the style envelope, no pairing artists he admired from other genres with appropriate songs. He'd had a small mountain of beats submitted by some of the best producers in the industry during the creation of *Revival*. He would go through them, solicit some more, and give the world an album of just beats and rhymes, jabs and uppercuts, Slim Shady spitting poison, straight from the dome. "Dre's input was all over the album. There were also a couple songs that he deaded," Em said. "He didn't have a good reaction to them, and he thought one of them was going a little too far. It definitely went too far."[8]

Considering what was released, that omitted track must be treacherous. *Kamikaze* is a lyrical Incredible Hulk, forty-five minutes and thirteen tracks of pointed anger and antagonism delivered in the most electrified method the world had heard from Eminem in years. And, as promised by the title, it was a sneak attack, aimed at metaphorically killing his career while taking everything he hated about contemporary rap and American society with him.

On August 30, Eminem teased the release of the song "Venom," included on *Kamikaze* as the last track and written for the Marvel film of the same name starring Tom Hardy: he posted a fifteen-second clip featuring the song and an animated title picturing the Venom title with an *e* that was

---

8. "Eminem x Sway—The Kamikaze Interview (Part 2)."

turned backward and red. A few hours later, at midnight, *Kamikaze* was released without promotion or announcement to digital music stores and streaming services. It was sold on Eminem's website in physical form, along with some themed merchandise.

"I feel like the way the climate is right now, giving them no warning was the best thing to do," Eminem said. "If you give people enough time to have preconceptions, if they get into the mind-set that it's gonna suck, even if they kinda don't feel that way but they've already formed those opinions in front of their friends, nobody wants to be wrong about it. When the *Revival* song list came down the pipe, it was over-whelmingly 'This shit is gonna be trash.' Nobody wanted to be wrong about it. A lot of people had already formed their opinions . . . I felt a bunch of different ways. Maybe because it didn't sound like everything else and what most people are doing, maybe that is what tainted their ear. I remember a time in hip-hop where you had to be so different from the next person or you were trash. A shift happened to where if you don't sound like everyone else, you're trash automatic-ally. It's not like I can't take constructive criticism, but I think it went beyond constructive criticism."[9]

The album is as old-school Eminem as he can possibly be at this stage in his life, short of becoming twenty-seven and abusing drugs again. It is a furious tirade and a detailed take-down of all that he sees wrong with hip-hop culture and, to

---

9. "Eminem x Sway—The Kamikaze Interview (Part 2)."

a lesser degree, society. He names trends and imitates other rappers' styles, his mockery all the more lethal because he infuses his parodies with far superior lyrics and delivery. The effect of hearing a high-grade talent ape a lesser form of rap is arresting, like watching a pro tight end run a set of downs in a high school game. Once upon a time, Eminem took aim at rappers and pop stars he didn't think deserved their success, everyone from MC Hammer and Vanilla Ice to Britney Spears and N'Sync. On *Kamikaze* he does the same, setting his sights on mumble rappers who built their following online by lifting from Lil Wayne, right down to their names, all of which start with Lil.

In five and a half minutes, the opening track, "The Ringer," accomplishes all of Eminem's goals with *Kamikaze*. If he had done nothing but release this single, his mission would have been accomplished. It is a scorching send-up of the state of hip-hop, not to mention an invigorating listen. Devoid of overly complex musical melodrama, the dank and brooding track hilariously mocks mumble rappers like Lil Xan, Lil Pump, and Migos while utilizing the triplet flow ubiquitous in the genre.

The triplet flow is a rap style based on the musical concept of triplets, in which one beat is divided into three notes rather than two or four, as it is within a four-four time signature. The oldest piece of famous music that employs triplets is probably the first movement of Beethoven's *Moonlight Sonata* (1801), while African music (West African particularly) is dominated by triplet rhythms—a direct tie to the roots of hip-hop. The first use of this cadence in rap can be traced to Chuck D on Public Enemy's "Bring the Noise" (1987). Over the next few years, with hip-hop evolving most rapidly on the east and west coasts, the style was used by various rappers in short bursts and less frequently full verses. In the midnineties, however, triplets became entrenched in the emerging southern style, most notably due to Memphis rapper Lord Infamous and the group he cofounded, Three 6 Mafia, who employed the flow for their choruses and often entire songs. At the same time, on the West Coast, Bone Thugs-n-Harmony expertly employed the style but were the only ones to do so regionally. It was Three 6 Mafia's influence, as well as the lean-sipping scene they celebrated, that had the most influence on new-school southern rappers from Migos to Future to Young Thug. Though it is far from true, Migos claims that they invented the slightly modified, now ubiquitous version of the triplet flow they popularized with their viral hit "Versace" in 2013.

There is absolutely nothing wrong with the triplet flow; it instantly brings energy and excitement to a beat, quite literally snatching the listener's ear. In the way that the placement of a drum sound, or the lack of one where it is expected within a measure, can make a song sound faster or slower than its tempo, the triplet flow challenges the accepted convention of how rap has been delivered for the better part of forty-four years. Chuck D knew what he was doing; when a triplet flow is applied to incendiary lyrics, the effect is formidable. Take Kendrick Lamar's burst of triplets in "D.N.A." (2017): "This is my heritage, all I'm inheritin' / Money and power, the maker of marriages."[10] The shift in his delivery highlights the segue to the most powerful, final verse of the song.

In trap music's laconic world of stretched-out beats and warped synths, triplets make complete sense. The hi-hats are arranged to punctuate the beats and where the words will land, while the space between the beats has been maximized to allow rappers more room to lay down their lines. Given the monotonous tone of trap, triplet flows rev up the proceedings. Migos didn't invent it, but they did popularize it and bring it to the mainstream. By illustrating how well triplets work with the uncomplicated beats of trap music, they spawned a nation of copycats, most with less style and technical skill.

What Eminem and many lyrical-minded hip-hop fans can't stand is the fact that contemporary rappers have utilized triplets to grant their songs excitement where there would otherwise be none. That and the fact that in contemporary hip-hop, for fans and artists alike, the vibe and mood of a song matters more than any of the words. After stating that he hates "this choppy flow everyone copies," Eminem makes this abundantly clear in "The Ringer":

> *So finger-bang, chicken wang, MGK, Igg' Azae' Lil Pump, Lil Xan imitate Lil Wayne*
> *I should aim at everybody in the game, pick a name . . .*
> *I heard your mumblin' but it's jumbled in mumbo-jumbo*
> *The era that I'm from will pummel you, that's what it's comin' to.*

---

10. Caswell Estelle, "How the Triplet Flow Took Over Rap," *Vox*, September 18, 2017, https://www.vox.com/2017/9/18/16328330/migos-triplet-flow-rap.

Em also says that he sees why people like Lil Yachty, though it's not for him because he's "simply just an MC."

Later in the album, on "Not Alike (featuring Royce da 5'9")," he slams this point home with a song that employs two different beats, both by producers (Tay Keith and Ronny J) who have made a name for themselves in the trap and SoundCloud rap world. Even his choice of words, chosen to mock the chorus of Migos's hit "Bad and Boujee," sounds random but related.

> *Brain dead, eye drops*
> *Pain meds, cyclops*
> *Daybed, iPod*
> *May back, Maybach*

Brain dead and pain meds correspond to eye drops and cyclops, but the most humorous line is the one that refers to the luxury Mercedes line (pronounced My-Bach) that rappers frequently mispronounce. For the rest of the song, Royce and Em decimate everything wrong with lyrically lazy trap music from all angles, while Em reserves a particularly vicious verse for white rapper Machine Gun Kelly (born Colson Baker).

The assault continues on "The Greatest," where Eminem once again utilizes a hi-hat-heavy trap beat to show younger rappers how triplets are done. When basic rhyme patterns are used in a triplet flow, they sound more complex; when Eminem's effortlessly complicated, reference-laced schemes are employed, keeping up with him is like treading water in a current. The humor that informed his earliest work is evident here ("So you sold ten million albums, eh? / Only problem is you put out ten million albums, eh?") as is his penchant for comparing his lyrical intensity to the worst of society's homicidal misanthropes, like Stephen Paddock, the man who killed fifty-eight concertgoers during a music festival in Las Vegas in October 2017, and James Holmes, the man who killed twelve people in Aurora, Colorado, at a movie theater during a screening of *The Dark Knight Rises* in 2012.

On the title track, "Kamikaze," Eminem uses what is commonly considered the worst song he's ever made, "FACK" (2005) from *Curtain Call*, and turns it into a hilariously bratty chorus and an opportunity to further mock trap artists. He references rappers who use ghostwriters and producers who play reference tracks for artists, which encourages further carbon-copy product.[11] He proclaims that since he had a bad year, he's killing his career and taking everyone he hates with him.

Smash into everyone, crash into everything
Back and I've just begun, "FACK" 2017
Fack, fack on everyone

His most concise takedown of mumble rap, however, comes in the melodiously moody "Fall," which features a hook sung by Justin Vernon of indie rock band Bon Iver. After it was released, Vernon publicly denounced the song for its negative message and slurs and said that he asked Eminem's

---

11. It is a common practice for a producer to send an artist they want to work with a "reference track," which is a track they've already done with another artist. Usually these are successful hits that encourage both parties to agree on creating a song that sounds similar, which in turn creates more music that sounds the same.

management to have his voice removed from the track.[12] They did not comply.

Em's expert lines in "Fall" say it all, as he compares mumble rappers to contestants fighting to survive in the young adult sci-fi book series *Hunger Games*, criticizing them for both mocking their elders like Jay-Z and Tupac, as well as J. Cole, and mimicking successful current artists like Migos and Drake.[13] Eminem also humorously pins everything to the reaction he got to "Walk on Water."

These rappers are like Hunger Games, one minute they're mocking Jay
Next minute, they get their style from Migos or they copy Drake.
Maybe I just don't know when to turn around and walk away,
But all the hate, I call it "Walk on Water" gate.

"Lucky You (featuring Joyner Lucas)," which sold platinum and gave Eminem his first number one debut on the *Billboard* Streaming Songs chart, is a relentless showcase of two rappers taking apart current hip-hop in a rapid-fire, lyric-heavy mode.

'Cause half of these rappers have brain damage
All the lean rappin' face tats, striped out like tree sap

---

12. Justin Vernon tweeted the following about the song after its release: "Eminem is one of the best rappers of all time, there is no doubt. I have and will respect that. Tho, this is not the time to criticize Youth, it's the time to listen. To act. It is certainly not the time for slurs. Wish they would have listened when we asked them to change it," Justin Vernon (@blobtower), Twitter, August 31, 2018, 9:14 a.m., https://twitter.com/blobtower/status/1035561538701156352?lang=en.

13. Rapper Lil Xan called Tupac "boring" and was so swiftly attacked by the hip-hop community that he tried to backpedal by covering a Tupac song in concert. Lil Yachty has been flippant about the legacy and rap talent of both Tupac and Biggie Smalls. Lil Pump and Smokepurpp had a long history of attacking lyrical North Carolina rapper J. Cole online. Pump even recorded a song called "Fuck J. Cole." Cole eventually responded, destroying them with the track "1985" (2018).

I don't hate trap, and I don't wanna seem mad
But in fact, where the old me at?
The same cat that would take that feedback and aim back, I need that.

Those last three lines point to the essence of *Kamikaze* more than anything else. The album is primarily a vehicle to get back at a list of about seventeen people and groups specifically name-checked by Eminem (more on this later), but its other intent is to regain the attention and currency that Eminem usually enjoys upon the release of an album. He didn't receive it upon the release of *Revival*. By reverting to the strategy that made him a household name in the first place—making fun of popular trends in music and society in the bulletproof lyrical manner that made him a legendary battle rapper—he once again stole the spotlight. This is perhaps the strongest response to critics who claimed that his sound, style, and entire career were so far out of whack with contemporary hip-hop that Eminem's music in 2017 was, according to Jon Caramanica's review of *Revival* in the *New York Times*, "outsider art."[14] Caramanica's assertion was ridiculous, the equivalent of calling a new Bruce Springsteen album outsider art because it didn't sound like Imagine Dragons. There will always be a current sound in any genre, but the artists whose work have defined the genre repeatedly over time at the highest level live outside that, not as outsiders but as the standard by which all others should be judged.

---

14. Jon Caramanica, "Hip-Hop Changes. Eminem Doesn't," *New York Times*, December 18, 2017, https://www.nytimes.com/2017/12/18/arts/music/eminem-revival-review.html.

Kamikaze did what *The Slim Shady LP* did: employing indefensible mockery, it brought the cultural conversation back to Eminem. Between the album's surprise arrival, the diss tracks, and the responses to the diss tracks, *Kamikaze* did what *Revival* didn't: it went viral. Every headline online and in real life that referred to those Eminem targeted had a built-in follow-up component—the inevitable article that covered the target's response to Em's barb. It ensured a never-ending loop of coverage that centered around Eminem and his new album. Considering that the general consensus was that Eminem was isolated and out of touch, as he had admitted to avoiding online culture as much as possible, he proved himself to be very in touch, aware of everyone who had spoken out against him and the details of the *Revival* backlash. It also revealed that for such a supposedly corny old man, Eminem knew a lot more about current hip-hop and manipulating the online nature of its consumption than he let on. "We've never felt closer to our favorite artists, and Em—not a fan of posting personal messages on social media—has drawn fans around him in a typically eccentric way," Jordan Bassett wrote on NME.com. "If you're with him, you're in the gang."[15]

"When people started talking about *Revival* the way they did, I think it was good for that to happen," Mr. Porter says. "It put a fire in Em that some people didn't think he had anymore.

15. Jordan Bassett, "We Need to Talk About: The Sheer Genius of Eminem's 'Kamikaze' Diss-track Feedback Loop," *NME*, September 7, 2018, https://www.nme.com/blogs/we-need-to-talk-about-the-genius-of-eminems-kamikaze-feedback-loop-2375234.

What came next with *Kamikaze* was a great moment for fans, but I don't think it should happen again. I want to see him get to a point where he understands that it's all just people talking and most of it don't matter. Most of it is just some kid in their basement!"

The sound of *Kamikaze* is entirely current, yet evocative of old-school Eminem. Four of the tracks were produced by Floridian Illadaproducer (born Illya Fraser), who did the beat for "Offended" on *Revival* but is better known for his work with Lil Pump, Smokepurpp, Kent Jones, and Chief Keef. "I was trying to make something for the club," he says of the beat that became "The Ringer." "Something for either Migos, Pump or Smokepurpp . . . I sent [Eminem] a bunch of different sounds: Atlantic-sounding shit, Miami-sounding shit, up-north-sounding shit, West-Coast shit. He picked that beat." Across most of the record, Eminem picked beats associated with the contemporary style he finds so much fault in lyrically and also jumped in the ring, rapping and singing in that style as well as effortlessly flowing into one of his many signature modes—often within the same song. "There's lyrical hip-hop, which always reigned supreme," Fraser said. "Then there's what they call mumble rap, which is feel-good music. It's more about the feelings than the lyrics. They can both coincide. When I'm hearing [Eminem] going at the younger guys, I'm like, 'This is the game you're in.' If you say you're a rapper, if another rapper goes at you, even if it's the G.O.A.T.,[16] either you're gonna take some bars or you're gonna give some

---

16. G.O.A.T. means "Greatest of All Time."

back. Most of 'em just gonna take 'em. 'Cause there's nothing you can do. What are you gonna do, battle rap Eminem?"[17]

"I'm not gonna be America's punching bag and let motherfuckers think it's cool to say whatever the fuck they want about me," Eminem said after *Kamikaze* was released. "If you don't give a fuck, you also will fire back at somebody who says something about you. I picked and chose who I wanted to say my piece with. A lot of those things were personal, but there are a lot of things that aren't personal on *Kamikaze*. A lot of it is just the game and competition. That's the spirit of the MC."[18]

Eminem indulged that spirit fully on *Kamikaze*, letting everyone have it to the limit of his lyrical abilities (which is to say a lot). The list of figures called out is numerous and diverse, from the aforementioned Lil mumble rappers to hip-hop talking heads like Charlamagne tha God; to former Shady signee Joe Budden and his podcast cohost DJ Akademiks; to race-appropriating Australian pop singer Iggy Azalea; South African alternative hip-hop group Die Antwoord; rappers Tyler, the Creator, Vince Staples, Earl Sweatshirt, and Machine Gun Kelly; the Recording Academy (the institution that controls the Grammy Awards); journalists and fans who unfairly judged *Revival* or didn't support his BET cypher; and of course President Donald Trump and Vice President Mike Pence.

17. Elias Leight, "Eminem Producer Explains Why 'Kamikaze' Is a Throwback to Slim Shady," *Rolling Stone*, August 31, 2018, https://www.rollingstone.com/music/music-news/eminem-kamikaze-slim-shady-producer-718242/.
18. "Eminem x Sway—The Kamikaze Interview (Part 2)."

Thankfully, there is the internet should you care to follow each of these various skirmishes down their respective rabbit holes. The commonalities among them (aside from Trump and Pence) have to do with Eminem feeling slighted or insulted. Some of them are definitely personal. Tyler, the Creator, for example, cites Eminem as a major influence and came out in support of *Relapse* even when Eminem didn't. His group, Odd Future, was chosen to open for Eminem during his two historic shows at Wembley, but he was very publicly vocal about his dislike of both *Shady XV* and *Revival*. "I know with a lot of this shit I could come across being very petty, but at a certain point in time, everyone has their breaking point," Eminem said. "When Tyler tweeted that 'Walk on Water' was fucking horrible, I was like, all right, I need to say something now. This is fucking stupid . . . Every time I saw this kid he was always so cool to me. I loved his energy; he was a funny dude, super charismatic and shit, but at what point do I have to say something to defend myself?"[19] That said, Em did admit that calling Tyler, who has identified as both gay and bisexual, a "faggot" on the song "Fall" was a step too far. "The word I called him on that song was one of the things where I felt like it might be too far. In my quest to hurt him I realize that I was hurting a lot of other people by saying it. At the time I was so mad that it was just, whatever. In the kinds of all the things required to pull this album together, it got lost. And in the end we spun the word back but people can hear what I'm saying anyways."[20]

19. "Eminem x Sway—The Kamikaze Interview (Part 2)."
20. "Eminem x Sway—The Kamikaze Interview (Part 2)."

The other personal diss worth mentioning involved Ohio rapper/actor Machine Gun Kelly (born Colson Baker), an Eminem stan who made the mistake of hollering at Hailie. In 2012, when Hailie was just sixteen, MGK tweeted: "Ok, so I just saw a picture of Eminem's daughter . . . and I have to say, she is hot as fuck, in the most respectful way possible cuz Em is king." Over the next few years, MGK threw a few subliminal barbs at Eminem, insinuating during an interview on influential hip-hop radio station Hot 97 that his sophomore album *General Admission* wasn't getting covered because he had insulted Em. He then released a song with Missouri rapper Tech N9ne (born Aaron Yates) called "No Reason," where he dissed Eminem for calling himself a rap god. And that was the last straw.

"The thing he was saying about my daughter I didn't know about until a year and a half later. It didn't even hit my radar," Eminem said. "One day you go down a wormhole on You-Tube I see 'MGK talks about Eminem's daughter.' Clicked on it, then I see he started doing a press run, basically about Hailie. That's not why I dissed him. The reason why I dissed him is a lot more petty than that. He said he was the greatest rapper alive since his favorite rapper banned him from Shade 45, like I'm trying to hinder his career or something. Do you know how many rappers are actually better than you? You're not even in the fucking conversation. I don't care if you blow or if you don't blow. It doesn't matter to me. But when he gets on Tech N9ne's album and he's sending shots, now I gotta answer this motherfucker. And every time I do that, as 'irrelevant' as people say I am in hop-hop, I make them bigger by getting into this thing. I want to destroy them, but I'm just going to make them bigger."[21]

Proving Eminem's point completely, just after *Kamikaze* dropped, MGK posted a tweet of himself listening to himself being insulted on "Not Alike," while shirtless, cheering, and spraying a bottle of champagne. He responded just a few days later with "Rap Devil," which he claimed to have recorded in a few hours. Considering his back catalog and that "Rap Devil" is his best work to date, it would seem that the champagne was to celebrate that the likely already-recorded-in-hopes-Em-would-diss-him track wasn't a waste of time and money. The fact that MGK had uploaded "Rap Devil" to his SoundCloud account six months before its release under a "private" setting supports this theory.

Eminem put an end to things with "Kill Shot," a blistering takedown named for a film of the same name shot in Detroit in which the protagonist, Carmen Colson, is targeted by an experienced, psychopathic hitman, which more or less sums up the song. With lines like "But I'm forty-five and I'm still outselling you / By twenty-nine I had three albums that had blew," and "I'd rather be eighty-year-old me than twenty-year-old you," he left his opponent with no choice but to call it quits. MGK did milk his moment for all it was worth, though, by wearing a "Killshot" shirt on stage and disparaging Em any chance he got. Once again, on Hot 97, he claimed to have another diss track at the ready but for the time being was shelving it.

---

21. "Eminem x Sway—The Kamikaze Interview (Part 2)."

"It's water under the bridge now, but I was one of the people who told him, 'Sit on your throne and be royalty,'" Royce da 5'9" says. "That's all he's got to do, man. It is not necessary for him to give all of this light out to all of these people. Their agenda is very, very different from his. But you know how he is, man. Over the years, throughout his career, he gets inspired by people throwing fuel in his fire. You throw fuel in that fire, you get the monster going. The monster is always going to be there, no matter what, because he's never going to be the guy that holds himself to some high regard, sitting on a pedestal pretending he doesn't hear what people are saying. He's never, ever, going to be that guy. We asked him to leave it alone, but I understood one hundred percent why he went out and made the album. I don't know what it feels like to be him, to be an artist on that level. Nobody does; there's a handful of artists alive who know what it's like to be in his shoes. At the end of the day he's going to do what he's going to do, and I'm going to support him, whatever it is."

For all its poison darts, *Kamikaze* does have a sincere and tender moment in "Stepping Stone." On the self-produced track, Eminem wistfully recounts his history with the members of his group D12. He regrets not being able to do more for their careers and faces the reality that Proof was the glue holding them together. He declares his undying love and friendship for his fellow members before pronouncing the group disbanded.

> But the longer we spend livin' this lie that we live,
> The less is left for closure, so let's let this go
> It's not goodbye to our friendship, but D12 is over

There are other places on the album where Eminem does more than just take shots at the world, but they are few. He made a point to name-drop the rappers he deems worthy of carrying the crown of hip-hop. The list is short: Joyner Lucas, Kendrick Lamar, J. Cole, Big Sean, and, it goes without saying, Eminem's nearest and dearest, Mr. Porter and Royce da 5'9". He also mentions LA rapper Hopsin (born Marcus Hopson) and Maryland rapper Logic (born Robert Bryson Hall II) as acts that he has inspired to the benefit of the culture.

Eminem's gripes with mumble rap on *Kamikaze* are completely valid and well articulated. He repeatedly demonstrates how easy it is to copy the musical style and co-opt the song structure and delivery of successful trap artists, not to mention how little value fans of the genre place on lyrics. It wasn't his focus, but it would have been nice if Eminem had included some up-and-coming talent that he does value in the next generation of hip-hop rather than just dole out compliments to established artists. The side effects of the viral tidal waves generated by his diss tracks could have been used to further up-and-comers deserving of the attention. "If Em must send shots, he should at least invite some new-school cats to be his young gunners," wrote Donna-Claire Chesman on DJBooth.net. "Aside from upping Eminem's philosophical consistency, the move would have scaled back the album's grouchy air. Displeasure does not need to invite more displeasure."[22] Chesman points to several new Shady

---

22. Donna-Claire Chesman, "'Saving Hip-Hop': Where Eminem Went Wrong," *DJ-Booth*, September 10, 2018, https://djbooth.net/features/2018-09-10-eminem-saving-hip-hop.

artists—Westside Gunn (born Alvin Worthy) and his brother Conway (born Demond Price) as well as Compton's Boogie (born Anthony Dixon)—who were fit for the task. There is, of course, always the next album.

"Current hip-hop is cool," Royce says. "We got some heavy lyricists out there and guys holding the flag. I love J. Cole, I love Kendrick, even younger guys like YBN Cordae and Nick Grant, their minds are in the right place to take the torch and make sure that the culture stays in the right form, the right place, and in the right shape. Due to technology we're looking through a different lens now that forces us to see everything. The good part is that we don't have to look at it. We can look at what we like and that's it. That's a good thing because there's a lot of bullshit out there, which there has always been but wasn't as easy to find. Now there's bullshit all over the place; you barely have to look."

Negative as it was, people do love when artists get mad. *Kamikaze* debuted at number one on the *Billboard* 200 with 434,000 album equivalent units (consisting of 252,000 traditional album sales and 225 million streams), giving Eminem his career-high number of streams in a week. It became his ninth consecutive number one in the United States. All eleven songs placed in the *Billboard* Hot 100 with "Lucky You" and "The Ringer" debuting in the top ten simultaneously, making Eminem the fifth artist in history to do so. By October 2018, it was the best-selling hip-hop album of the year. As of January 2019, it was the only album to sell more than five hundred thousand copies in pure sales and was the ninth-best-selling album globally in 2018. Eminem might have overextended himself on *Revival*, trying too hard to deliver what he thought was expected. It didn't work, because you can't please all the people all the time. But he knew what to do with his disappointment. He played to his strengths, letting his rage spill over the page, turning his frown into a joyously irresponsible upturned middle finger.

Conclusion

Greatest in the World

Eminem is an artist and a person characterized by dichotomy: a loving father who fantasizes about killing his daughter's mother, a victim of abuse who verbally abuses his own mother, a profanity-spewing MC who doesn't allow cursing in his home, a quiet family man who makes his living courting controversy, a white rapper in a black medium who knows his place but relishes what he can get away with saying because he's white. Watching him walk that tightrope is the thrill of being an Eminem fan.

He has a showman's flair for the dramatic and a poet's gift for storytelling. He is capable of creating films in rhymed verse, of taking the listener on a journey via their headphones. Through force of will and desperate necessity, he arose from a creatively free underground to the heights of a mainstream industry overnight, with little time to learn the rules. If he had, he probably wouldn't have followed them anyway. He is a true outsider, a citizen of a proud city unlike any other in

America; in music, art, and design, Detroit has always moved to the beat of its own drummer, and Eminem is no different.

He has evolved, yet remained the same: forever rebellious, rambunctious, bold, and empowered. He changed the music that gave him a reason to live, first as the one-step-ahead-of-you battle-rap wiseass who charmed his way into culture by photobombing the popular kids, then as a master raconteur, equally capable of pathos and psychosis. Along the way, his obsession with his art transformed the medium itself. Eminem has forever altered the way the world sees rap because he was a critical force in making the language a global phenomenon. Today, with every accolade under the sun under his belt, he continues to push rap to its very limits because that's all he's ever done it for. "I would say that he is the most obsessive artist, maybe, that I have met in any genre. He is very, very dedicated to his craft. To the point where it seems like there is nothing else in his life. It truly is a 24-7 thing for him," Rick Rubin said. "He really is an MC first. And, where so many artists get wrapped up in celebrity, he doesn't. He leads a very simple life at home in Detroit and tours very little. Basically he is a full-time, full-on hip-hop head. I think it's amazing. It's amazing that he's unfazed by all the amazing things that have happened to him. Less fazed than anyone."[1]

Marshall Mathers's love for the game causes him to pour over rhyme schemes for the sake of it longer than most

1. Rob Kenner, "Interview: Rick Rubin Talks About the Making of 'The Marshall Mathers LP2,'" *Complex*, November 8, 2013, https://www.complex.com/music /2013/11/rick-rubin-eminem-marshall-mathers-2-interview.

rappers spend on an entire album. His passion has driven him to move the foundation of lyricism forward just to find new challenges. No one else in hip-hop possesses his ability to slip between rhythmic flows, expelling intricate, interwoven rhyme patterns packed with assonance, homophones, subliminal (and not so) references, and every degree of entendre known to man. His zealous pursuit of that crystalline line where language reveals its essence is tangible. You can hear it driving him on like Galahad in search of the Holy Grail, that perfect verse to unlock the prism of infinite linguistic knowledge. Eminem in his second act has sometimes spit verses that are more arduous than enjoyable, seemingly more fun for him to say than they are for fans to hear. But even in those moments, while haters claim he's saying things just to be saying them, there's a technical proficiency to his ability that is awe inspiring. Listening to him at those moments is like watching a prodigy guitar player run scales: even when the musician is just warming up, witnessing such talent in action is still incredible. When Em's technical abilities are fused to a moving story line, like the best pieces of his life he's pulled from his soul and made into records, the result is breathtaking.

"He has made changes in how he makes music," Royce says. "He records during the day now. I don't know if that's an absolute thing, but that's how he's done it since he got off the pills. I do know that he's very meticulous now, and I don't remember him being that meticulous when we were recording back in the day. His thought process is always tight and perfect, and I don't remember him being like that when we were younger. Everything is well thought out, sometimes to his detriment. For me, sometimes everything can be a little too perfect. People love it when he appears human, because, let's face it, lyrically he's God level. When people hear a flaw here and there, it actually looks good on him. I always tell him, 'You don't have to be so perfect all the time.'"

An MC must be a master of words, because manipulating language is the spirit of rap. The MC's lyrical genius was what separated hip-hop from R&B and rock and roll. The sheer joy of words, the power of communication in a different style to an undeniable beat, was what launched a revolution. Anger, frustration, humor, love, loss, pride, prejudice—all of it has been sent forth in bars for the past forty-plus years. Things have changed drastically, and contemporary hip-hop favors mood over message, medium over meaning, but like everything else, that has its place. "Hip-hop has always been like that, if you really think about it." Eminem says. "Back when I was growing up, there was LL and Run-DMC, and then there was Big Daddy Kane, KRS One, you know, the few and far between what actually made the game what it was. If there weren't other rappers who were kind of wack, then you wouldn't appreciate the good ones so much. If there was no variety of what was going on, then you wouldn't actually know when you heard somebody that was really good. Hip-hop is always ever-changing, and you know, you're always going to have the people who are separate from the pack. We need that."

"Em isn't the kind of artist that puts out an album every year. Sure, he's done that, but he's a particular artist," Mr. Porter says.

"He is always recording and trying new things, so any album can change direction real quick. It's a tricky thing sometimes. After *Kamikaze* he's seen that he can put out music faster with no warning, no nothing. I think the machine around him has to adapt so that he can release things when he's ready. And he should be doing that to stay relevant, because these younger kids, their loyalty is shorter than a firecracker wick."

For his part, as his friend of over three decades, Mr. Porter would like to see Em collaborate with Royce on a full-length Bad Meets Evil project as well as let the public see his many other sides. "I know Em has ideas for another Bad Meets Evil," he says. "He's no one-trick pony, and I have some ideas for him to try for his next album. I'm always the one pushing the left-field ideas to him, and I'll keep doing it because just seeing where those suggestions take him is exciting to me. I'd love to see him spread his wings. I'd love to see him act again. He's such an incredible person. People are so in awe of his talent as a rapper, but the dude is fucking talented! He's super funny, and he has a lot of other interests people don't even know about that I'd love to see him bring into the light. There are things that will come out later, I think, that will make people realize that he's not just the Superman of rap. From his jokes to his impressions, he's a super intelligent dude. Even his political views, they're so cut and dried that he'd be the perfect guy to be a commentator. For me, I think he should produce some shows and explore those interests, then do another album."

The love of lyricism will never die, and too many rappers bragging about swag will surely turn the tide back to headier content—which they should, because with America and the world in the state they're in, there is much to talk about. Regardless, Eminem will be there, as he always has been, representing the way of life that made his worth living. "Hip-hop was the most important thing to empower me as a kid. It made me feel tough when I wasn't," he said. "When I was a scrawny kid growing up on 8 Mile, walking up the fucking block, put headphones on and it made me feel powerful. Hip-hop was like my dad. It was the only thing that made me feel empowered, that made me feel good about myself, and when I realized I could write rhymes and figured out I could do it? That's where the feeling comes from for me. The excitement is being able to come up with the shit. It gave me the confidence to throw my first punch."[2]

As for the future, one thing is certain. With his self-destructive days behind him and eleven years of sobriety under his belt, Eminem has a lot to live for. "Marshall has a huge heart," Mr. Porter says. "I had an incredible father and mother. I probably got some whupping I didn't deserve, but I have an incredible family. But Marshall taught me what it is to be a father, and he didn't even have one. Aside from my own father and my uncle, Marshall and Royce are my role models. My biggest goal in life is to be a father because of them, because of seeing how they each came out of fucked-up situations to become the greatest fathers I've ever met."

Eminem is lucky to have emerged from such darkness, having found a way to live with his dysfunction and demons, with

---

2. "Eminem x Sway—The Kamikaze Interview (Part 2)."

his family, careers, and passion intact. "I'm always doing something to do with work," he says. "Aside from spending time with my kids, everything I do is about work." It's an unlikely outcome, but hip-hop's loosest cannon has settled into a nine-to-five, logging his time at the office, crafting rhymes to tweak our ears and alight our minds. And by all indications, one listen to the single "Homicide," by Logic, featuring Eminem, from Logic's album *Confessions of a Dangerous Mind* (2019) is proof that the bonfire that fueled *Kamikaze* isn't close to being put out. Logic, a twenty-nine-year-old Maryland native who cites Em as a major influence, has been signed to Def Jam since 2014, and since his debut, *Under Pressure* (2014), has been lauded for taking his cues from the golden age of hip-hop lyricism. He is the perfect ally for Em. On this relentless track, the pair continue the trend of drawing a line in the sand between lyrical content and rap skill and hip-hop that captures a mood and reflects an aspirational lifestyle. This division in hip-hop has become Em's latest opponent, and one he hasn't yet let off the hook. It will be interesting to see how long he finds inspiration there. Whenever that might be, one thing is certain: the world will be ready, waiting, and listening.

"There will always be a silver lining with Em," Royce says. "He's the type of guy who is gonna figure out what he needs to do. He had a disconnect with the fans, and now he's just figuring out exactly what kind of music he needs to be making at this juncture in his life. He has touched upon so many styles and done them all so well. He's touched so many different types of people in different ways all around the world. He's changed the world three times over, won every award you can think of. Where do you go from there?" Royce takes a moment to chuckle at the magnitude of it all. "It's a tough situation to be in, but he signed up for it. And it's nothing to get mad about—these are good problems! Nobody in this camp is hanging they head; we are fucking happy over here! We gonna figure it out and that's it. The best part is that I don't even know what he's going to do next. *Kamikaze* came out of nowhere. He still has that kind of fire in him where it gets so hot you don't know what his next move might be. When you can't predict it and you the dude standing right next to him? Yo, that means it's still fun and it's still hip-hop."

Epilogue

No one has worked more closely with Marshall Mathers than Paul Rosenberg, a Detroit native who was studying to be a music lawyer when he bought a cassette copy of Infinite *from Mathers for six dollars back in 1997. The two have been friends ever since and collaborators since the* Slim Shady EP, *from the many skits featuring Paul on Em's albums over the years to their mutual business ventures: Shady Records and Shade 45. No one has helped implement Mathers's creative vision more than Paul, and no one can better speak to Em's artistic and personal evolution over the past fifteen years. Here, in an interview exclusive to this book, Rosenberg reflects on how much his friend has changed and how he's very much stayed the same.*

There was never a conscious decision made to stop doing songs that dealt with the inner workings of his past and family life, but that change did occur. Marshall never said to me, "Hey, man, I'm not doing songs about this or that anymore," but at some point, for the most part, he was moving on in his life from those particular problems and those relationships. Even with his mother, the references changed; they became playful—like "my mom took Valium and lots of drugs" in the song "My Mom," on *Relapse*, which was a more playful record referencing his mother. I do know that at a certain point, he felt that talking about his daughters had exposed them in a way that he didn't intend to, so he decided to move away from that. He had put a lot of his personal life out there and realized that enough was enough. What he decides to expose to the public with regard to his personal relationships with his family is his decision. He felt that he'd exposed enough of it through his music and had no obligation to do anything any further. He also realized that he didn't have to answer anyone's questions about his personal life or family ever again if he didn't want to, because the world is not entitled to that information. He had already given what he decided was the appropriate amount to give, and that was that.

Of course, what he gave wasn't enough, because the more you give, the more the public wants. I would imagine there are some fans whose favorite thing about him is hearing about his family and his personal life. Hopefully that's not all they care about, but if it is, I guess they can go listen to only those records.

Marshall is a private person, and he's certainly shied away from the things that a lot of other celebrities do on a regular basis. He's not someone who is tremendously social in a traditional sense. He's not the kind of person who wants to host dinner parties or go out to see and be seen. It's just not who he is, and I think he would be the same whether he was famous or not. The level of attention that he receives putting himself in certain scenarios makes those situations different for him than they would be for a regular person. Some celebrities really enjoy that public admiration and adoration. It's maybe what feeds them or makes them feel good. For Marshall it just makes him feel uncomfortable—like he's being observed and watched in a way that isn't entertaining to him.

The way Marshall creates has changed over the years, but it's been very gradual. He's always been a hard worker, and that's never really changed. But his hard work doesn't just come from the fact that he's got an incredible work ethic; it's more the fact that when he's passionate about something, that is what he enjoys doing more than anything else. Yes, making music is his work, but it's also his passion and his hobby. It's what makes him tick. That hasn't changed; the real change has just been his schedule. He used to go into the studio in the afternoon and stay there real late, like younger artists do, particularly in hip-hop. These days he's on more of a nine-to-five. I don't mean specifically 9:00 a.m. to 5:00 p.m., just that he goes to the studio in the morning and leaves in the early evening. But although he treats it like it's his job, we should all be so lucky to have our job be the kind of thing that we care most about and that we're most passionate about. In that sense he's in a really enviable place.

One thing that hasn't changed is that Marshall is most inspired when he's got something that serves to antagonize him and that he can bounce off creatively. It helps guide his process. It could be a person, a situation, or a group of people, but it's got to be something that serves as an antagonizer, because he's much better as a protagonist when there's an antagonist.

He comes from a place in hip-hop where you worked very hard on your craft, and if you didn't write your own lyrics, then people didn't take you seriously. To him, if somebody is saying lyrics they didn't write, he does not understand how an audience can feel those words, knowing that the person may not have written the lyrics themselves. He doesn't want to be seen as somebody who is against adapting with the times or the modernization of an art form, because there's plenty of new stuff that he thinks is great. But when he encounters something that is a combination of an artist who maybe didn't write the song and a song that is an example of one of those haphazard, simple production efforts—of which there are a lot going around today—those two qualities, especially when they're combined, really don't work for him. They make him step back and say, "Man, I really don't know how people are getting away with this." If an artist did that in the scene where Marshall came from, they wouldn't be taken seriously for half a second. That is what is driving him when he criticizes newer stuff. It's not that he doesn't understand what this new wave of people are doing creatively; it's that he takes what he does very seriously and works hard on his music. He simply can't understand how anybody can care about or feel records that are made through any lesser of a process.

Kamikaze was his statement on that—and his statement on something else. He said publicly that he didn't understand at what point people decided that it was okay for them to say whatever they wanted to say about him, thinking that he wasn't going to do shit about it. He sat back and acted like he was a more mature artist and tried to chill out a little bit for a while, but he's still who he is and who he always was. If people keep poking him and poking him, he's going to come at them. And he did. *Kamikaze* was designed, no pun intended, to drop out of the sky. It was designed with that purpose, right down to the title; everything was related to how it was delivered. That doesn't mean every record he does from here on out is going to be delivered that way. That worked for that time; maybe we'll do that again one day, and maybe we won't. But if we do a more traditional-style album rollout, the window between when the announcement about the project is made and when it comes out is going to be much shorter. It just has to be these days. The window leading up to promoting albums has gotten much shorter just because of the way that music is distributed and consumed and how much of a short-attention economy we're in.

Marshall has evolved so much, but every time I feel that he's moved on from all the different personalities that embodied his earlier music, right when I think they're all just one now, he does something and pulls out Slim Shady again. He's kinda unpredictable. He's very capable of playing me a record and having that same evil grin on his face, and I'm like, "Okay, I know what's about to happen." I can't say too much about what's coming next other than there's not any plan for a drastic departure from who Marshall is as a person or artist. He's pretty set in his ways and who he is at this point. He's going to continue to create in the manner that he is comfortable creating. I wouldn't necessarily rule anything out, but we're not in the process of making a feature film or a similar project. We've always got our eyes open, and Marshall could return to the big screen one day. We'll see.

Look, Marshall's version of happiness is something that most people wouldn't think of as happiness at all, but I do think that today he is very content. He's content in where his life is and where he's at artistically. That's how I would describe it. I wouldn't describe him as happy in the traditional sense. I don't know if he's capable of being happy in the traditional sense—or if he wants to be.

Acknowledgments

I would like to thank my agent, Lisa Gallagher; my manager, Shawn Dailey; my editors, Ben Schafer and Oliver Holden-Rea; and everyone at Bonnier and Da Capo. Thanks also to all of the copyeditors, designers, and every single member of the production staff. It takes a village to make a book. Most of all, a huge thanks to Dennis Dennehy, Paul Rosenberg, and Marshall Mathers for allowing me the freedom and granting me the access necessary to write this book.

Index

A$AP Yams, 126–127n9

Aaron, Charles, 151

"Above the Law (ft. Claret Jai)" (Bad Meets Evil), 163

accents, 58–59, 60, 110, 115, 116, 171

accountability, 95–96

Aceyalone, 107

acid rap, 83

advertising industry, 99, 109–110. *See also* marketing

AdWeek, 211

AEG Presents, 211

Aesop Rock, 104

African Americans: Black Lives Matter movement, 216n14; fraternities, 73; hip-hop culture and, 70, 75–77, 91–92 (*see also* cultural appropriation); hip-hop genre and, 2–3, 75–77, 91–92, 113–114; police violence and, 206–207, 214–224; slavery and, 77, 90, 91. *See also* race

African music, 247–248

Aftermath, 156–157

Aguilera, Christina, 77n2

"Airplanes" (B.o.B), 140

"Airplanes, Part II" (Eminem), 197

Akon, 38, 123

albums, production cycle, 204, 233–234, 267–268, 277. *See also specific albums*

Alchemist, 14

alcohol, 35, 37, 100, 164–165

Aldean, Jason, 90

Alex Da Kid (Alexander Grant), 139–140, 145

Alexander, Don, 216n14

aliases. *See* alter egos

All Things Considered, 123

alter egos: Insane Clown Posse, 81; Mac Miller, 101–102; narrative point of view and, 18; in rap genre, 81; Slim Shady (*see* Slim Shady persona); Slim Shady/Marshall Mathers/Eminem persona, 18, 40, 59–60, 63–66, 141–143

alternative hip-hop genre, 103–104, 256

alternative rock genre, 74–75

Ambien, 36, 37, 42, 46

American Idiot (Green Day), 176n7

Anderson, Sean Michael Leonard (Big Sean), 206

Anger Management Tour, 3, 13, 14–17, 20, 38

"Animal" (Harry Shotta), 187n15

Antares Auto-Tune, 119–122, 127

anti-Semitism, 205–206

anti-Trump themes, 204–205, 207–208, 212–213, 219–221, 226, 256

"Arose" (Eminem), 229

Asleep in the Bread Aisle (Asher Roth), 96

"Ass Like That" (Eminem): lyrics and delivery, 59

"Assassins" (Geto Boys), 81

"Asshole" (Eminem), 182

Atha, Michael Wayne (Yelawolf), 92, 209

Atlantic Records, 87, 110

Atmosphere, 103

authenticity: Eminem and, 3, 84, 85, 86, 89; frat rap, 111; hip-hop culture and, 103; hip-hop genre and, 89; Proof and, 34; white rap and, 70, 75, 86, 89

autobiographical themes, 172–173, 178–181, 188

Auto-Tune, 91, 97, 111, 118–130, 206

award shows, viewership, xv–xvi. *See also specific awards*

awards and nominations: Eminem generally, 3, 237n2; *The Eminem Show* (Eminem), 151–152; "Lose Yourself" (Eminem), 1–2; "Love the Way You Lie" (Eminem), 152; *The Marshall Mathers LP* (Eminem), 151–152; "My Name Is" (Eminem), 3; "Not Afraid" (Eminem), 144n1, 152; *Recovery* (Eminem), 144n1; *Relapse* (Eminem), 146; *The Slim*

Shady LP (Eminem), 3. *See also* commercial success
AZ, 84
Azalea, Iggy, 105–107, 112, 256

B.G., 130
B.o.B., 90, 92, 140
"Back Down" (50 Cent), 158
"Bad and Boujee" (Migos), 250
Bad Boy Records, 94, 104
"Bad Guy" (Eminem), 173–176
Bad Meets Evil, 152–153, 157, 159–166, 268
"Bad Meets Evil" (Eminem), 153, 156
Bailey, D'Angelo, 9–10
Baker, Colson (Machine Gun Kelly), 94, 250, 256, 258–259
Banks, Azealia, 106
Banks, Lloyd, 14, 30, 44
Bar Exam (Royce da 5'9"), 159
Bar Exam 2, The (Royce da 5'9"), 159
Bass Brothers, 57
Bassett, Jordan, 254, 255
battle raps, xvii, xviii, 23, 171, 172, 199
Beastie Boys, xii, 70–72, 86, 177, 178, 184, 221
Beatles, 105, 189
beats: alternative rap, 103; "Arose" (Eminem), 229; "Ass Like That" (Eminem), 59; "Believe" (Eminem), 223–224; DJ Kool Herc and, 150n7; Dr. Dre and, 57–58, 117, 157; *Eminem Presents: The Re-Up*, 39; gangsta rap, 152; "The Greatest" (Eminem), 250; hick-hop, 90; Just Blaze and, 133; "Kings Never Die" (Eminem), 204; lo-fi, 224, 225; lyrics and, 53, 58, 61, 156, 188, 204, 206, 223–224, 226; Mr. Porter and, 218; "Offended" (Eminem), 255; "Phenomenal" (Eminem), 203; "Rap God" (Eminem), 188; *Recovery* (Eminem), 146–147; *Revival* (Eminem), 245; "The Ringer" (Eminem), 255; Royce da 5'9" and, 152; selection, 146–147, 255; trap-style rap, 223–224, 249–251; "25 to Life" (Eminem), 137; triplet flow and, 249–251; "Untouchable" (Eminem), 216–217
"Beautiful" (Eminem), 57, 61, 64–65
"Beef Is Ova" (Proof), 158
Beerbongs and Bentleys (Post Malone), 111
"Believe" (Cher), 121–122
"Believe" (Eminem), 223
Bender, Keith, Jr., 27–30
benzodiazepines, 42, 43
Berry, Chuck, 76n1
"Berzerk" (Eminem), 184, 186
"Best Friend" (Yelawolf), 92

BET: Eminem's *106 and Park* (2005) performance, 44–45; Hip Hop Awards, xv–xxiv, 106, 207–208, 234, 256; hip-hop culture and, 75; "Just Lose It" video, 12; YouTube channel, 208
Bhad Bhabie, 110
Big Boy, 136
Big Daddy Kane, 226
Big Sean, 206, 261
Biggie Smalls, 226, 252n12
Billboard charts, xvii, 72, 111–112, 200–201, 233n1, 252
Billboard Hot 100, 74, 91, 105, 110, 122, 125, 132, 139, 161, 187
Billboard Streaming Songs chart, 252
Billboard 200, 87, 88, 101,109, 131, 200–201, 262
Birdbox, 94
Birdman, 184
Bizarre, 157
Black Lives Matter movement, 216n14
Bland, Sandra, 207
Blige, Mary J., 52n15
"Bling Bling" (Hot Boys), 130
Blondie, 70
Blue Slide Park (Mac Miller), 101
Blueprint, The (Jay-Z), 153, 155
blues genre, 75–76
boastful lyrics, 135–136, 154–155, 161, 187–188, 197–198
Boi-1da, 145
Bon Iver, 251
Bone Thugs-n-Harmony, 91, 248
Boogie, xix, 262
Boogie Nights, 221–222
Book of Ryan (Royce da 5'9"), 161n17, 165–166
Boomin' Words from Hell (Esham), 82–83
Born in the U.S.A. (Bruce Springsteen), 214
"Born to Roll (Jeep Ass Niguh Remix)" (Masta Ace), 216
"Both of Us" (Taylor Swift), 90
Bowie, David, 72
"Brain Damage" (Eminem), 9–10, 182
"Brainless" (Eminem), 181–182
Bregoli, Danielle, 109–110
"Bring the Noise" (Public Enemy), 248
Brown, Chris, 140, 140n20
Brown, Foxy, 155, 155n13
Bryson Hall II, Robert (Logic), 261
Bubba Sparxxx, 87–89
Budden, Joe, 159, 238n3, 256
Bump Show, The, 186
Bush, George W., 12, 13
Busta Rhymes, 97, 185, 185n13

Ca$his, 38, 44

Cactus Album, The (3rd Bass), 71

Calloway, Sway, 180

"Calm Down" (Busta Rhymes), 185n13

"Campaign Speech" (Eminem), 204–205, 206–207

Campbell, Clive (DJ Kool Herc), 150, 150n7

Cannon, Nick, 136n17

Carey, Mariah, 136n17

Caramanica, Jon, 253

Cardi B, xvi

Carey, Mariah, 136n17

Carmen: A Hip Hopera, 176n7

Cash Money Records, 87, 130

Castile, Philando, 207

"Castle" (Eminem), 228–229, 230

"Caterpillar" (Royce da 5'9"), 165–166

CCC Club, 26–30

Chamillionaire, 87

Chance the Rapper, 188

Charlamagne tha God, 256

Charm, The (Bubba Sparxxx), 88

Cheech and Chong, 216, 217

Cher, 121–122

"Cher Effect, The," 122

Chesman, Donna-Claire, 261–262

Chicago Tribune, 189

Chief Keef, 255

Childish Gambino, 126

Childrey, Akino, 156, 156n14

"Chloraseptic" (Eminem), 224–225, 224n18

"Chloraseptic Remix (featuring 2 Chainz and Phresher)" (Eminem), 240–241

Christgau, Robert, 39, 192

Chuck D, 248

civil rights movement, 91, 217

"Cleanin' Out My Closet" (Eminem), 151, 171, 178

Cobain, Kurt, 93

cocaine, 100, 133n13

codeine, 126–127n9

"Cold Wind Blows" (Eminem), 117, 128, 141

Coldplay, 149

Cole, J., 188, 252, 252n12, 261, 262

comedy rap, 98–99

commercial success: Beastie Boys, 71; *Blue Slide Park* (Mac Miller), 101; Cher, 122; controversy and, 13; country rap/hick-hop, 90–93, 91n7; cultural appropriation and, 72–73, 93; *Curtain Call: The Hits* (Eminem), 21; *Dark Days, Bright Nights* (Bubba Sparxxx), 88; *8 Mile*, 17–18; *808s & Heartbreak* (Kanye West), 126; Eminem generally, xxii, 85–86, 188, 237; *The Eminem Show* (Eminem), 144n1; *Encore*

(Eminem), 13, 15; frat rap, 101; *Get Ya Mind Correct* (Paul Wall and Chamillionaire), 87n5; *Hell: The Sequel* (Bad Meets Evil), 161; hip-hop genre, 113–114; Home and Home Tour, 149; Insane Clown Posse, 77; *Kamikaze* (Eminem), 262; "Lighters" (Bad Meets Evil), 163; "Love the Way You Lie" (Eminem), 19, 139–140, 141, 144; "Lucky You (featuring Joyner Lucas)" (Eminem), 252–253, 262; *Marshall Mathers LP, The* (Eminem), 17; *Marshall Mathers LP2, The* (Eminem), 187, 189; "The Monster" (Eminem), 170–171; Monster Tour, 197; mumble rap, 224–225; "No Love" (Eminem), 131–133; "Not Afraid" (Eminem), 19, 144; *People's Champ, The* (Paul Wall), 87; pop rap, 105, 107–109, 110, 111–112; race and, xii–xiii, 2–3, 70, 71, 72–73, 74, 85–86, 87, 87n5, 88, 101; rap genre and, 91–92; "Rap God" (Eminem), 187; *Rebirth* (Lil Wayne), 131; *Recovery* (Eminem), 144; *Relapse* (Eminem), xxii, 65–66, 67–68; *Revival* (Eminem), xxii, 211–212, 240; "The Ringer" (Eminem), 262; *Shady XV* (Eminem), 200–201; *The Slim Shady LP* (Eminem), 17; social media and, 96; T-Pain, 123–124; Vanilla Ice, 72–73; white privilege and, xix–xx, 93, 99, 100, 108–109, 110, 113–114, 217; white rap, 2–3, 70, 71, 72–73, 74, 85–86, 87, 87n5, 88, 101; Yelawolf, 92

concerts. *See* performances; tours

Confessions of a Dangerous Mind (Logic), 270

Consequence of Sound, 150

Conway, xvii, xix, 262

Conway, Kellyanne, 226

Cook, David, 118

"Cooky Puss" (Beastie Boys), 71

Cool G Rap, 226

Cooper, Anderson, 172n3

Copycat Beauty, 110

Cosby, Bill, 226

Coulter, Ann, 206–207

country genre, 90, 92, 122

Country Music Television Music Awards, 90

country rap genre, 90–93, 199

"Cowboy" (Kid Rock), 88

Cowell, Simon, 225

Cranberries, 227, 227n21

creative process: beats and lyrics, integration, 53, 58, 61, 156, 188, 204, 206, 223–224, 226; beats selection, 146–147, 255; "Framed" (Eminem), 226; freestyle lyrics vs. writing, 41, 58–59; ghostwriting and, 106, 156, 251, 276; inspiration and, 269; *Marshall Mathers*

LP2, The (Eminem), 170; Paul Rosenberg on, 275; post-*Revival*, 244–245; "Rap God" (Eminem), 188; *Relapse* (Eminem), 50–55; *Revival* (Eminem), 240–241; rhyme scheme, 265–266; Royce da 5'9" on, 266–267; substance use and, 40–41, 43, 50–56, 60, 64–65, 135–136, 165; writing process, 41–42

credibility: Eminem and, 44n8, 72, 85–86, 89, 146; Paul Wall and, 87, 89; social media and, 95–96; white rap, generally, 44n8, 70, 72, 73, 86, 95–96

"Criminal" (Eminem), 54, 176–177

criticism/reviews: BET Awards (2017) performance, xix; Bubba Sparxxx, 88; *Curtain Call: The Hits*, 21; Eminem generally, xxi–xxiii, 235; Eminem as producer, 38–39; *Eminem Presents: The Re-Up*, 38–39; Eminem tour (2005), 15–16; Eminem's reaction to, 66–68, 246, 256, 257; *Encore* (Eminem), 15–17, 170, 189; *Hell: The Sequel* (Bad Meets Evil), 161; Home and Home Tour, 150–151; Iggy Azalea, 105–107; Joe Budden and, 238n3; from LGBT community, 172; *Kamikaze* (Eminem) and, 276–277; "Like Home" (Eminem), 219–220; Macklemore, 108–109; *The Marshall Mathers LP2* (Eminem), 172, 189–192; reaction videos, 239, 242–244; *Rebirth* (Lil Wayne), 131; *Recovery* (Eminem), 115–116, 170, 189; *Relapse* (Eminem), 64–68, 146, 170; *Revival* (Eminem), 219, 220–221, 231, 238n3, 240–244, 253, 254–255, 257, 262; *Shady XV* (Eminem), 201–202, 257; "Untouchable" (Eminem), 219

Crooked I, 159

"Crossroads" (Bone Thugs-n-Harmony), 91

Crowe, Cameron, 94

"Cruise" (Florida Georgia Line), 90–91, 91n7

cultural appropriation: commercial success and, 72–73, 93; hick-hop and, 90–93; Iggy Azalea and, 105–107, 256; shared cultural influence vs., 75–77; white rap and, 70, 72–73, 75–77

Curtain Call: The Hits (Eminem), 21, 251

Curtis, Jamie Lee, 206, 207

Cypher, xvii

cyphers, xvii–xviii, 234, 256

Cypress Hill, 74, 175n4

"D.N.A." (Kendrick Lamar), 248

D12: Anger Management Tour (2005), 14; Eminem and, xiii, 11, 16, 21–22, 38, 157; Home and Home Tour, 149; Proof and, 24, 31–32, 33, 147, 148, 260; Royce da 5'9"

and, 157–159, 158n15; "Stepping Stone" (Eminem) and, 260; tours, 158n15

D12 World (D12), 10

Danny Boy, 74

Dark Days, Bright Nights (Bubba Sparxxx), 88

Dark Side of the Moon (Pink Floyd), 63

Das EFX, 175n4

Davis, Jonathan, 76

De La Soul, 103, 185

"Death Day" (Royce da 5'9"), 158

Death Row, 73

Def Jam Records, 70–71, 851, 177, 270

Definitive Jux, 103

"Deja Vu" (Eminem), 64–65

Deliverance (Bubba Sparxxx), 88

delivery. *See* vocal delivery

Delusional Thomas, 102

Dennehy, Dennis, 211

depression, 42, 43, 62, 94, 101, 198n2

Derelicts of Dialect (3rd Bass), 71

Desiigner, 224

Detox (Dr. Dre), 52n15

Detroit: crime (1980s), 82–83; as Eminem's hometown, 2, 3–4, 21, 193–195, 265; hip-hop scene, 23, 25; horrorcore and, 63n20, 80–81

Detroit Federation of Musicians, 23

Detroit Free Press, 16

Devil's Night Mixtape, The (D12), 158n15

Diddy, 94, 104, 125, 159

Die Antwoord, 256

direct-to-consumer marketing, 93

"Dirt Road Anthem" (Jason Aldean), 90

Dirt, The, 94

diss tracks, 20, 75, 80, 130, 155–156, 157–159, 254, 256–260

Divine Feminine, The (Mac Miller), 102

Dixon, Anthony (Boogie), 262

DJ Akademiks, 256

DJ Jazzy Jeff and the Fresh Prince, 82

DJ Khaled, xvi

DJ Kool, 101

DJ Kool Herc (Clive Campbell), 150, 150n7

DJ Lethal, 74–75

DJ Muggs, 74

DJ OC, 25

DJ Premier, 159

DJBooth.net, 261–262

Dogg Food (Tha Dogg Pound), 101

domestic violence, 139–141

Donaldson, Lou, 175, 175n4

Doubt Me Now (Lil Wyte), 95

Dr. Dre: Alex Da Kid and, 140; beats library, 58, 157; copyright infringement lawsuit, 9; *Detox*,

Dr. Dre (*Cont.*)
52n15; Eminem and, 38, 52–58, 85–86, 235–236, 244–245; Home and Home Tour, 149; "I Need a Doctor" (Dr. Dre), 210; *Kamikaze* (Eminem) and, 245; LL Cool J and, ix; as producer, 13, 14, 57–58, 57n18, 67, 144–145, 156, 234; *Relapse* (Eminem) and, 57–58, 57n18, 67, 141; *Relapse 2* (Eminem) and, 67; *Revival* (Eminem) and, 244–245; Royce da 5'9" and, 156; "Untouchable" (Eminem) and, 215

Dr. Lecter (Action Bronson), 104
Dr. Phil, 109
Drake: BET Hip Hop Awards and, xvi; commercial success of, 144, 188, 233n1; Eminem and, 223, 224n18, 252; G-Eazy and, 111; Home and Home Tour, 149; Kanye West and, 126; Mike Stud and, 97
DreamWorks, 202, 203
"Drop the World" (Lil Wayne), 131
"Drug Ballad" (Eminem), xxii
drugs/drug use. *See* substance use
Dupri, Jermaine, 156, 176n7
Durst, Fred, 76

"Earache My Eye" (Cheech and Chong), 216
Earl Sweatshirt, 188, 256
East Coast rap, 74, 82, 107, 216, 248
"Echo" (Bad Meets Evil), 160
Ecstasy, 43, 133n13
Effigy Studios, 56–57, 131
8 Mile: Eminem and, xxiii, 10–11, 17–18, 36; LL Cool J on, xiii; Proof's role in, 24; soundtrack, 1–2, 115, 138
8 Mile Road, ix, 26
808s & Heartbreak (Kanye West), 125, 134
El-P, 103
Eminem (Marshall Mathers): alter egos (*see* alter egos; Slim Shady persona); authenticity of, 3, 84, 85, 86, 89; Auto-Tune and, 129; Bad Meets Evil and, 152–153, 157, 159–166, 268; BET 2017 Hip Hop Awards and, xv–xxiv; Busta Rhymes and, 185, 185n13; childhood/upbringing, xxi, 35, 183–184, 209, 237, 269; commercial success of (*see* commercial success); credibility and, 44n8, 72, 85–86, 89, 146; criticism of (*see* criticism/reviews); D12 and, xiii, 11, 16, 21–22, 38, 157; daughter(s) of, 20, 22, 94, 228–230, 234, 258–259, 274; David Duke and, 205–206; depression and, 42–43, 62; Detroit home of, 2, 3–4, 21, 193–195, 265; dichotomous nature of, 264; Dr. Dre and, 38, 52–58, 85–86, 235–236, 244–245; Elton John and, 49; Everlast and,

75; evolution of, xxi, 58–60, 66–67, 146, 273–278; fame and, 1–13, 17–18, 183, 235, 237–240, 274–275; family of, 178, 179–180, 230, 230n23, 270; 50 Cent and, xiii, 38; future directions, 277–278; honesty and, xiii, xx, 85, 115, 140–141, 180, 182, 198; insomnia and, 35–36; inspirations, ix, 62, 184, 232; Jay-Z and, 149–151, 153; Kanye West and, 129–130, 134, 135, 149; Kimberley Scott and, xxi, 9, 21–22, 140n20, 180–181, 181n11, 226–227, 234; legal issues, 9–10, 14–15, Lil Wayne and, 130–133; LL Cool J and, ix–xiv; "lost years," 60–61; lyrics of (*see* lyrics); Machine Gun Kelly and, 94; Paul Rosenberg (manager) and, 31, 209, 273–278; as perfectionist, 146–147, 231; philanthropy of, 62; polarizing nature of, xxii–xxiii, 2, 66, 143, 169, 235; politics and (*see* politics); private life of, 3, 61–62, 141–142, 195, 274–275; Proof and, 22–26, 31, 34; publicist of, 211; race and, xxii, 2–3, 85–86; racism and, 11–12, 18–19, 221; radio interviews, 166, 225; rap style (*see* lyrics; vocal delivery); retirement rumors, 15–17; Rick Rubin and, 178, 182, 184–185, 215, 221, 223, 229, 244, 265; Royce da 5'9" and, 158–166, 268, 270–271; Sirius station, 166, 180, 225; status and influence of, xxiii–xxiv, 237, 264–271; substance use and (*see* substance use); trauma history and, xxi, 35, 64, 171, 172–173, 181, 193, 237; Trump and, xvii–xviii, 204–205, 207–208, 212–213, 219–221, 226, 256; Tyler, the Creator and, 257; underground rap scene and, 63, 236–237, 238, 264
Eminem, as producer: "Believe" (Eminem), 223; controversy and, 13; *D12 World*, 10; *Eminem Presents: The Re-Up*, 38–41; freestyle singles and, 204; *Loyal to the Game* (Tupac Shakur), 10; *Recovery* (Eminem), 142–143; retirement rumors and, 16–17; Shady Records and, 10; Slaughterhouse 238n3; "Stepping Stone" (Eminem), 260; substance use and, 38, 40–41
Eminem Presents: The Re-Up, 38–40
Eminem Show, The (Eminem), 17, 57n18, 117, 144n1, 151–152
Emmy Awards, xvi
emo rap genre, 93, 125–126
"Empire State of Mind" (Jay-Z), 219
empowerment, xiii, xiv, 14, 269
Encore (Eminem): in album cycle, 192; analysis of, 18–20; commercial success of, 13, 15; criticism/reviews, 15–17, 170, 189; Dr. Dre production work on, 57n18; effects of fame theme, 183–184; "Just Lose It" video

controversy, 12; lyrics and delivery, xxii, 59; *Relapse* (Eminem) vs., 65; retirement rumors and, 15–17
entrepreneurism, 83
EPMD, 225
Epps, Tauheed (2 Chainz), 240–241
Equalizer, The, 199
Eric B and Rakim, 32
Esham, 78, 82–83
Esquire TV, 97–98
"Ether" (Nas), 155–156
Etheridge, Mario, 27–30
Eve, 52n15
Everlast, 74–75
Evidence, 104
"Evil Deeds" (Eminem), 18
"Evil Twin" (Eminem), 177n8
Eyedea and Abilities, 103–104

F.B.T. Studios, 57
Facebook, 6–7, 96. *See also* social media
"FACK" (Eminem), 251
"Fall" (Eminem), 251–252, 252n12, 257
fame: effect of as lyrical theme, 183, 199–200, 228; impact on Eminem, 1–13, 17–18, 235, 237–240, 274–275; psychological effects of, 21, 142; social media and, 6–7
"Fancy" (Iggy Azalea), 105
fans: feedback from, 66–68, 219, 244; music evolution and, 78–79; post-*Revival* era, 234–235; social media and, 6–7, 69, 254–256; "stan" and, 176, 176n6; Trump supporters and, 79, 100, 208
"Fast Lane" (Bad Meets Evil), 161
"Feel Me Flow" (Naughty by Nature), 184
Fennessey, Sean, 21
fentanyl, 93, 100
Fergie, 206, 207
feuds: Eminem and, generally, 136n17; Eminem and Machine Gun Kelly, 258–259; Jay-Z vs. Nas, 155–156; Lil Pump and J. Cole, 252n12; Royce da 5'9" and D12, 157–159, 158n15
50 Cent: Anger Management Tour (2005), 14, 15; Dr. Dre and, 52n15; D12 vs. Royce da 5'9" and, 158; Eminem and, xiii, 38; *Get Rich or Die Tryin'*, 15; Home and Home Tour, 149; mixtapes, 130; *106 and Park* (2005), 44–45; Proof and, 31
54 Sound, 57
"Fight for Your Right to Party" (Beastie Boys), 178, 184
"Fine Line" (Eminem), 199–200
Fisherman, Larry (Mac Miller), 102

5 Ela, 25, 31
Flatlinerz, 85
Flo Rida, 125
Florida Georgia Line, 90–91
Fontana, Wayne, 185
45 King, 101
Fox, Megan, 141
"Framed" (Eminem), 225–226
Francis, Sage, 104
Fraser, Illya (Illadaproducer), 255–256
frat rap genre, 95, 96–104
Freestyle Fellowship, 107
Freestyle Friday, xvii
freestyle rap, xviii–xx, 25, 204, 207–208, 212, 217
Frere-Jones, Sasha, 189
"Frick Park Market" (Mac Miller), 101
Frukwan, 84–85
"Fuck J. Cole" (Lil Pump), 252n12
Future, 127, 224, 233n1, 248

Galordi, Tina, 37, 40, 42, 49–50, 51, 138, 146, 195
"Game of Love" (Wayne Fontana and the Mindbenders), 185
Game, 52n15, 156
Game Recordings, 152
gangs, 79–80
gangsta rap, 81–83, 92, 103
G-Eazy, 110–111
Gemini (Macklemore), 109
General Admission (Machine Gun Kelly), 258
Genuine Article, The (Remedy), 95
Get Money, Stay True (Paul Wall), 87
Get Rich or Die Tryin' (film), 15
Get Ya Mind Correct (Paul Wall and Chamillionaire), 87n5
Geto Boys, 81–82
ghostwriting, 106, 156, 251, 276
"Girls" (Beastie Boys), 221
GO:OD AM (Mac Miller), 102
"Good Vibrations" (Marky Mark and the Funky Bunch), 73–74
Goon Sqwad, 25, 31
GQ, 113
Grammy Awards: Azealia Banks on, 106; "Believe" (Cher), 122; Best New Artist, xv; Eminem generally, 237n2; *The Heist* (Macklemore), 107–108; "My Name Is" (Eminem), 3; race and, 107–108; Recording Academy, 256; *Recovery* (Eminem), 144, 144n1; *Relapse* (Eminem), 146, 146; Rick Rubin and, 177–178; *The Slim Shady LP* (Eminem), 3; viewership, xvi

Grand Don't Come for Free, A (the Streets), 176n7
Grand Hustle, 105
Grande, Ariana, 105
Grandmaster Kaz, 108
Grant, Alexander (Alex da Kid), 139–140, 145
Grant, Nick, 262
Gravediggaz, 84–85
Green Day, 176n7
Grey, Skyler, 140
Guardian, 28, 39
Gucci Mane, 224
G-Unit, 14, 30, 149
"Guts Over Fear" (Eminem and Sia), 199
Gyllenhaal, Jake, 202, 203

Haddaway, 133–134
Hafermann, Holly (Skyler Grey), 140
"Hailie's Song" (Eminem), 20
Halloween, 206
Hamilton, 176n7
Hand 2 Hand: Official Mixtape Instruction Manual, 23
hardcore rap genre, 78, 103, 145
Hardy, Tom, 245
Harry, Debbie, 70
Harvey, Steve, 12
hate crimes, 74
Haystak, 88
Hazlett, Shelly, 193
HBO Blaze Battle, 103
"Headlights" (Eminem), 179–180
"Heat" (Eminem), 221
Heist, The (Macklemore and Ryan Lewis), 107, 109
Hell: The Sequel (Bad Meets Evil), 160–166
heroin, 46
hick-hop genre, 89–93
Hieroglyphics, 107
Hildebrand, Andy, 119–120, 127
Hill, Lauryn, 175n4
Hip Hop Shop, 25, 33
hip-hop collectives, 95
hip-hop culture: African Americans and, 70, 75–77, 91–92; authenticity and, 103; Detroit scene, 23; Eminem entry into, 17, 70; frat rap and, 95–96; gatekeepers of, 2, 70, 90; influence of, 75–77; *Kamikaze* (Eminem) commentary on, 246–247; LL Cool J on, x–xi, xiii–xiv; as lyrical theme, 136–137; pop rap and, 105–113; race and, 2–3, 86, 89, 106, 113–114; rap vs., xi; "Renegade" and, 154–155; respect and, 252, 252n12; roots and, xiii,

72, 75–76, 88–90, 104, 107; violence and, 19, 25–30, 31–32; whitewashing of, 89, 106
hip-hop genre: African Americans and, 2–3, 75–77, 91–92, 113–114; alternative hip-hop, 103–104, 256; authenticity and, 89; Auto-Tune and, 122–130; commercial success, 113–114; country rap and, 93; empowerment and, xiii, xiv, 14, 269; evolution of, 69–70, 236, 261–262, 267, 270; hip hopera, 176n7; hip-hop collectives, 95; popularity of, xvi; respect and, 89; roots of, 247–248; sellouts and, 238; white hip-hop, 77–83. *See also* white rap
hip-hop/rap industry: country rap and, 89–93; hip-hop collectives, 95; race and, xii–xiii, 2–3, 108, 109, 110. *See also* music industry
hip hopera, 176, 176n7
Hispanic Americans, 76
Hogan, Brooke, 118
Hogan, Hulk, 118
Hollywood Reporter, 151
Holmes, James, 251
Holton, DeShaun "Proof." *See* Proof (DeShaun Holton)
Home and Home Tour (2010), 149–151
"Homicide" (Logic), 270
homophobic lyrics, 54, 169, 171, 172, 191, 257
Hoodie Allen, 97
Hopsin, 261
Hopson, Marcus (Hopsin), 261
horrorcore rap, 63–64, 63n20, 80–81, 84–85, 101–102, 163, 225–226
Hot 97, 106, 224, 258, 259
Hot Boys, 130
House of Pain, 74–75, 77
How to Make Money Selling Drugs, 46, 47
Hughes, Howard, 195
Hunger Games, 252
Hyde Park festival, 196

I Decided (Big Sean), 206
"I Love Rock and Roll" (Joan Jett and the Blackhearts), 221
"I Need a Doctor" (Dr. Dre), 52n15, 140, 210
"I'm Not Racist" (Joyner Lucas), 215
"I'm On Everything (ft. Mike Epps)" (Bad Meets Evil), 163
"I'm the King" (Royce da 5'9"), 152
"Ice Ice Baby" (Vanilla Ice), 72–73
"Ida Red" (Bob Wills and Texas Playboys), 76n1
"If I Had" (Eminem), xxi
Illadaproducer, 255
imagery, 54, 81–83, 152, 154, 172, 225–226
Imagine Dragons, 140, 253
"In Your Head" (Eminem), 227–228

Incredible True Story, The (Logic), 176n7
independent rap labels, 78, 79, 83, 87, 101,
   103–104
Infinite (Eminem), 84, 85, 273
Inglis, Fred, 5, 6
Insane Clown Posse (ICP), 77–83
insomnia, 35–36, 50
Instagram, 6–7, 105, 112, 125. *See also* social
   media
institutionalized racism, xx, 217
internet: bubble culture, 95–97; fame and, 6–13.
   See also social media
Interscope Records, 9, 12, 21, 67, 88, 153, 186,
   210, 211
"Intro (Feel the Heat)," 221
Iovine, Jimmy, 88, 206, 215
Iron Fist, 23
Island Records, 107
"It's My Thing" (EPMD), 225
iTunes, 102, 141

J. Cole, 252, 252n12, 261, 262
J Dilla, 175n4
Jackson, Michael, xiii, 12, 112, 237
Jay-Z: awards and nominations, xvi, 3;
   commercial success of, 144, 188; criticism
   and reviews 190; *Detox* (Dr. Dre), 52n15;
   Eminem and, 149–151, 153; "Empire State of
   Mind" (Jay-Z), 219; freestyle rap, 41; Home
   and Home Tour, 149–151; iconic status of,
   xii, 219, 252; Kayne West and, 126; Nas and,
   155–156; "Renegade" and, 153–155; Rick
   Rubin and, 178
Jean, Wyclef, 176n7, 185n13
Jin, xvii
Joan Jett and the Blackhearts, 221
Joey Bada$$, 156
John, Elton, 49, 237
Johnson, Mario "Chocolate," 73
Jones, Kent, 255
Jonsin, Jim, 145
Jordan, Michael, 239
Jordan, Sly, 161
"Jump Around" (House of Pain), 74
"Jumping the Shark" (fun.), 179
Just Blaze (Justin Smith), 133–134, 145
"Just Don't Give a Fuck" (Eminem), 236
"Just Lose It" (Eminem), 12
Juvenile, 130

Kamikaze (Eminem): analysis of, 245–262;
   Joyner Lucas and, 215; name-checking, 253,
   256–260; Paul Rosenberg on, 276–277;
   release of, 233–235 246, 277

"Kamikaze" (Eminem), 251
Keith, Tay, 250
Kelly, R., 176n7
Keys, Alicia, 219
Khalifa, Whiz, 224
Khan, Joseph, 141
Kid Cudi, 126
Kid Rock, 80, 88, 92
Kid Vishis, xix
Kiedis, Anthony, 93
"Kill Shot" (Eminem), 259
"Kill You" (Eminem), xxii, 9, 178
"Kim" (Eminem), 20, 181
"King of Rock" (Run-DMC), 221
"Kings Never Die" (Eminem), 203–204
Kluger, Adam, 109–110
Knight, Suge, 73
Knowles, Beyoncé, 149, 176n7, 212
Kon Artis, 22–23
Konvict Muzik, 123
Kool Keith, 175n4, 198, 198n2
Kool Moe Dee, 108
Kot, Greg, 189
KRS-One, xi, xiii
Ku Klux Klan, 205
"Kush" (Dr. Dre), 52n15
Kweli, Taleb, 107
KXNG Crooked, 238n3

Lamar, Kendrick: awards and nominations,
   xvi; Eminem and, 184–185, 186, 192, 261;
   Grammy Awards and, 106, 108; style and
   vocal delivery of, 111, 186, 248–249
Lamont, Bishop, 52n15
Larry Lovestein and the Velvet Revival, 102
"Lazy Sunday" (Lonely Island), 98
"Legacy" (Eminem), 187
legal issues: Chris Brown, 140n20; Eminem,
   9–10, 14–15; Insane Clown Posse, 79–80;
   Proof and Royce da 5'9" feud, 158; Royce da
   5'9", 159
"Let Me Clear My Throat" (DJ Kool), 101
Lewis, Ryan, 107–109
LGBT community, 107–108, 172
License to Ill (Beastie Boys), 71
"Life's Been Good" (Joe Walsh), 183
"Like Home" (Eminem), 214, 219–221
"Like Toy Soldiers" (Eminem), 19, 151
Lil B, 102, 111
Lil Dicky, 99–100
Lil Jon, 14
Lil Peep, 93–94, 224, 225
Lil Pump, 224, 247, 252n12, 255
Lil Uzi Vert, 127, 224

Lil Wayne: *Detox* (Dr. Dre) and, 52n15; Eminem and, 129–133, 135; imitators of, 247; T-Pain and, 125, 126–127
Lil Wyte, 95
Lil Xan, 224, 247, 252n12
Lil Yachty, 224, 252n12
Limp Bizkit, 75
"Lion's Roar" (Asher Roth), 97
"Living Proof" (Bad Meets Evil), 160
LL Cool J, ix–xi, 70, 177, 178, 184
Logic, 176n7, 261, 270
Lonely Island, 98–99
Lord Infamous, 248
"Lose Yourself" (Eminem): awards and nominations, xx, 1–2, 60, 138–139, 171
Loussier, Jacques, 9
"Love Game" (featuring Kendrick Lamar) (Eminem), 184–185, 186
Love Story (Yelawolf), 92
"Love the Way You Lie" (Eminem), xxii, 19, 139–141, 144, 151, 152, 197
"Low" (Flo Rida), 125
Low-End Theory, The (A Tribe Called Quest), 185
Loyal to the Game (Shakur), 10
Lucas, Gary Maurice, Jr. (Joyner Lucas), 215, 252–253, 261
"Lucky You (featuring Joyner Lucas)" (Eminem), 215, 252–253
Ludacris, 90, 92
Lynskey, Dorian, 39
lyrics: alternative hip-hop, 103–104; antagonistic/aggressive, xx–xxi, 145, 245; anti-Trump, 204–205, 207–208, 212–213, 219–221, 226, 256; "Asshole" (Eminem), 182; autobiographical, 116, 178–180, 228–230, 273–274; "Bad Guy" (Eminem), 173–176; Bad Meets Evil, 152–153, 160; beats and, 53, 58, 61, 156, 188, 204, 206, 223–224, 226; "Beautiful" (Eminem), 61, 64–65; Bible references, 78, 199–200; boastful, 135–136, 154–155, 161, 187–188, 197–198; "Campaign Speech" (Eminem), 206–207; "Castle" (Eminem), 228–229, 230; "Chloraseptic" (Eminem), 225; cinematic, 92, 138, 139, 155, 169; confessional, xxi, 64, 115; "Criminal" (Eminem), 54; "Deja Vu" (Eminem), 64–65; delivery (*see* vocal delivery); diss tracks, 20, 75, 80, 130, 155–156, 157–159, 254, 256–260; double entendres, 154, 182, 222; Eminem style and, xxii, xiii, xviii, xxi, 41–42, 58, 145, 204, 266, 268–269; emotional, xxi, 93, 137; *Encore* (Eminem), 15–16, 18–20;

"Evil Deeds" (Eminem) 18; evolution of, xxi–xxii; fame's effect theme, 183, 199–200, 228; frat rap, 96–99; freestyle, xviii–xx, 25, 41, 58–59, 204, 207–208, 212, 217; ghostwriting, 106, 156, 251, 276; "The Greatest" (Eminem), 250; "Headlights" (Eminem), 179–180; homophobic, 54, 169, 171, 172, 191, 257; honesty in, 115, 140–141, 180, 182; horrorcore, 225–226; humorous, 183–184, 250–251, 252; imagery in, 54, 81–83, 152, 154, 225–226; Insane Clown Posse, 79, 80–81; "Kings Never Die" (Eminem), 203–204; LGBT rights themes, 107–108; "Like Home" (Eminem), 219–221; "Like Toy Soldiers" (Eminem), 19; "Lucky You (featuring Joyner Lucas)" (Eminem), 252–253; lyrical flow and, 84 (*see also* vocal delivery); Mac Miller, 101–102; *The Marshall Mathers LP2* (Eminem), 171–172; mental illness themes, 82; metaphors, 62–63, 80–81, 104, 116, 136, 137, 140, 203, 209; misogynist, 54, 117, 162, 169, 171, 172–173, 191, 206, 221, 222; mumble rap, 224–225; name-checking, 253, 256–260; name-dropping, 261; narrative point of view, 18 (*see also* alter egos; Slim Shady persona); narrative/storytelling, 18, 52, 92, 153, 169, 173–177, 177n8, 218–219, 265; "No Favors" (Big Sean), 206; "No Love" (Eminem), 131–133; number of words, 187, 187n15; offensive, 117, 152, 154, 172, 178, 196, 226; origin stories, 18, 70; paranoia themes, 81–83; parodies, 247; political, 19, 213, 214–224, 226, 256 (*see also* politics); pop culture references, 118, 141, 144–145, 253; pop rap and, 111; product placement and, 110; race themes, 107–108; *Recovery* (Eminem), 115, 171; *Relapse* (Eminem), 50–56, 58–64, 171; relationship themes, 139–141, 172–173, 185, 226–227; "Renegade" (Jay-Z), 154; revenge themes, 85, 182; "Rhyme or Reason" (Eminem), 178–179; rhyme scheme and, 187–188; "The Ringer" (Eminem), 249–250; roasts/roasting, 72; Royce da 5'9", 159; satirical, 98–99, 138, 141; "Seduction" (Eminem), 136; self-absorbed, 111; self-deprecating, 96, 99, 184; self-doubt theme, 197–198, 199, 212; *Shady XV* (Eminem), 197–199; Slim Shady/Marshall Mathers/Eminem persona and, 18, 40, 59–60, 63–66, 141–143 (*see also* Slim Shady persona); social justice themes, 107–108, 213; "Stepping Stone" (Eminem), 260; "Still Don't Give a Fuck" (Eminem),

54; substance use vs. sobriety and, 50–56, 60, 64–65, 135–136, 165; supernatural and occult themes, 81–83; "Taken from Me" (Bad Meets Evil), 161; "Underground" (Eminem), 53–55; "Untouchable" (Eminem), 214–224; Vanilla Ice, 72–73; violent, 81–83, 84–85, 162; "Walk on Water" (Eminem), 212; "We as Americans" (Eminem), 12; "White America" (Eminem), 19; wordplay, 19, 40, 169, 171, 187–188, 203–204, 226; Yelawolf, 92; "Yellow Brick Road" (Eminem), 18–19

Mac Miller (Larry Fisherman), 100–104
Machine Gun Kelly (MGK), 94, 250, 256, 258–259
Macklemore, 106–109
Madison Square Garden 2005 concert, 14–15
Magna Carta Holy Grail (Jay-Z), 190
Making Trouble (Geto Boys), 81
"Malcolm X" (Royce da 5′9″), 157–158
Malone, Maurice, 25
"Many Men (Wish Death)" (50 Cent), 158
"Many Men" (Proof), 158
marginalization, 224n13
marijuana, 43, 84, 132–133n13
marketing: country rap, 93; Dr. Dre and, 52; 50 Cent and, 15; hick-hop and, 90; product placement, 110; race and, 102–103; *Revival* (Eminem) viral campaign, 209–211, 213; social media and, 97, 98
Marky Mark and the Funky Bunch, 73–74
Mars, Bruno, 163
Marshall Mathers LP, The (Eminem): awards and nominations, 151–152; on cassette, 194; commercial success of, 17; "Criminal," 54; Dr. Dre production work on, 57n18; emotional intensity, 115, 137; "Kill You" legal issues, 9; *The Marshall Mathers LP2* and, 169; original title of, 43n7; Slim Shady/Eminem/Marshall Mathers persona, 141–143; substance use and, 43
Marshall Mathers LP2, The (Eminem): in album cycle, 192; analysis of, 169–193; autobiographical themes, 172–173, 178–181, 188; commercial success, 187, 189; criticism/reviews, 172, 189–192; effects of fame theme, 183–184; Kendrick Lamar and, 186; Rapture Tour, 196; Rick Rubin and, 177–178; self-doubt theme, 197–198; Slim Shady/Eminem/Marshall Mathers persona, 177, 177n8
"Marshall Mathers" (Eminem), 178
Martin, Chris, 149
Martin, Trayvon, 207

"Massive Attack" (Niki Minaj), 140
Masta Ace, 216
Mathers, Debbie, 178
Mathers, Hailie, 20, 22, 94, 228–230, 234, 258–259, 274
Mathers, Marshall. *See* Eminem (Marshall Mathers)
"Maybelline" (Chuck Berry), 76n1
MC Breed, 78
MC Hammer, 72, 247
MC Ren, 184
MC Serch, 70
McCain, John, 223
McConnell, Mitch, 226
McGraw, Tim, 91
media, 5–13, 75. *See also* social media
Melle Mel, 108
Memphis Bleek, 149
mental health: fame and, 4–13; substance use and, 21, 37, 40, 42, 49–50, 51, 138, 146, 195–196
mental illness themes, 82
"Mess" (Lil Wayne), 127
"Message, The" (Dr. Dre), 156
metaphors, 62–63, 80–81, 104, 116 136, 137, 140, 203, 209
methadone, 46–47
Method Man, 25
Midler, Bette, 229
Midnight Memories (One Direction), 189
Migos, 223, 224, 247, 248, 252
Mike D, 33
Mike Stud, 97–98, 111
Millard, Drew, 99
Miller, Mac (Larry Fisherman), 100–104
Minaj, Nicki, 106, 140, 149
"Mind Playing Tricks on Me" (Geto Boys), 82
misogynist themes, 54, 117, 162, 169, 171, 172–173, 191, 206, 221, 222
Mitchell, Matthew, 174
mixtapes, 38–39, 87, 101, 111, 126, 130, 156, 159
Molly, 43
Monaghan, Dominic, 141
Monster Tour, 197
"Monster, The" (Eminem), xxii, 171
Montgomery, Ryan (Royce da 5′9″). *See* Royce da 5′9″ (Ryan Montgomery)
Mos Def, 176n7
"Mosh" (Eminem), 13, 19
Motown, xiii
Mr. Porter (Denaun Porter): "Believe" (Eminem) and, 223; album release timing and, 267–268; Eminem and, 43–44, 48, 56, 67, 231,

Mr. Porter (*Cont.*)
    242–243; fatherhood and, 269; *Kamikaze*
    (Eminem) and, 261; performances and,
    147–149; as producer, 160, 165–166; Proof
    and, 22–23, 43–44; *Recovery* (Eminem), 116,
    118; *Relapse* (Eminem), 115–117; *Revival*
    (Eminem), 254–255; self-doubt and, 235;
    "Untouchable" (Eminem) and, 214–216,
    218–219
Mr. Shing-a-Ling (Lou Donaldson), 175, 175n4
MTV: awards, xvi, 144; hip-hop culture and, 75;
    "Just Lose It" video, 12; *TRL*, 44n8
MTV News, 16, 20, 95
Mudd, 25
mumble rap, 224–225, 247, 251–252, 255, 261
music festivals, 74–75, 111, 149, 196–197
music industry: Auto-Tune and, 118–121, 128;
    digital distribution era and, 86, 88–90, 94,
    113, 200–201, 233n1, 239–240; early 2000s,
    94–95; Nashville and, 89–90, 91; social media
    and, 96
music streaming, xvi, 69, 94, 201, 233n1
music videos: "Berzerk" (Eminem), 184; Dr. Dre,
    52n15; "Just Lose It" (Eminem) 12; "Love
    the Way You Lie" (Eminem), 141; "Lucky
    You" (Eminem), 215; "Mosh" (Eminem), 13;
    product placement, 110; "Started from the
    Bottom" (Drake), 224n18
Musikmesse, 120n3
"My Kinda Lover" (Billy Squier), 198
"My Mom" (Eminem), 274
"My Name" (Xzibit), 156
"My Name Is" (Eminem), 3, 143, 151, 184

N.W.A, ix, 32, 87
Najm, Faheem Rasheed (T-Pain), 122–125
name-checking, 253, 256–260
name-dropping, 261
narcissism, 7, 95
Nas, 52n15, 84, 155–156
Nate Dogg, 161
National Association of Music Merchants
    (NAMM) Show, 120, 120n3
Native Americans, 77
Naughty by Nature, ix, 31, 184, 226
Nelly, 90–91, 92
New Classic, The (Iggy Azalea), 105
New York Times, 16, 83, 253
Nice, Pete, 71
Nightmare on Elm Street, 82
"Nightmare on My Street" (DJ Jazzy Jeff and
    the Fresh Prince), 82
"900 Number, The" (45 King), 101
"99 Problems" (Jay-Z), 178

"'97 Bonnie and Clyde" (Eminem), 20
"1985" (J. Cole), 252n12
Nirvana, 95
NME.com, 254
"No Favors" (Big Sean), 206
No Limit, 79, 87
"No Love" (Eminem), 131–134
"No Reason" (Tech N9ne), 258
Noisey, 99, 100
"Not Afraid" (Eminem), xxii, 19, 131, 138–139,
    144, 151, 152
"Not Alike (featuring Royce the 5'9")"
    (Eminem), 250, 259
Notorious B.I.G., 25, 150
"Nowhere Fast" (Eminem), 214
NPR, 123
nu metal genre, 75–77
"Nuttin' to Do" (Bad Meets Evil), 152, 153

O'Riordan, Dolores, 227n21
occult themes, 81–83
Ocean, Frank, 126
Odd Future, 257
"Ode to Billie Joe" (Lou Donaldson), 175
"Offended" (Eminem), 225–226, 255
"On Point" (House of Pain), 74
101Barz, 36
106 and Park, 44–45
Onyx, ix, 175n4
opiates, 37, 42, 43
Organized Noize, 88
Ortiz, Joell, 159, 238n3
Oscar Awards, xv, xvi, 1–2
Outkast, 87, 103
outsider art, 253
"Over and Over" (Tim McGraw), 91

Paddock, Stephen, 251
paranoia themes, 81–83
"Parking Lot" (Eminem), 176, 177
parodies, 12, 247
"Party on Fifth Ave." (Mac Miller), 101
patriotism, 214, 214n13
Paz, Vinnie, 104
Pence, Mike, 256
People's Champ, The (Paul Wall), 87
performances: Beastie Boys, 71–72; BET 2017
    Hip Hop Awards, xv–xxiv, 207–208; Madison
    Square Garden 2005, 14–15; MetLife
    Stadium, 197; Motor City Casino, 147–149;
    Mr. Porter and, 147–149; music festivals,
    74–75, 196–197; Proof and, 147; Wembley
    Stadium, 196, 257. *See also* tours
"Phenomenal" (Eminem), 203

Phifer, Alexis, 125
Phifer, Mekhi, 24, 176n7
Phresher, 224, 241
Pick, the Sickle and the Shovel, The
  (Gravediggaz), 85
Pimp C, 126–127n9
Pink Floyd, 176n7
Pitchfork, xix, 21, 201
Poetic, 85
police violence, 214–224
political correctness, 77n2, 222
politics: "Campaign Speech" (Eminem), 204–
  205; Eminem and David Duke, 205–206;
  Eminem and Donald Trump, xvii–xviii, 204–
  205, 207–208, 212–213, 219–221, 226, 256;
  hick-hop genre and, 90; hip-hop culture and,
  113–114; "Mosh" video, 13, 19; "No Favors"
  (Big Sean), 206–207; rap music and, xii,
  xvii–xviii; *Revival* (Eminem) and, 214–224;
  "Untouchable" (Eminem), 214–224; "We as
  Americans" (Eminem) and, 12
pop culture: Eminem's role in, xxii–xxiii;
  influence of hip hop, 75–77; lyrical references
  to, 118, 141, 144–145, 253; race and, 91–92
pop genre, 69–70, 90, 95, 104–105, 124, 128
pop rap, 103, 105–113, 145, 163
"Pop the Trunk" (Yelawolf), 92
Popsomp Hills, 210–211
Porter, Denaun. See Mr. Porter (Denaun Porter)
Post Malone, 111–113, 233n1
poverty, 78, 81, 173
Press Play (Diddy), 159
Price, Demond (Conway), 262
Prince Among Thieves, A (Prince Paul), 176n7
Prince Paul, 84, 176n7
Prince Paul and the Bomb Squad, 71
"Problem" (Ariana Grande), 105
Professional Rapper (Lil Dicky), 100
Promatic, 31
promethazine, 126–127n9
Proof (DeShaun Holton): Bad Meets Evil and,
  152, 153; childhood and family of, 24–25, 31;
  D12 and, 260; Detroit hip-hop scene and, 23,
  25; *8 Mile* representation, 24; Eminem and,
  21, 22–26, 31, 34; funeral of, 30–33; as hype
  man, 157; Insane Clown Posse and, 80; MC
  style and inspiration, 24; as mentor, 23–24;
  Mike D and, 33–34; murder of, 22, 25–30;
  performances and, 147; Royce dà 5′9″ feud,
  157–159
"Protecting Ryan" (Royce da 5′9″), 161n17
psychedelic mushrooms, 94
Psychopathic Records, 78, 79
Public Enemy, 184, 248

"Puke" (Eminem), 20
"Pulsion" (Loussier), 9
purple drank, 126–127n9
Purple Gang, 158
"Purple Pills" (D12), 33

Q-Tip, 105–107
Queen, 72

R&B genre, 122, 124
race: commercial success and, xii–xiii, 2–3, 70,
  71, 72–73, 74, 85–86, 87, 87n5, 88, 101;
  cultural appropriation and (*see* cultural
  appropriation); Grammy Awards and,
  107–108; hick-hop and, 90; hip-hop culture
  and, 2–3, 86, 89, 106, 113–114; hip-hop/
  rap industry and, xii–xiii, 2–3, 108, 109,
  110; image and, 112–113; as lyrical theme,
  107–108; marketing and, 102–103; pop
  culture and, 91–92; pop rap and, 112–
  113; "Untouchable" (Eminem) and, 218–219;
  white privilege and, xix–xx, 93, 99, 100,
  108–109, 110, 113–114, 217
racism: Black Lives Matter movement,
  216n14; Eminem and, 11–12, 18–19, 221;
  institutionalized, xxi, 217; Lil Dicky and,
  99; as lyrical theme, 208; police violence,
  214–224; Trump and, xx–xxi, 208; white rap
  and, 76–77
radio: celebrity status and, 6; Eminem
  interviews, 166, 225; hip-hop culture and, 75
Radio (LL Cool J), 184
Radioactive (Yelawolf), 92
"Radioactive" (Imagine Dragons), 140
Rag and Bone, 238
Rah Digga, 176n7
Raheem, 81
Rakim, xiii–xiv
"Rap Devil" (Machine Gun Kelly), 94, 259
rap genre: acid rap, 83; alter egos in, 81 (*see also*
  alter egos); battle raps, xvii, xviii, 23, 171,
  172, 199; commercial success and, 91–92;
  country rap, 89–93, 199; cyphers, xvii–xviii;
  East Coast rap, 74, 82, 107, 216, 248; emo
  rap, 125–126; freestyle rap, xviii–xx, 25, 204,
  207–208, 212, 217; gangsta rap, 81–83, 92,
  103; hardcore rap, 78, 103, 145; hick-hop
  and, 90–93; hip-hop vs., xi; horrorcore rap,
  63–64, 63n20, 80–81, 84–85, 101–102, 163,
  225–226; independent rap labels, 78, 79, 83,
  87, 101, 103–104; mumble rap, 224–225,
  247, 251–252, 255, 261; politics and (*see*
  politics); pop rap, 103, 105–113, 145, 163;
  rap-rock, 88; rock and, 184–185; southern,

rap genre (*Cont.*)
  248; trap-style rap, 206, 223–225, 249–252; underground, 63, 107, 236–237, 238, 264; West Coast, 248; white rap, 69–114 (*see also* white rap)
"Rap God" (Eminem), 187
Rap Olympics, 3
rapcent, 110
rap-rock genre, 88
"Rapture" (Blondie), 70
Rapture Tour, 196
Rawling, Brian, 121
"Real Slim Shady, The" (Eminem), 143, 151
Rebirth (Lil Wayne), 131
Recording Academy, 256
Recovery (Eminem): acknowledgment of other artists, 129–130; in album cycle, 192; analysis of, 117–118, 135–143; commercial success, xxii, 144; cover of, 214; criticism/ reviews, 115–116, 170, 189; effects of fame theme, 183–184; Eminem age and, 137; lyrics, 171; *The Marshall Mathers LP2* and, 170–171; Mr. Porter on, 116, 118; *Relapse* vs., 67, 134; serious tone of, 138, 142–143, 173; singles from, 144–146; Slim Shady/ Eminem/Marshall Mathers persona, 141–143; songwriting and production, 145–148
Red Hot Chili Peppers (RHCP), 93
Redrum, 85
Reel Life Productions, 83
reference tracks, 251n11
Refill (Eminem), 134, 146
reggae genre, 122
Relapse (Eminem): in album cycle, 192; analysis of, 63–64, 116, 117–118; beats, 117; commercial success of, xxii, 65–66, 67–68; criticism/reviews, 64–68, 146, 170; Dr. Dre as producer, 57–58; effects of fame theme, 183–184; *Encore* (Eminem) vs., 65; metaphor use, 62–63; Mr. Porter on, 115–117; "My Mom" (Eminem), 274; origination of idea for, 51–52; prerelease marketing, 210–211; production of, 56; *Recovery* (Eminem) vs., 134; *Refill* (Eminem) and, 67; release performances, 147–149; Slim Shady/Marshall Mathers/Eminem persona and, 59–60, 63–65, 137, 162; Tyler, the Creator and, 257; writing and recording process, 50–55; lyrics and delivery, 58–64, 171
Relapse 2 (Eminem), 67, 118
relationship themes, 139–141, 172–173, 185, 226–227
Relief (Mike Stud), 97
Remedy, 95
"Remind Me" (Eminem), 221
"Renegade" (Jay-Z), 153–155
"Renegade" (Royce da 5'9" and Eminem), 153–154
response tracks, 59
Return of the Dozen (D12), 158n15
"Reunion, The" (Bad Meets Evil), 162, 163
revenge themes, 85, 182
Revival (Eminem): analysis of, 211–232; commercial success, xxii, 211–212, 240; confused themes, 213–214, 231; cover of, 213–214; criticism/reviews, 218, 219, 220–221, 231, 238n3, 240–244, 253, 254–255, 257, 262; Tyler, the Creator and, 257; viral campaign, 209–211, 213
"Rhyme or Reason" (Eminem), 177–178, 186
Rhymesayers, 103, 104
RIAA Diamond certification, 91, 151–152
"Ridaz" (Eminem), 141
"Right for Me" (Eminem), 200
Rihanna, 140–141, 140n20, 171, 197
"Ringer, The" (Eminem), 247, 249–250, 255
RJ-D2, 104
Roadies, 94
"RoboCop" (Kanye West), 125
"Rock Bottom" (Eminem), xxi, 61
Rock City (Royce da 5'9"), 153
"Rock City" (Royce da 5'9" and Eminem), 153
rock genre, 75–77, 92, 184, 199
"Rock the Bells" (LL Cool J), 178
rock-rap genre, 95
Rockwell, Donna, 4, 7, 8, 21, 142
Rocsi, 45
Roker, Steven, 14
"Role Model" (Eminem), x
Rolling Stone, xxiii, 39, 102
Ronny J, 250
"Rose, The" (Bette Midler), 229
Rosenberg, Paul: Action Bronson and, 104; David Duke and, 206; *Encore* (Eminem) and, 17; interview with, 273–278; Joe Budden and, 238n3; Mr. Porter and, 148; Proof and, 31; *Recovery* (Eminem) and, 166; *Revival* (Eminem) campaign and, 209, 211; Slaughterhouse and, 159
Rostrum, 101
Roth, Asher, 96–97
Royal Court Theatre, 72
Royce da 5'9" (Ryan Montgomery): Bad Meets Evil, 152–153, 157, 159–166, 268; BET Awards performance, xix; D12 feud, 157–159, 158n15; diss tracks and, 260; Dr. Dre and, 156–157; Eminem and, 158–166, 268, 270–271; hip-hop genre and, 262;

Kamikaze (Eminem) and, 261, 262; manager, 156–157, 156n14; "Not Alike" (Eminem), 250; "Renegade" and, 152–153, 155; Slaughterhouse and, 238n3

Rubin, Rick: Beastie Boys and, 70–71; as Eminem producer, 182, 184–185, 215, 221, 223, 229, 244, 265; as producer, commercial success and, xii, 177–178

Ruess, Nate, 179

Run the Jewels, 188

Run-DMC, xii, 7, 810, 177, 221

Rutling, Kashaun Rameek (Phresher), 224

RZA, 84–85

"Sabrina" (Yelawolf), 92

Samberg, Andy, 98–99

Same as It Ever Was (House of Pain), 74

"Same Love" (Macklemore and Ryan Lewis), 108

samples/sampling: "Arose" (Eminem), 229; "Bad Guy" (Eminem), 175; "Berzerk" (Eminem), 184; "Chloraseptic" (Eminem), 225; "Cooky Puss" (Beastie Boys), 71; "Heat" (Eminem), 221–222; "Ice Ice Baby" (Vanilla Ice), 72–73; "In Your Head" (Eminem), 227–228; "Kill You" (Eminem) 9; "Lose Yourself" (Eminem), 9; "Love Game (featuring Kendrick Lamar)" (Eminem), 185; "Love the Way You Lie" (Eminem) 9; Mac Miller, 101; *The Marshall Mathers LP2* (Eminem), 178; "My Brother's a Basehead" (De La Soul), 185; "My Name" (Xzibit), 156; "No Love" (Eminem), 133–134; "Not Afraid" (Eminem) 9; "Remind Me" (Eminem), 221; "Rhyme or Reason" (Eminem), 178; "Shady XV" (Eminem), 198–199; "So Far" (Eminem), 183

Sanneh, Kelefa, 16

satire, 98–99, 138, 141, 209–211, 213

"Say Goodbye to Hollywood" (Eminem), 20

Scarface, 81–82

Scary Movie, 153

"Scary Movies" (Bad Meets Evil), 152, 153

"Scenario" (A Tribe Called Quest), 185

Schaffer, Akiva, 98–99

Scott, Kimberly, xxi, 9, 20, 21–22, 140n20, 180–181, 181n11, 226–227, 234

Scott, Raymond "Benzino," 19

Searching for Jerry Garcia (Proof), 24

sedatives, 42

"Seduction" (Eminem), 136

serial killers, 62

Servitto, Deborah, 9–10

Sever, Sam, 71

Shade 45, 166, 180, 225, 258, 273

Shady Records: commercial success of, 23; Eminem album releases, 166, 203; Joe Budden and, 238n3; mixtapes, 38; Paul Rosenberg and, 273; signed artists, xix, 14, 92, 159

Shady XV (Eminem), 197–201, 257

"Shady XV" (Eminem), 198–199

Shaggy 2 Dope, 79, 80

Shakur, Tupac, 10, 226, 252, 252n12

"Shit on You" (Royce da 5'9"), 157

Short History of Celebrity, A (Inglis), 5

Shotta, Harry, 187n15

Sia, 199

Simmons, Jamel (Redrum), 85

Simmons, Russell, 70–71, 85

"Sing for the Moment" (Eminem), 20, 138, 151

Sir Rap-a-Lot, 81

Sire Jukebox, 81

Sirius, 166, 180, 225

6 Feet Deep (Gravediggaz), 85

Slaughterhouse, 159, 166, 238n3

slavery, 77, 90, 91

Slim Shady LP, The (Eminem): awards and nominations, 3; "Bad Meets Evil," 153, 156; "Brain Damage" lawsuit, 9; Busta Rhymes and, 185n13; commercial success of, 17; Dr. Dre production work on; Eminem's age and, 137; as Eminem's entry point, 17; as first major label album, 1; *Kamikaze* (Eminem) and, 254; Paul Rosenberg and, 273; "Rock Bottom," 62; "Still Don't Give a Fuck," 54

Slim Shady persona: Bad Meets Evil, 152; *Encore* and, 18, 59–60, 65; end of, 13; *Hell: The Sequel* and, 161–162; horrorcore and, 81, 84–85; Paul Rosenberg on, 277; Proof and, 31; Recovery and, 115, 137–138, 141; *Relapse*, 63, 64, 65, 137–138, 162; *Revival*, 226, 227–228, 231; *The Marshal Mathers LP 2*, 177, 179, 182, 183, 186, 192

Slim Shady/Marshall Mathers/Eminem persona: lyrics and, 18, 40, 59–60, 63–66, 141–143; *Relapse* and, 59–60, 63–65, 137, 162; *The Marshall Mathers LP2* and, 177

Slum Village, 31

"Smack Down" (D12), 158

Smith, Justin (Just Blaze), 133–134, 145

Smith, Rashaam Attica, 82

Smokepurpp, 252n12, 255

Snoop Dogg, xii, 105–106, 205

Snow, 59

"So Bad" (Eminem), 141

"So Far" (Eminem), 182–184, 186

social media: award shows and, xv–xvi; celebrity status and, 6–13; commercial success and,

social media (*Cont.*)
    96; fans and, 254–256; feuds and, 105–107;
    Kamikaze (Eminem) and, 254–256;
    marketing and, 97, 98; reaction videos, 239;
    relationships with fans, 69; 2017 BET Awards
    and, xix
"Soldier" (Eminem), 20
songs. *See* lyrics; *specific songs*
Sons of Anarchy, 202
SoundCloud, xvii, 88–89, 94, 100, 224, 250,
    259
Source, The, 11, 12, 19, 92
southern rap genre, 248
southern rap-rock-country genre, 92
Southpaw, 202–203
Southpaw soundtrack (Eminem), 203–204
Spears, Britney, 77n2, 111, 247
Spin, 151
"Spring Break Anthem" (Lonely Island), 99
Springsteen, Bruce, 214, 253
Squamish Valley Music Festival, 197
Squier, Billy, 184, 198
"Stan" (Eminem), xxii, 173–174, 176, 176n6,
    197
Staples, Vince, xix, 102, 256
"Started from the Bottom" (Drake), 224n18
Stat Quo, 14, 21, 38
Staten, Vanessa, 112
Stefani, Gwen, 203
Stephen, Bijan, 113
"Stepping Stone" (Eminem), 260
"Still Don't Give a Fuck" (Eminem), 54
Stillmatic (Mas), 155
Stingley, Mick, 151
Stoney (Post Malone), 111–112
"Storm, The" (Eminem), xvii–xxiv, 207–208
Street Hop (Royce da 5'9"), 159
Streets, the, 176n7
"Stroke, The" (Billy Squier), 184
"Stronger Than I Was" (Eminem), 180–181, 227
Stylz, 25
substance use: Bubba Sparxxx and, 88; "Castle"
    (Eminem) and, 228–229; creative process
    and, 40–41, 43, 50–56, 60, 64–65, 135–136,
    165; depression and, 42, 43, 62; *8 Mile* and,
    36; Eminem and, 20, 21, 35–68, 135–136,
    139, 165, 228–230; fame and, 21; horrorcore
    and, 81; "I'm On Everything (ft. Mike Epps)"
    (Bad Meets Evil), 163; influence on lyrics,
    50–56, 60, 64–65, 135–136; insomnia and,
    35–36, 50; Kimberly Scott and, 20; Lil Peep
    and, 93–94; Lil Wayne and, 132–133n13;
    Lil Xan and, 225; Mac Miller and, 100, 101;
    psychological aspects of, 21, 37, 40, 42,

49–50, 51, 138, 146, 195–196; relapse and,
    37; Royce da 5'9" and, 164–165; sedatives, 42;
    tours and, 149, 195; weight gain and, 44, 45
Sunderland, Mitchell, 80
supernatural themes, 81–83
Sutter, Kurt, 202–203
Swift, Taylor, 90
Swimming (Mac Miller), 102
Swishahouse, 87
Sydney Herald, 10
"Syllables" (Dr. Dre), 52n15
SZA, 102

T.I., 105, 106, 135
Taccone, Jorma, 98–99
Tahiem Smith, Trevor, Jr. (Busta Rhymes),
    185n13
"Taken from Me" (Bad Meets Evil), 161
"Talkin' 2 Myself" (Eminem), 130
Tate, James, 26
Taylor, Mark, 121, 122
Tech N9ne, 258
Tekashi 6ix9ine, 224, 225
television: celebrity status and, 6; reality shows,
    73, 98, 118, 209
"Tell Me" (Diddy), 159
Terrence, 45
Tha Block Is Hot (Lil Wayne), 130
Tha Carter (Lil Wayne), 130
Tha Carter V (Lil Wayne), 127
Tha Dogg Pound, 101
3rd Bass, 71, 72, 86
This Is Mike Stud, 98
This Unruly Mess I've Made (Macklemore and
    Ryan Lewis), 108, 109
Thomaz, Cameron (Whiz Khalifa), 224
Three 6 Mafia, 95, 248
Thriller (Michael Jackson), 112
Thyme, 25
"'Till I Collapse" (Eminem), 20
Timbaland, 88
Timberlake, Justin, 77n2, 189
"Time of the Season" (Zombies), 178
Time, 128
TMZ, 207
To the Extreme (Vanilla Ice), 72
Tommy (the Who), 176n7
Tommy Boy Records, 156
Too Short, 87
tours: Anger Management Tour (2005), 3, 13,
    14–17, 20, 38; D12, 158n15; digital era and,
    69, 113; direct marketing and, 98; European
    festivals, 149; frat rap and, 98; Home and
    Home Tour (2010), 149–151; Iggy Azalea,

107; Mac Miller, 101, 102–103; Monster Tour, 197; Rapture Tour, 196; Smokin' Grooves, 185n13; substance use and, 149, 195; television promos, 44–45, 44n8; Vans Warped Tour, 111, 157
Tow Down, 88
Tower of Power, 24
"Toy Soldiers" (Martika), 19
T-Pain, 122–130
Trapped in the Closet (R. Kelly), 176n7
trap-style rap, 206, 223–225, 249–252
Treach, 31, 226
Trial by Fire (Yelawolf), 92, 209
Tribe Called Quest, A, 103, 175n4, 185
Trice, Obie, 14, 23, 31–32, 33
Trick Trick, 25, 149
triplet flow, 247–251
Triumph the Insult Comic Dog, 59
TRL, 44n8
Trojanowicz, Robert, 82–83
Trump, Donald: BET Awards (2017) and, xvii–xviii; "Campaign Speech" (Eminem) and, 204–205; Eminem and, xvii–xviii, 204–205, 207–208, 212–213, 219–221, 226, 256; "Like Home" (Eminem) and, 219–221; racism and, xx–xxi, 208; Snoop Dogg and, xii, 205; supporters of, 100, 208
Trunk Muzik 0-60 (Yelawolf), 92
T-Wayne, 126
20/20 Experience, The (Justin Timberlake), 189
"25 to Life" (Eminem), 137
21 Savage, 224
Twitter, 6, 105, 210, 252n12, 258, 259. *See also* social media
Twiztid, 78
2 Fast 2 Furious, xvii
2 Live Crew, 87
2001 (Dr. Dre), 156
Tylenol PM, 36
Tyler, the Creator, 256, 257

U.S.A. (Under Satan's Authority) (Flatlinerz), 85
Under Pressure (Logic), 270
"Under Pressure" (Dr. Dre), 52n15
"Under Pressure" (Queen and David Bowie), 72
"Underground" (Eminem), 53–55
"Untitled" (Eminem), 141
"Untouchable" (Eminem), 214–224
"Unwind Yourself" (Marva Whitney), 101
"Up All Night" (Mac Miller), 101
Up in Smoke, 216
Upchurch, Ryan, 90
Usher, 153

Valium, 37, 42, 46
Vanilla Ice (Robert Van Winkle), 72–73, 247
Vans Warped Tour, 111, 157
Venom (film), 245–246
"Venom" (Eminem), 245–246
Vernon, Justin, 251–252, 252n12
"Versace" (Migos), 248
Vice, 80
Viceland TV, 104
Vicodin, 36–37, 42, 46
violence: in Detroit (1980s), 82–83; hip-hop culture and, 19, 25–30, 31–32; horrorcore and, 80–81; as lyrical theme, 81–83, 84–85, 162; mass shootings, 251; police, 206–207, 214–224
Violent J, 79
vocal delivery: a cappella, xvii, 19, 207; use of accents, 58–59, 60, 115, 116, 171; Auto-Tune and, 118–130, 206, 220, 224; "Bad Guy" (Eminem), 174; "Campaign Speech" (Eminem), 204–205; "Chloraseptic" (Eminem), 224–225, 224n18, 243–244; cyphers, xvii–xviii, 234, 256; Eminem's style, generally, 58–60, 132–133, 171, 202; *Encore* (Eminem), 59; *Infinite* (Eminem), 84; Jay-Z vs. Eminem, 154–155; Joyner Lucas, 215; Kendrick Lamar, 186, 248–249; Lil Wayne, 126–127, 128, 130, 132–133; "Love Game" (Eminem), 185–186; Mac Miller, 101; mumble rap, 224–225; "Phenomenal" (Eminem), 203; *Recovery* (Eminem), 137; *Relapse* (Eminem), 58–64; "Renegade" (Jay-Z), 154–155; rhyme schemes, 54–55, 60, 171, 187–188; Slim Shady persona and (*see* Slim Shady persona); Slim Shady/Marshall Mathers/Eminem persona and, 59–60, 63–66; third-verse climax, 54–55; triplet flow, 247–251; Vanilla Ice, 72–73; "Walk on Water" (Eminem), 212; Yelawolf, 92

Wack Album, The (Lonely Island), 99
Wahlberg, Mark, 44n8, 74, 221
"Walk on Water" (Eminem), 212, 214, 240, 252, 257
Wall, Paul, 86–87, 89
Wall, The (Pink Floyd), 176n7
Wallace, Carvell, 95
Walsh, Joe, 183
"Way I Am, The" (Eminem), 173, 178
Wayne Fontana and the Mindbenders, 185
Weeknd, 126
Welcome to: Our House (Slaughterhouse), 166, 238n3
Well Done (Action Bronson), 104
Wembley Stadium, 196, 257